Faces of Environmental Racism

Studies in Social, Political, and Legal Philosophy
General Editor: James P. Sterba, University of Notre Dame

Faces of Environmental Racism

Confronting Issues of Global Justice

Edited by
Laura Westra
and
Peter S. Wenz

Foreword by Eugene Hargrove

Rowman & Littlefield Publishers, Inc.

ROWMAN & LITTLEFIELD PUBLISHERS, INC.

Published in the United States of America
by Rowman & Littlefield Publishers, Inc.
4720 Boston Way, Lanham, Maryland 20706
3 Henrietta Street
London, WC2E 8LU, England

British Cataloging in Publication Information Available

Library of Congress Cataloging-in-Publication Data

Faces of environmental racism : confronting issues of global justice /
edited by Laura Westra and Peter S. Wenz.
p.   cm. — (Studies in social, political, and legal philosophy)
Includes bibliographical references and index.
1. Environmental policy—United States. 2. Environmental policy—
North America. 3. Racism—United States. 4. Racism—North
America. I. Westra, Laura. II. Wenz, Peter S.   III. Series.
GE180.F33 1995   363.7'00973—dc20   95-22209   CIP

ISBN 0–8476–8045–2 (cloth : alk. paper)
ISBN 0–8476–8046–0 (pbk. : alk. paper)

Printed in the United States of America

∞™ The paper used in this publication meets the minimum requirements of
American National Standard for Information Sciences—Permanence of
Paper for Printed Library Materials, ANSI Z39.48–1984.

For my sons,
Peter Christopher and
Mark Tjalling Westra

For my daughters,
Ami Rachael, Karen Miriam,
and Felicia Naomi Wenz

Contents

Part Three: Racism in Africa

Foreword

Environmental racism, or more generally environmental justice, is a major but largely unnoticed problem in environmental ethics. This book is an important contribution to recent efforts to begin addressing this issue. Indeed, it can correctly be called a pioneering effort.

One reason that environmental racism has been ignored is that environmental ethics literature, for the most part, reflects environmentalist concerns, and these have not included concerns about human welfare. Environmentalism is focused rather narrowly on the protection of natural systems and species—on the nonhuman world. Environmentalists are not especially interested in talking about human rights, preferring to speak about rights for nature instead, and environmental ethicists, who have been unable to come up with a theory of rights for nature, are busy trying to develop alternative terminology to express the environmentalists' intuitions. To date, the effort to replace talk about the rights of nature with talk about the intrinsic value of nature is not going well. Advocates of the civil rights movement, on the other hand, though they have spent a great deal of time defending a host of human rights, have seldom focused on the right to a safe and healthy environment and have seen little need to work with environmentalists, whom they frequently consider to be part of the system to which they are opposed.

There is a historical basis for this belief, and similar criticisms against the major environmental organizations have frequently been made from within the environmental movement by such grassroots groups as the Earth First! movement. Although most movements started slowly and with difficulty, the environmental movement sprang into existence in the mid-nineteenth century without any preliminary struggles, immediately producing a spate of environmental legislation beginning with the creation of Yellowstone and Yosemite as national parks. The environmental movement arose quite naturally out of changes in attitude toward nature as a result of developments in landscape painting and photography, nature poetry, landscape gardening, and biological and botanical classification activities in the natural sciences. The people who supported environmentalism in those early years were the best educated and most powerful people in the United States. There was no significant opposition, because they, for the most part, controlled the government. Except for the Hetch Hetchy battle, which is usually viewed as a disagreement between two groups of environmentalists, the preservationists and the conservationists, there was little conflict between environmentalists and the government until the 1950s when the Sierra Club had a falling out with the U.S. Forest Service. It is because environmentalists have such a brief history as an opposition group that they so often settle their disputes through compromise, clumsily giving away too much, as many critics claim. Civil rights advocates, who have fought long and hard for their political victories, are reluctant to become associated with a movement that characteristically resolves its battles by giving in.

Although an alliance of environmentalists and civil rights advocates is probably the best way to pursue the problems of environmental racism, such an alliance is not likely in the foreseeable future, given the differences in style and approach of the two movements. Paradoxically, the environmentalists most likely to match the political style of the civil rights groups are the radical environmentalists, whose interests and sympathies are primarily with the nonhuman rather than the human. The mainstream groups could deal more easily with human environmental problems; however, with their history of compromise, they would have the most difficulty finding a common strategy with the civil rights movement. Until common ground can be found between the environmental and the civil rights movements, environmental racism will remain an issue that falls through the cracks.

Moving from practice to theory, there are also problems with environmental ethics as a professional field within philosophy that make research into environmental racism difficult. The most important of these is the focus of environmental philosophy research on nonanthropocentrism and holism. When environmental ethics first began in the 1970s, environmentalists thought the underlying philosophical problem was anthropocentrism. Decades have been devoted to the analysis of this problem and many attempts have been made to develop a system of nonanthropocentric environmental ethics. Anthropocentrism as it was conceived at that time was supposed to be a traditional position that viewed nature as being solely instrumentally valuable to humans. To counter this position, nonanthropocentrists have developed theories to permit the valuing of nature for its own sake without reference to human benefit by establishing the presence of objective intrinsic value in nature independent of human judgment.

The dangers of this approach are reflected in the misanthropy that emerges now and then in the writings of most environmental ethicists—and indeed frequently in the writings of the radical environmentalists. One early example is J. Baird Callicott's remark in his seminal paper, "Animal Liberation: A Triangular Affair," that "the extent of misanthropy in modern environmentalism . . . may be taken as a measure of the degree to which it is biocentric." As support for this assertion, Callicott pointed to Edward Abbey's often quoted remark that he would rather shoot a human than a snake and to Garrett Hardin's recommendation that people who have accidents in wilderness areas not be rescued because doing so would violate the pristine purity of wilderness areas and ruin the experience for others. As Hardin put it, "Making great and spectacular efforts to save the life of an individual makes sense only when there is a shortage of people. I have not lately heard that there is a shortage of people." Similar statements appear in Paul Taylor's *Respect for Nature,* where he writes that "in the contemporary world the extinction of the species *Homo sapiens* would be beneficial to the Earth's Community of Life as a whole." He concludes that "our presence, in short, is not needed." The next step on the slippery slope is Rik Scarce's *Eco-Warriors,* which advocates the extermination of humankind as an "environmental cure-all." Scarce quotes with approval a remark by an anonymous writer using the pseudonym "Miss Ann Trophy," that "if radical environmentalists were to invent a disease to bring human population back to ecological sanity, it would probably be something like AIDS."

To be sure, environmental ethicists have taken quite a few knocks for their expressions of misanthropy and have almost always backed away from their misanthropic remarks in response to their critics. For example, Callicott, to atone for his earlier misanthropy, made it clear in "Animal Liberation and Environmental Ethics: Back together Again" that "the acknowledgement of a holistic environmental ethic does not entail that we abrogate our familiar moral obligations to family members, to fellow citizens, to all mankind, *nor* to fellow members, individually, of the mixed community, that is, to domesticated animals." Holmes Rolston, III, who is perhaps the most human-oriented of the nonanthropocentrists, takes similar pains to avoid any misanthropic confusion about the human/nature relationship he advocates in his book, *Environmental Ethics,* stressing that "duties to other humans remain all they have ever been, but 'the land' now counts too." Taylor never recants his misanthropy; nonetheless, by the end of the book he advocates letting human ethics override his environmental ethics when the nonbasic needs of humans (for example, the building of an art museum) are considered to be of such high value within human culture that they trump the basic needs of nonhumans. Although Miss Ann Tropy has also never recanted, no one among the environmentalists have as yet carried out his or her suggestions. Earth First! misanthropy is usually confined to monkey wrenching—for example, damaging construction equipment and spiking trees. The point of most misanthropic statements, moreover, seems to be to shock people into reassessing the human/nature relationship so that they will come to see that nature should count too. The rhetoric, nevertheless, makes it more difficult for environmentalists and environmental ethicists to think about and feel genuine concern for humans who have been marginalized environmentally. It is not that they are consciously discriminating against environmentally disadvantaged humans. They simply have formulated the problems they want to deal with in such a way that environmental racism does not appear on their agenda.

The holistic aspects of environmental ethics, which stress the good of the whole or the system over the individual, create similar problems. The health of an ecosystem is maintained through the suffering and death of countless individuals every day. Likewise, the good of a species is independent of the good of its individual members and, in accordance with the theory of evolution, routinely requires the untimely death of many of its members. This low regard for the individual in environmental ethics literature is another reason why civil rights advocates can rightly be nervous about environmentalist objectives. To be sure, there is one ethical/political theory in human ethics with good credentials, Plato's theory, which supports this conception of the relationship of individual to the whole. In it, however, the good of the individual is always sacrificed for the good of the state. It is for this reason that Karl Popper long ago denounced Plato's ethics and politics as a form of fascism. Similar claims have been made about environmentalists and environmental ethicists (for example, by the animal rights advocate Tom Regan).

The fear that environmentalists will apply their holistic ethic to humans or dilute human ethics by extending it to include the environment is never completely assuaged by disclaimers that traditional ethics will be left in place. In most systems of environmental ethics, the good of the individual is not important; only the good of the ecosystem or the species matters. Those individuals that are fit survive. Those that are not do not; yet their fate and that of the fit promotes the good of the whole. In accordance with human ethics, all humans are considered equal. As persons, they have certain rights. The good of the whole is promoted by proper respect for those basic rights. So it goes in theory. Practice, however, is another matter. Under environmental racism, some humans are treated worse than others. They are forced to live under environmental conditions that the more powerful (perhaps "the more fit") would never accept, and would never be required to accept. It is not enough simply to say that the disdain for the individual in environmental ethics will not be applied to humans, because the reality of environmental racism already says otherwise.

This book is an attempt to go beyond the usual disclaimer, to try to do something about a real problem. If it is successful, perhaps it will lead not only to new theory, but also to new practice.

— Eugene Hargrove,
Editor, *Environmental Ethics*;
Chair, Department of Philosophy
and Religion Studies, University
of North Texas

Introduction

Laura Westra and Peter S. Wenz

Today we enthusiastically participate in what is in essence a massive
and unprecedented experiment with the natural systems of the global
environment, with little regard for the moral consequences.

Al Gore, *Earth in the Balance*

Since the first Earth Day a quarter of a century ago, people have
worried about human impact on the nonhuman environment. Issues
range from desertification and species extinctions to acid rain, ozone
depletion, and global warming. However, in the initial zeal to publi-
cize holistic negative effects of human activities, the distribution of
effects among human beings was little noted.

More recently, people have recognized that in the United States,
poor people, African Americans, Hispanic Americans, and Native
Americans suffer disproportionate exposure to environmental pollution.
Because affected minorities are considerably poorer than average
Americans, some people have argued that minorities experience dis-
proportionate burdens due not to racism, but to poverty alone.[1]

However, most studies that have investigated the relative influence
of income and race on exposure to environmental toxins, including
all three of the studies of national scope, conclude that race is a more
influential factor.[2] For example, the *United Church of Christ Study of
1987* concludes: "The proportion of minority members in communities with commercial hazardous waste facilities is double that of communities without such facilities. Where two or more such facilities are
found, the proportion of minority members is nearly triple that in otherwise comparable communities. In fact, the best predictor of where
to find hazardous waste is to classify communities by race, not in-

come or real estate values." The study's director, Benjamin Chavis, coined the term "environmental racism."[3] Other studies reveal that damage awards for violations of environmental standards are lower in minority communities and government mandated cleanup efforts are slower and less thorough.[4] Among the moral consequences of the human assault on earth's ecosystems, then, is racist distribution of environmental hazards.

This racism exists internationally as well as nationally. On 12 December 1991, Lawrence Summers, chief economist of the World Bank, argued in a memo to colleagues that toxic pollution should be located in poor countries. Many such countries currently have little such pollution, and the first increments may not impair human health. And where human health is impaired, it should be in the poorest countries, he argued.

> The measurement of the costs of health-impairing pollution depends on the forgone earnings from increased morbidity and mortality. From this point of view a given amount of health-impairing pollution should be done in the country with the lowest cost, which will be the country with the lowest wages. I think the economic logic behind dumping a load of toxic waste in the lowest-wage country is impeccable and we should face up to that.[5]

Editors at the *Economist* found that "on the economics, [these] points are hard to answer."

The element of racism appears from the fact that poor countries are overwhelmingly nonwhite, by current American definitions at least. So the above proposal amounts to this: Toxic hazards should be located among nonwhites, even though they are generated by whites in industrial processes mostly invented by whites and employed by corporations owned predominantly by whites to provide products and services overwhelmingly for whites. Mainstream economics, also invented by whites, gives this proposal "racially neutral" support.

Few people of influence today openly advocate racism, yet it persists, hidden behind several masks. These include community revenue enhancement, job opportunities, efficiency, urban planning, international balance of trade, Third World development, and even environmental protection. The present volume attempts to unmask some of these strategies to reveal the faces of environmental racism.

Concentrating on race relations between blacks and whites, this volume explores environmental racism in North America and between the Caucasian world and Africa. Part one, "Foundations," introduces basic concepts and concerns and suggests fundamental intellectual, moral, and legal strategies to combat environmental racism. Parts two and three concentrate on case studies. These essays unmask racism by pulling off its disguises one by one. Part two, "Racism in North America," includes four case studies of environmental racism, one in Canada and three in the United States. Part three, "Racism in Africa," includes three studies detailing Africa's environmental burdens in the wake of colonialism and neocolonialism.

Part One: Foundations

Environmentalism and Justice

People concerned with racial justice have often been suspicious of environmentalists. Major environmental organizations, such as Sierra Club, Friends of the Earth, and the Wilderness Society, have traditionally had few minority members on their staffs and consulted little with minority members about matters affecting their communities.[6] This led one community leader in Birmingham, Alabama, to write, "if it does not hoot in the night, or swim upstream, environmentalists are not interested."[7]

Laura Westra maintains, however, that holistic environmental ethics permits and fosters a complementary ethic of justice among human beings. Human beings are first and foremost biological beings, in the sense that their cultural, intellectual, and spiritual aspects exist in and through actual living individuals and communities. So holistic, deep environmental thought that concentrates on the integrity of all biotic systems supports human life along with all other life forms.[8]

A "deep green" stance potentially supports all people, because no one group can long be isolated from the effects of its own, or anyone else's, assaults on the environment. Scientific evidence abounds that what happens in Brazil, Sicily, or Russia can have worldwide significance. At bottom, we have but *one world, one earth,* and environmental concern about protecting life-support systems is for everyone, in fact, is for everything. There is no inherent discrimination on the basis of gender, ethnicity, or race.

Because environmental ethics primarily sets limits on human actions as they affect the integrity of biotic communities, it must be supplemented by human ethics, which concerns principally interrelationships among human individuals and communities. All leading theories of interpersonal ethics (Kantian, contractarian, utilitarian, feminist, etc.) agree that racism is wrong and should be fought. Our attention here to the masks that racism presents in environmental contexts is part of that fight.

It is particularly important that environmentalists join the fight against racism. Changes in behavior required of almost all people for environmental reasons need widespread cooperation, and most people on earth are nonwhite. Environmentalists can expect needed worldwide cooperation only if the environmental agenda is seen clearly to respect all people, regardless or gender, ethnicity, or race.

Theoretical Perspectives

In "Decision Making," sociologist Robert D. Bullard discusses examples of environmental racism and some legal remedies that exist, or have been proposed. He then summarizes and explains five principles of environmental justice: (1) to guarantee the right to environmental protection; (2) to prevent harm before it occurs; (3) to shift the burden of proof to polluters; (4) to obviate proof of intent to discriminate; and (5) to redress existing inequities. This is the only essay in the present volume that has appeared elsewhere.

Clarice Gaylord, director of the Office of Environmental Justice at the United States Environmental Protection Agency, and Elizabeth Bell review laws that exist currently and recent administrative initiatives and programs designed to ameliorate environmental racism. In "Environmental Justice: A National Priority," they explain obstacles to environmental justice but maintain that considerations of justice can be, and increasingly are, integrated into many EPA programs.

Philosopher Bill Lawson notes in "Living for the City: Urban United States and Environmental Justice" that until recently, mainstream environmentalists have been unresponsive to the needs of city residents who are overexposed to environmental hazards. Lawson maintains that the association in popular culture of cities with both corruption and black people, and blacks with moral, cultural, and physical impurity, makes it seem that cities are inherently polluted. When places are considered polluted already, it seems reasonable to add pollution to them, rather than pollute a different place that is considered relatively pure. Thus, prejudice against cities and African Americans explains the disproportionate exposure of black and urban dwellers to toxic hazards.

Peter S. Wenz addresses in "Just Garbage" an apology sometimes given by economists for the disproportionate exposure of African Americans to pollution. The economic argument is that people of color are exposed by reason of poverty, not race. Where there is chemical pollution, land values are low, making the area attractive to people who cannot afford to spend money on real estate or housing.

Wenz argues that even if their overrepresentation among the poor accounted for the overexposure of blacks to pollution, the situation would be unjust because disproportionate exposure of the poor is unjust. Wenz proposes a system to redress current injustices. This system would also drastically reduce the overexposure of African Americans and discourage the manufacture, use, and disposal of dangerous substances.

Part Two: Racism in North America

The first case concerns Africville, Nova Scotia, Canada, which is depicted on the cover of this book. Howard McCurdy outlines the history of this black settlement near Halifax. He says that from the 1840s through the 1950s Halifax city officials imposed on the community "human waste disposal pits," an infectious disease hospital, a trachoma hospital, an open city dump, an oil plant/storage complex, a fertilizer plant, two slaughter houses, a coal-handling facility, a tar factory, a tannery, and a shoe factory. These were all locally undesirable land uses (LULUs) that whites of South Halifax did not want in *their* backyards. This historical study belies the claim that poor blacks are exposed to environmental hazards because, being poor, they move to already polluted areas where land is cheap. In this case, blacks settled on perfectly clean land that was progressively polluted due to land-use decisions of white political officials.

In the second case study, "Evanston Community and Environmental Racism: A Case Study in Social Philosophy," Richard Phillips explains and analyzes the plight of a black community, Evanston, Ohio. A BASF Inmont toxic and hazardous (ninety-day) treatment disposal and storage facility exploded there on 19 July 1990. Environmental racism is evident in the placement of the facility. There is no buffer between it and Evanston, but there is between it and the predominantly white communities of Norwood and Walnut Hill. Many infractions of environmental regulations and guidelines characterized the daily operation of the facility. After the explosion, relief was made available to the white communities long before the black community's problems were even considered. To this date, it is not clear how many different toxic substances were buried underground and what their effects on the life and health of the community may be.

In "The Faces of Environmental Racism: Titusville, Alabama, and

BFI," Laura Westra analyzes an attempt by Browning-Ferris Industries (BFI) to mechanically reduce wastes in Titusville, Alabama, a predominantly black community in Birmingham. Public notices and hearings about the project omitted mention of its nature, so planning was nearly complete before the community was aware that it was going to be dumped on again. Zoning procedures specific to waste disposal were not followed. Synergistic effects of proposed and existing pollutants were never considered. Even though BFI has a long history of violating the law and targeting black communities for waste disposal, no independent studies of the project's safety were ordered by responsible government officials. This case is unusual and gives hope for the future because a citizens' association took BFI to court and won. Greenpeace has now issued a video on this case entitled "Not in Anyone's Backyard: The Victory Over Browning-Ferris Industries."

The final case in this section, "Consent, Equity, and Environmental Justice: A Louisiana Case Study," concerns Louisiana Energy Services' (LES's) moves to build and operate a uranium enrichment facility. They needed a geophysically appropriate site where the nearest communities would be supportive. It is no surprise that white, middle-class communities would not welcome the proximity of nuclear materials and radiation, so LES sought an economically depressed area with high unemployment, poor rate of high school completion, and low per capita income. It found these conditions at Center Springs and Forest Grove, two African American settlements near Homer, Louisiana. Daniel C. Wigley and Kristin Shrader-Frechette argue that, contrary to Kantian requirements, people in these communities were treated by LES merely as means to the ends of others, that is, communities of richer, more powerful, better-educated people who wanted to avoid the burdens of hazardous radioactive facilities or wastes in their own neighborhoods. "Therefore," they conclude, "allegedly maximizing the overall good cannot justify the uncompensated, avoidable inequalities resulting from the LES plant."

Part Three: Racism in Africa

The strategy for imposing dangers on poor, relatively powerless people of color is similar whether the context is intranational or international. Writing about international relations, Shrader-Frechette has called it the "isolationist strategy," whereby people who create and profit from dangerous substances and processes are isolated from negative consequences through export. "Perhaps the dominant attitude toward transfers of hazardous technologies is that the ethics of risk evaluation in developed nations is isolated or separate from analogous moral requirements in developing countries."[9]

The North American cases in part two of this volume illustrate the same isolationist strategy in a domestic setting. Environmental racism both in North America and elsewhere is the practice of viewing minority communities as means to the majority's ends, and of burdening the disempowered with what no one else is prepared to accept, or of furthering the economic success of some at their expense. Shrader-Frechette presents four arguments often offered in support of the transfer of hazardous technologies, and we have already seen some versions of the same arguments in our cases. They are (1) the Social Progress Argument, (2) the Countervailing Benefit Argument, (3) the Consent Argument, and (4) the Reasonable Possibility Argument. We have already spoken of the social progress argument and its failings in this context; and we have also noted that the "countervailing benefits" are most often nonexistent, particularly for the affected communities; that the "consent" claimed is either nonexistent, culpably forced, or manipulated; and that environmental racism cases are *all* preventable assaults on specific communities. Hence, it is not true that "it is impossible to prevent them," and therefore, "reasonable possibility" does not accurately describe a harm not only vaguely possible, but actually imposed.

It might give us pause, in that case, to notice that the North and West's interaction not only with Africa, but also with African Americans at home, can be classed as just another environmental-specific case of the "isolationist strategy." One wonders, in that case, how close are the concepts and the practice of "isolation" and "segregation," and how it can be that so many regular citizens and socially aware (as well as "politically correct") corporate citizens, who would not dream of openly hiring or promoting in a discriminatory manner, or speaking for or supporting school or housing segregation practices, have no qualms about following these practices environmentally.

It is for this reason that we have spoken of "masks" and hidden "faces": once one begins to scratch below the surface, the same ugly attitudes and practices that are universally condemned by morality and proscribed by the law are still present, although they manifest themselves in new and different ways. This will be equally clear when we analyze some cases and issues in the African continent.[10]

Omari H. Kokole provides an overview of African environmental issues in "The Political Economy of the African Environment." Widespread environmental difficulties can be tied to colonial and neocolonial relationships between African peoples and industrial powers of the North and West. European powers disrupted traditional patterns of social and economic life when they imposed production for export, for example, by establishing coffee plantations and cattle ranches. Such production degraded ecosystems and left people dependent on imports for vital needs. The loss of security in traditional ways of life led to population increases that continue today.

In the process of finally relinquishing political control in Africa, colonial powers established states on the Western model. Political power is given to African elites who desire the same imports from industrial countries as did their colonial forebears, so ecologically degrading, economically servile, and socially disruptive production for export continues. Because the needs of many people are not met by this system, revolt is a constant danger. So elites maintain large armies, import modern weapons, and employ great violence.

In "Somalia: Environmental Degradation and Environmental Racism," Hussein M. Adam explains how Somalia illustrates these patterns. He stresses the disruption following the European establishment of inappropriate national borders in Africa. These borders divide ethnic group members from one another, truncate seasonal migrations of herding people, and place members of rival clans under a single jurisdiction. Worse than this, the European model of a state, an organization claiming to determine how violence is used in society, is more centralized than is functional in the Somali context, where decentralized control worked for centuries. The result, again, is military violence, which is less in the north, former British Somaliland. There, traditional centers of consensus-building political power were not eradicated completely. Cultural imperialism is thus a form of cultural pollution that leads to violence, environmental pollution, and death.

Adam stresses also the cultural pollution of Western ideas about humanity's relationship to the earth. Traditional Somali literature exhibits a respect for the earth incompatible with the degradation created by production for export.

Robert Goodland's "South Africa: Environmental Sustainability Needs Empowerment of Women" stresses another of the issues introduced by Kokole. Population increase is a serious problem that makes sustainable development impossible. Goodland stresses the need to address this problem through the empowerment of women. He rightly rejects draconian methods, such as enforced sterilization, and cautions against use of contraceptives that local people cannot control themselves, such as six-month injectables.

Western and Northern concern over population increases in developing countries is one of the most insidious masks of environmental racism because it reflects genuine environmental concern. Yet few in the industrial world recognize that modest population increases in their own countries (the United States population is projected to be 392 million in the year 2050) have greater environmental impact than do larger increases elsewhere. The industrial ways of life are so environmentally destructive that one person in the United States may consume more resources and produce more pollution in a lifetime than fifty people in some parts of Africa. Racism lurks in self-righteous calls for population limits for Africans while high-tech infertility cures abound for Americans.

The faces of environmental racism unmasked in this volume are only some of those hiding behind considerations of environmentalism, urban planning, economic rationality, energy security, Third World development, and jobs. We hope their presentation here leads to the unmasking of many more.

Notes

1. Vicki Been, "Market Forces, Not Racist Practices, May Affect the Siting of Locally Undesirable Land Uses," in *At Issue: Environmental Justice*, ed. Jonathan Petrikin (San Diego: Greenhaven Press, 1995).

2. Paul Mohai and Bunyan Bryant, "Demographic Studies Reveal a Pattern of Environmental Injustice," in Petrikin, 16.

3. Mohai and Bryant, 10–11.

4. Marianne Lavelle and Marcia Coyle, "Unequal Protection: The Racial Divide in Environmental Law," *National Law Journal*, 21 September 1992, S2.

5. Laura Westra, "A Transgenic Dinner? Ethical and Social Issues in Biotechnology and Agriculture," *The Journal of Social Philosophy* 24, no. 3 (Winter 1993): 215–32.

6. "A Sierra Club Roundtable on Race, Justice, and the Environment," *Sierra*, May/June 1993, 51–58 and 90–91.

7. W. Battle, letter to the editor, *Birmingham Post Herald*, 1994.

8. Laura Westra, *An Environmental Proposal for Ethics: The Principle of Integrity* (Lanham, Md.: Rowman & Littlefield, 1994), 21–78.

9. Kristin Shrader-Frechette, *Risk and Rationality* (Berkeley: University of California Press, 1991), 147–66.

10. Laura Westra, "Ecosystem Integrity and Sustainability: The Foundational Value of the Wild," in *Ethical and Scientific Perspectives on Integrity*, ed. Laura Westra and John Lemons (Dordrecht, The Netherlands: Kluwer Academic Publishers, 1995).

Part One

Foundations

1

Decision Making

Robert D. Bullard

Despite the recent attempts by federal agencies to reduce environmental and health threats in the United States, inequities persist.[1] If a community is poor or inhabited largely by people of color, there is a good chance that it receives less protection than a community that is affluent or white.[2] This situation is a result of the country's environmental policies, most of which "distribute the costs in a regressive pattern while providing disproportionate benefits for the educated and wealthy."[3] Even the Environmental Protection Agency (EPA) was not designed to address environmental policies and practices that result in unfair outcomes. The agency has yet to conduct a single piece of disparate impact research using primary data. In fact, the current environmental protection paradigm has institutionalized unequal enforcement, traded human health for profit, placed the burden of proof on the "victims" rather than on the polluting industry, legitimated human exposure to harmful substances, promoted "risky" technologies such as incinerators, exploited the vulnerability of economically and politically disenfranchised communities, subsidized ecological destruction, created an industry around risk assessment, delayed cleanup actions, and failed to develop pollution prevention as the overarching and dominant strategy. As a result, low-income and minority communities continue to bear greater health and environmental burdens, while the more affluent and white communities receive the bulk of the benefits.[4]

The geographic distribution of both minorities and the poor has been found to be highly correlated to the distribution of air pollution, mu-

This article previously appeared in *Environment* 36, no. 4 (May 1994): 11–20, 39–44.

nicipal landfills and incinerators, abandoned toxic waste dumps, lead poisoning in children, and contaminated fish consumption.[5] Virtually all studies of exposure to outdoor air pollution have found significant differences in exposure by income and race. Moreover, the race correlation is even stronger than the class correlation.[6] The National Wildlife Federation recently reviewed some sixty-four studies of environmental disparities; in all but one, disparities were found by either race or income, and disparities by race were more numerous than those by income. When race and income were compared for significance, race proved to be the more important factor in twenty-two out of thirty tests.[7] And researchers at Argonne National Laboratory recently found that

> in 1990, 437 of the 3,109 counties and independent cities failed to meet at least one of the EPA ambient air quality standards. . . . 57 percent of whites, 65 percent of African-Americans, and 80 percent of Hispanics live in 437 counties with substandard air quality. Out of the whole population, a total of 33 percent of whites, 50 percent of African-Americans, and 60 percent of Hispanics live in the 136 counties in which two or more air pollutants exceed standards. The percentage living in the 29 counties designated as nonattainment areas for three or more pollutants are 12 percent of whites, 20 percent of African-Americans, and 31 percent of Hispanics.[8]

The public health community has very little information on the magnitude of many air pollution-related health problems. For example, scientists are at a loss to explain the rising number of deaths from asthma in recent years. However, it is known that persons suffering from asthma are particularly sensitive to the effects of carbon monoxide, sulfur dioxide, particulate matter, ozone, and oxides of nitrogen.[9]

Current environmental decision making operates at the juncture of science, technology, economics, politics, special interests, and ethics and mirrors the larger social milieu where discrimination is institutionalized. Unequal environmental protection undermines three basic types of equity: procedural, geographic, and social.

Procedural Equity

Procedural equity refers to fairness—that is, to the extent that governing rules, regulations, evaluation criteria, and enforcement are applied in a nondiscriminatory way. Unequal protection results from nonscientific and undemocratic decisions, such as exclusionary practices, conflicts of interest, public hearings held in remote locations and at inconvenient times, and use of only English to communicate with and conduct hearings for non-English-speaking communities.

A 1992 study by staff writers from the *National Law Journal* uncovered glaring inequities in the way EPA enforces its Superfund laws: "There is a racial divide in the way the U.S. government cleans up toxic waste sites and punishes polluters. White communities see faster action, better results and stiffer penalties than communities where blacks, Hispanics and other minorities live. This unequal protection often occurs whether the community is wealthy or poor."[10]

After examining census data, civil court dockets, and EPA's own record of performance at 1,177 Superfund toxic waste sites, the authors of the *National Law Journal* reported the following:

- Penalties applied under hazardous waste laws at sites having the greatest white population were 500 percent higher than penalties at sites with the greatest minority population. Penalties averaged out at $335,566 at sites in white areas but just $55,318 at sites in minority areas.

- The disparity in penalties applied under the toxic waste law correlates with race alone, not income. The average penalty in areas with the lowest median income is $113,491—3 percent more than the average penalty in areas with the highest median income.

- For all the federal environmental laws aimed at protecting citizens from air, water, and waste pollution, penalties for noncompliance were 46 percent higher in white communities than in minority communities.

- Under the Superfund cleanup program, abandoned hazardous waste sites in minority areas take 20 percent longer to be placed on the National Priority List than do those in white areas.

- In more than half of the ten autonomous regions that administer EPA programs around the country, action on cleanup at Superfund sites begins from 12 to 42 percent later at minority sites than at white sites.

- For minority sites, EPA chooses "containment," the capping or walling off of a hazardous waste dump site, 7 percent more frequently than the cleanup method preferred under the law: permanent "treatment" to eliminate the waste or rid it of its toxins. For white sites, EPA orders permanent treatment 22 percent more often than containment.[11]

These findings suggest that unequal environmental protection is placing communities of color at risk. The *National Law Journal* study supplements the findings of several earlier studies and reinforces what grassroots activists have been saying all along: Not only are people of color differentially affected by industrial pollution but also they can expect different treatment from the government.[12]

Geographic Equity

Geographic equity refers to the location and spatial configuration of communities and their proximity to environmental hazards and locally unwanted land uses (LULUs), such as landfills, incinerators, sewage treatment plants, lead smelters, refineries, and other noxious facilities. Hazardous waste incinerators are not randomly scattered across the landscape. Communities with hazardous waste incinerators generally have large minority populations, low incomes, and low property values.[13]

A 1990 Greenpeace report (*Playing with Fire*) found that communities with existing incinerators have 89 percent more people of color than the national average; communities where incinerators are proposed for construction have minority populations that are 60 percent higher than the national average; the average income in communities with existing incinerators is 15 percent lower than the national average; property values in communities that host incinerators are 38 percent lower than the national average; and average property values are 35 percent lower in communities where incinerators have been proposed.[14]

The industrial encroachment into Chicago's Southside neighborhoods is a classic example of geographic inequity. Chicago is the nation's third largest city and one of the most racially segregated cities in the country. More than 92 percent of the city's 1.1 million African American residents live in racially segregated areas. The Altgeld Gardens housing project, located on the city's southeast side, is one of these segregated enclaves. The neighborhood is home to 150,000 residents, of whom 70 percent are African American and 11 percent are Latino.

Altgeld Gardens is encircled by municipal and hazardous waste landfills, toxic waste incinerators, grain elevators, sewage treatment facilities, smelters, steel mills, and a host of other polluting industries.[15] Because of its location, the area has been dubbed a "toxic doughnut" by Hazel Johnson, a community organizer in the neighborhood. There are 50 active or closed commercial hazardous waste landfills; 100 factories, including 7 chemical plants and 5 steel mills; and 103 abandoned toxic waste dumps.[16]

Currently, health and risk assessment data collected by the state of Illinois and the EPA for facility permitting have failed to take into account the cumulative and synergistic effects of having so many "layers" of poison in one community. Altgeld Gardens residents wonder when the government will declare a moratorium on permitting any new noxious facilities in their neighborhood and when the existing problems will be cleaned up. All of the polluting industries imperil the health of nearby residents and should be factored into future facility-permitting decisions.

In the Los Angeles air basin, 71 percent of African Americans and 50 percent of Latinos live in areas with the most polluted air, whereas only 34 percent of whites live in highly polluted areas.[17] The "dirtiest" zip code in California (90058) is sandwiched between South-Central Los Angeles and East Los Angeles.[18] The one-square-mile area is saturated with abandoned toxic waste sites, freeways, smokestacks, and wastewater pipes from polluting industries. Some eighteen industrial firms in 1989 discharged more than 33 million pounds of waste chemicals into the environment.

Unequal protection may result from land-use decisions that determine the location of residential amenities and disamenities. Unincorporated communities of poor African Americans suffer a "triple" vulnerability to noxious facility siting.[19] For example, Wallace, Louisiana, a small unincorporated African American community located on the Mississippi River, was rezoned from residential to industrial use by the mostly white officials of St. John the Baptist Parish to allow construction of a Formosa Plastics Corporation plant. The company's plants have been major sources of pollution in Baton Rouge, Louisiana; Point Comfort, Texas; Delaware City, Delaware; and its home country of Taiwan.[20] Wallace residents have filed a lawsuit challenging the rezoning action as racially motivated.

Environmental justice advocates have sought to persuade federal, state, and local governments to adopt policies that address distributive impacts, concentration, enforcement, and compliance concerns. Some states have tried to use a "fair share" approach to come closer to geographic equity. In 1990, New York City adopted a fair share legislative model designed to ensure that every borough and every community within each borough bears its fair share of noxious facilities. Public hearings have begun to address risk burdens in New York City's boroughs.

Testimony at a hearing on environmental disparities in the Bronx points to concerns raised by African Americans and Puerto Ricans who see their neighborhoods threatened by garbage transfer stations, salvage yards, and recycling centers.

On the Hunts Point peninsula alone there are at least thirty private transfer stations, a large-scale Department of Environmental Protection (DEP)
sewage treatment plant and a sludge dewatering facility, two Department of Sanitation (DOS) marine transfer stations, a city-wide privately regulated medical waste incinerator, a proposed DOS resource
recovery facility and three proposed DEP sludge processing facilities.
That all of the facilities listed above are located immediately adjacent
to the Hunts Point Food Center, the biggest wholesale food and meat
distribution facility of its kind in the United States, and the largest source
of employment in the South Bronx, is disconcerting. A policy whereby
low-income and minority communities have become the "dumping
grounds" for unwanted land uses, works to create an environment of
disincentives to community-based development initiatives. It also undermines existing businesses.[21]

Some communities form a special case for environmental justice.
For example, Native American reservations are geographic entities but
are also quasi-sovereign nations. Because of less-stringent environmental regulations than those at the state and federal levels, Native American reservations from New York to California have become prime
targets for risky technologies.[22] Indian natives do not fall under state
jurisdiction. Similarly, reservations have been described as the "lands
the feds forgot."[23] More than one hundred industries, ranging from solid
waste landfills to hazardous waste incinerators and nuclear waste storage facilities, have targeted reservations.[24]

Social Equity

Social equity refers to the role of sociological factors, such as race,
ethnicity, class, culture, lifestyles, and political power, in environmental
decision making. Poor people and people of color often work in the
most dangerous jobs and live in the most polluted neighborhoods, and
their children are exposed to all kinds of environmental toxins on the
playgrounds and in their homes and schools.

Some government actions have created and exacerbated environmental inequity. More stringent environmental regulations have driven noxious facilities to follow the path of least resistance toward poor,
overburdened communities. Governments have even funded studies that
justify targeting economically disenfranchised communities for noxious facilities. Cerrell Associates, Inc., a Los Angeles-based consult-
ing firm, advised the state of California on facility siting and concluded
that "ideally . . . officials and companies should look for lower socio-

economic neighborhoods that are also in a heavy industrial area with little, if any, commercial activity."[25]

The first state-of-the-art solid waste incinerator slated to be built in Los Angeles was proposed for the south-central Los Angeles neighborhood. The city-sponsored project was defeated by local residents.[26] The two permits granted by the California Department of Health Services for state-of-the-art toxic waste incinerators were proposed for mostly Latino communities: Vernon, near East Los Angeles, and Kettleman City, a farm-worker community in the agriculturally rich Central Valley. Kettleman City has 1,200 residents of which 95 percent are Latino. It is home to the largest hazardous waste incinerator west of the Mississippi River. The Vernon proposal was defeated, but the Kettleman City proposal is still pending.

Principles of Environmental Justice

To end unequal environmental protection, governments should adopt five principles of environmental justice: guaranteeing the right to environmental protection, preventing harm before it occurs, shifting the burden of proof to the polluters, obviating proof of intent to discriminate, and redressing existing inequities.

The Right to Protection

Every individual has a right to be protected from environmental degradation. Protecting this right will require enacting a federal "fair environmental protection act." The act could be modeled after the various federal civil rights acts that have promoted nondiscrimination— with the ultimate goal of achieving "zero tolerance"—in such areas as housing, education, and employment. The act ought to address both the intended and unintended effects of public policies and industrial practices that have a disparate impact on racial and ethnic minorities and other vulnerable groups. The precedents for this framework are the Civil Rights Act of 1964, which attempted to address both *de jure* and *de facto* school segregation, the Fair Housing Act of 1968, the same act as amended in 1988, and the Voting Rights Act of 1965.

For the first time in the agency's twenty-three-year history, EPA's Office of Civil Rights has begun investigating charges of environmental discrimination under Title VI of the 1964 Civil Rights Act. The cases involve waste facility siting disputes in Michigan, Alabama, Mississippi, and Louisiana. Similarly, in September 1993, the U.S. Civil

Rights Commission issued a report entitled *The Battle for Environmental Justice in Louisiana: Government, Industry, and the People.* This report confirmed what most people who live in "Cancer Alley"—the 85-mile stretch along the Mississippi River from Baton Rouge to New Orleans—already knew: African American communities along the Mississippi River bear disproportionate health burdens from industrial pollution.[27]

A number of bills have been introduced into Congress that address some aspect of environmental justice:

- The Environmental Justice Act of 1993 (H.R. 2105) would provide the federal government with the statistical documentation and ranking of the top one hundred "environmental high impact areas" that warrant attention.

- The Environmental Equal Rights Act of 1993 (H.R. 1924) seeks to amend the Solid Waste Act and would prevent waste facilities from being sited in "environmentally disadvantaged communities."

- The Environmental Health Equity Information Act of 1993 (H.R. 1925) seeks to amend the Comprehensive Environmental Response, Compensation, and Liability Act of 1990 (CERCLA) to require the Agency for Toxic Substances and Disease Registry to collect and maintain information on the race, age, gender, ethnic origin, income level, and educational level of persons living in communities adjacent to toxic substance contamination.

- The Waste Export and Import Prohibition Act (H.R. 3706) banned waste exports as of 1 July 1994 to countries that are not members of the Organization for Economic Cooperation and Development (OECD); the bill would also ban waste exports to and imports from OECD countries as of 1 January 1999.

The states are also beginning to address environmental justice concerns. Arkansas and Louisiana were the first two to enact environmental justice laws. Virginia has passed a legislative resolution on environmental justice. California, Georgia, New York, North Carolina, and South Carolina have pending legislation to address environmental disparities.

Environmental justice groups have succeeded in getting President Clinton to act on the problem of unequal environmental protection, an issue that has been buried for more than three decades. On 11

February 1994, Clinton signed an executive order entitled "Federal Actions to Address Environmental Justice in Minority Populations and Low-Income Populations." This new executive order reinforces what has been law since the passage of the 1964 Civil Rights Act, which prohibits discriminatory practices in programs receiving federal financial assistance.

The executive order also refocuses attention on the National Environmental Policy Act of 1970 (NEPA), which established national policy goals for the protection, maintenance, and enhancement of the environment. The express goal of NEPA is to ensure for all U.S. citizens a safe, healthful, productive, and aesthetically and culturally pleasing environment. NEPA requires federal agencies to prepare detailed statements on the environmental effects of proposed federal actions significantly affecting the quality of human health. Environmental impact statements prepared under NEPA have routinely downplayed the social impacts of federal projects on racial and ethnic minorities and low-income groups.

Under the new executive order, federal agencies and other institutions that receive federal monies have a year to implement an environmental justice strategy. For these strategies to be effective, agencies must move away from the "DAD" (decide, announce, and defend) modus operandi. EPA cannot address all of the environmental injustices alone but must work in concert with other stakeholders, such as state and local governments and private industry. A new interagency approach might include the following:

- Grassroots environmental justice groups and their networks must become full partners, not silent or junior partners, in planning the implementation of the new executive order.

- An advisory commission should include representatives of environmental justice, civil rights, legal, labor, and public health groups, as well as the relevant governmental agencies, to advise on the implementation of the executive order.

- State and regional education, training, and outreach forums and workshops on implementing the executive order should be organized.

- The executive order should become part of the agenda of national conferences and meetings of elected officials, civil rights and environmental groups, public health and medical groups, educators, and other professional organizations.

The executive order comes at an important juncture in this nation's history: Few communities are willing to welcome LULUs or to become dumping grounds for other people's garbage, toxic waste, or industrial pollution. In the real world, however, if a community happens to be poor and inhabited by persons of color, it is likely to suffer from a "double whammy" of unequal protection and elevated health threats. This is unjust and illegal.

The civil rights and environmental laws of the land must be enforced even if it means the loss of a few jobs. This argument was a sound one in the 1860s, when the Thirteenth Amendment to the Constitution, which freed the slaves in the United States, was passed over the opposition of proslavery advocates who posited that the new law would create unemployment (slaves had a zero unemployment rate), drive up wages, and inflict undue hardship on the plantation economy.

Prevention of Harm

Prevention, the elimination of the threat before harm occurs, should be the preferred strategy of governments. For example, to solve the lead problem, the primary focus should be shifted from treating children who have been poisoned to eliminating the threat by removing lead from houses.

Overwhelming scientific evidence exists on the ill effects of lead on the human body. However, very little action has been taken to rid the nation's housing of lead even though lead poising is a preventable disease tagged the "number one environmental health threat to children."[28]

Lead began to be phased out of gasoline in the 1970s. It is ironic that the "regulations were initially developed to protect the newly developed catalytic converter in automobiles, a pollution-control device that happens to be rendered inoperative by lead, rather than to safeguard human health."[29] In 1971, a child was not considered "at risk" unless he or she had 40 micrograms of lead per deciliter of blood (μg/dl). Since that time, the amount of lead that is considered safe has continually dropped. In 1991, the U.S. Public Health Service changed the official definition of an unsafe level to 10 μg/dl. Even at that level, a child's IQ can be slightly diminished and physical growth stunted.

Lead poisoning is correlated with both income and race. In 1988, the Agency for Toxic Substances and Disease Registry found that among families earning less than $6,000, 68 percent of African American children had lead poisoning, as opposed to 36 percent of white children.[30] In families with incomes exceeding $15,000, more than 38 percent of African American children suffered from lead poisoning, compared with 12 percent of white children. Thus, even when differences in income are taken into account, middle-class African American children are three times more likely to be poisoned with lead than are their middle-class white counterparts.

A 1990 report by the Environmental Defense Fund estimated that under the 1991 standard of 10 μg/dl, 96 percent of African American children and 80 percent of white children of poor families who live in inner cities have unsafe amounts of lead in their blood—amounts sufficient to reduce IQ somewhat, harm hearing, reduce the ability to concentrate, and stunt physical growth.[31] Even in families with annual incomes greater than $15,000, 85 percent of urban African American children have unsafe lead levels, compared to 47 percent of white children.

In the spring of 1991, the Bush administration announced an ambitious program to reduce lead exposure of children, including widespread testing of homes, certification of those who remove lead from homes, and medical treatment for affected children. Six months later, the Centers for Disease Control announced that the administration "does not see this as a necessary federal role to legislate or regulate the cleanup of lead poisoning, to require that homes be tested, to require home owners to disclose results once they are known, or to establish standards for those who test or clean up lead hazards."[32]

According to the *New York Times*, the National Association of Realtors pressured President Bush to drop his lead initiative because it feared that forcing homeowners to eliminate lead hazards would add from $5,000 to $10,000 to the price of those homes, further harming a real estate market already devastated by the aftershocks of Reaganomics.[33] The public debate has pitted real estate and housing interests against public health interests. Right now, the housing interests appear to be winning.

For more than two decades, Congress and the nation's medical and public health establishments have waffled, procrastinated, and shuffled papers while the lead problem steadily grows worse. During the years of President Reagan's "benign neglect," funding dropped very low. Even in the best years, when funding has risen to as much as $50 million per year, it has never reached levels that would make a real dent in the problem.

Much could be done to protect at-risk populations if the current laws were enforced. For example, a lead smelter operated for fifty years in a predominantly African American West Dallas neighborhood, where it caused extreme health problems for nearby residents. Dallas officials were informed as early as 1972 that lead from three lead smelters was finding its way into the bloodstreams of children who lived in two mostly African American and Latino neighborhoods: West Dallas and East Oak Cliff.[34]

Living near the RSR and Dixie Metals smelters was associated with a 36 percent increase in childhood blood lead levels. The city was urged to restrict the emissions of lead into the atmosphere and to undertake a large screening program to determine the extent of the public health problem. The city failed to take immediate action to protect the residents who lived near the smelters.

In 1980, EPA, informed about possible health risks associated with the Dallas lead smelters, commissioned another lead-screening study. This study confirmed what was already known a decade earlier: Children living near the Dallas smelters were likely to have greater lead concentrations in their blood than children who did not live near the smelters.[35]

The city only took action after the local newspapers published a series of headline-grabbing stories in 1983 on the "potentially dangerous" lead levels discovered by EPA researchers in 1981.[36] The articles triggered widespread concern, public outrage, several class-action lawsuits, and legal action by the Texas attorney general.

Although EPA was armed with a wealth of scientific data on the West Dallas lead problem, the agency chose to play politics with the community by scrapping a voluntary plan offered by RSR to clean up the "hot spots" in the neighborhood. John Hernandez, EPA's deputy administrator, blocked the cleanup and called for yet another round of tests to be designed by the Centers for Disease Control with EPA and the Dallas Health Department. The results of the new study were released in February 1983. This study again established the smelter as the source of elevated lead levels in West Dallas children.[37] Hernandez's delay of cleanup actions in West Dallas was tantamount to waiting for a body count.[38]

After years of delay, the West Dallas plaintiffs negotiated an out-of-court settlement worth more than $45 million. The lawsuit was settled in June 1983 as RSR agreed to pay for cleaning up the soil in West Dallas, a blood-testing program for children and pregnant women, and the installation of new antipollution equipment. The settlement was made on behalf of 370 children—almost all of whom were poor black residents of the West Dallas public housing project—and forty property owners. The agreement was one of the largest community lead-contamination settlements ever awarded in the United States.[39] The settlement, however, did not require the smelter to close. Moreover, the pollution equipment for the smelter was never installed.

In May 1984, however, the Dallas Board of Adjustments, a city agency responsible for monitoring land-use violations, asked the city attorney to close the smelter permanently for violating the city's zoning code. The lead smelter had operated in the mostly African American West Dallas neighborhood for fifty years without having the necessary use permits. Just four months later, the West Dallas smelter was permanently closed. After repeated health citations, fines, and citizens' complaints against the smelter, one has to question the city's lax enforcement of health and land-use regulations in African American and Latino neighborhoods.

The smelter is now closed. Although an initial cleanup was carried out in 1984, the lead problem has not gone away.[40] On 31 December 1991, EPA crews began a cleanup of the West Dallas neighborhood. It is estimated that the crews will remove between 30,000 and 40,000 cubic yards of lead-contaminated soil from several West Dallas sites, including school property and about 140 private homes. The project will cost EPA from $3 million to $4 million. The lead content of the soil collected from dump sites in the neighborhood ranged from 8,060 to 21,000 parts per million.[41] Under federal standards, levels of 500 to 1,000 parts per million are considered hazardous. In April 1993, the entire West Dallas neighborhood was declared a Superfund site.

There have been a few other signs related to the lead issue that suggest a consensus on environmental justice is growing among coalitions of environmental, social justice, and civil libertarian groups. The Natural Resources Defense Council, the National Association for the Advancement of Colored People Legal Defense and Education Fund, the American Civil Liberties Union, and the Legal Aid Society of Alameda County joined forces and won an out-of-court settlement worth between $15 million and $20 million for a blood-testing program in California. The lawsuit (*Matthews v. Coye*) arose because the state of California was not performing the federally mandated testing of some 557,000 poor children who receive Medicaid. This historic agreement will likely trigger similar actions in other states that have failed to perform federally mandated screening.[42]

Lead screening is important but it is not the solution. New government-mandated lead abatement initiatives are needed. The nation needs a "Lead Superfund" clean-up program. Public health should not be sacrificed even in a sluggish housing market. Surely, if termite inspections (required in both booming and sluggish housing markets) can be mandated to protect individual home investment, a lead-free home can be mandated to protect human health. Ultimately, the lead debate— public health (who is affected) versus property rights (who pays for cleanup)—is a value conflict that will not be resolved by the scientific community.

Shift the Burden of Proof

Under the current system, individuals who challenge polluters must prove that they have been harmed, discriminated against, or disproportionately affected. Few poor or minority communities have the resources to hire the lawyers, expert witnesses, and doctors needed to sustain such a challenge. Thus, the burden of proof must be shifted to the polluters who do harm, discriminate, or do not give equal protection to minorities and other overburdened classes.

Environmental justice would require the entities that are applying for operating permits for landfills, incinerators, smelters, refineries, and chemical plants, for example, to prove that their operations are not harmful to human health, will not disproportionately affect minorities or the poor, and are nondiscriminatory.

A case in point is Louisiana Energy Services' proposal to build the nation's first privately owned uranium enrichment plant. The proposed plant would handle about 17 percent of the estimated U.S. requirement for enrichment services in the year 2000. Clearly, the burden of proof should be on Louisiana Energy Services, the state government, and the Nuclear Regulatory Commission to demonstrate that local residents' rights would not be violated in permitting the plant. At present, the burden of proof is on local residents to demonstrate that their health would be endangered and their community adversely affected by the plant.

According to the Nuclear Regulatory Commission's 1993 draft environmental impact statement, the proposed site for the facility is Claiborne Parish, Louisiana, which has a per capita income of only $5,800 per year—just 45 percent of the national average.[43] The enrichment plant would be just one-quarter mile from the almost wholly African American community of Center Springs, founded in 1910, and one and one-quarter miles from Forest Grove, which was founded by freed slaves. However, the draft statement describes the socioeconomic and community characteristics of Homer, a town that is five miles from the proposed site and whose population is more than 50 percent white, rather than those of Center Springs or Forest Grove. As far as the draft is concerned, the communities of Center Springs and Forest Grove do not exist; they are invisible.

The racial composition of Claiborne Parish is 53.43 percent white, 46.09 percent African American, 0.16 percent American Indian, 0.07 percent Asian, 0.23 percent Hispanic, and 0.01 percent "other."[44] Thus, the parish's percentage population of African Americans is nearly four times greater than that of the nation and nearly two and one-half times greater than that of Louisiana. (African Americans composed 12 percent of the U.S. population and 29 percent of Louisiana's population in 1990.)

Clearly, Claiborne Parish's current residents would receive fewer of the plant's potential benefits—high-paying jobs, home construction, and an increased tax base—than would those who moved into the area or commuted to it to work at the facility. An increasing number of migrants will take jobs at the higher end of the skill and pay scale. These workers are expected to buy homes outside of the parish. Residents of Claiborne Parish, on the other hand, are likely to get the jobs at the low end of the skill and pay scale.[45]

Ultimately, the plant's social costs would be borne by nearby residents, while the benefits would be more dispersed. The potential social costs include increased noise and traffic, threats to public safety and to mental and physical health, and LULUs.

The case of Richmond, California, provides more evidence of the need to shift the burden of proof. A 1989 study, *Richmond at Risk*, found that the African American residents of this city bear the brunt of toxic releases in Contra Costa County and the San Francisco Bay area.[46] At least, thirty-eight industrial sites in and around the city store up to ninety-four million pounds of forty-five different chemicals, including ammonia, chlorine, hydrogen fluoride, and nitric acid. However, the burden of proof is on Richmond residents to show that they are harmed by nearby toxic releases.

On 26 July 1993, sulfur trioxide escaped from the General Chemical plant in Richmond, where people of color make up a majority of the residents. More than twenty thousand citizens were sent to the hospital. A September 1993 report by the Bay Area Air Quality Management District confirmed that "the operation was conducted in a negligent manner without due regard to the potential consequences of a miscalculation or equipment malfunction, and without required permits from the District."[47]

When Richmond residents protested the planned expansion of a Chevron refinery, they were asked to prove that they had been harmed by Chevron's operation. Recently, public pressure has induced Chevron to set aside $4.2 million to establish a new health clinic and help the surrounding community.

A third case involves conditions surrounding the 1,900 *maquiladoras*, assembly plants operated by U.S., Japanese, and other countries' companies along the 2,000-mile U.S.-Mexican border.[48] A 1983 agreement between the United States and Mexico requires U.S. companies in Mexico to export their waste products to the United States, and plants must notify EPA when they are doing so. However, a 1986 survey of 772 *maquiladoras* revealed that only twenty of the plants informed EPA when they were exporting waste to the United States, even though 86 percent of the plants used toxic chemicals in their manufacturing processes. And in 1989, only ten waste-shipment notices were filed with EPA.[49]

Much of the waste from the *maquiladoras* is illegally dumped in sewers, ditches, and the desert. All along the Rio Grande, plants dump toxic wastes into the river, from which 95 percent of the region's residents get their drinking water. In the border cities of Brownsville, Texas, and Matamoros, Mexico, the rate of anencephaly—being born without a brain—is four times the U.S. national average.[50] Affected families have filed lawsuits against eighty-eight of the area's one hundred *maquiladoras* for exposing the community to xylene, a cleaning solvent that can cause brain hemorrhages and lung and kidney damage. However, as usual, the burden of proof rests with the victims. Unfortunately, Mexico's environmental regulatory agency is understaffed and ill equipped to enforce the country's environmental laws adequately.

Obviate Proof of Intent

Laws must allow disparate impact and statistical weight—as opposed to "intent"—to infer discrimination because proving intentional or purposeful discrimination in a court of law is next to impossible. The first lawsuit to charge environmental discrimination in the placement of a waste facility, *Bean v. Southwestern Waste*, was filed in 1979. The case involved residents of Houston's Northwood Manor, an urban, middle-class neighborhood of homeowners, and Browning-Ferris Industries, a private disposal company based in Houston.

More than 83 percent of the residents in the subdivision owned their single-family, detached homes. Thus, the Northwood Manor neighborhood was an unlikely candidate for a municipal landfill except that, in 1978, it was more than 82 percent black. An earlier attempt had been made to locate a municipal landfill in the same general area in 1970, when the subdivision and local school district had a majority white population. The 1970 landfill proposal was killed by the Harris County Board of Supervisors as being an incompatible land use; the site was deemed to be too close to a residential area and a neighborhood school. In 1978, however, the controversial sanitary landfill was built only 1,400 feet from a high school, football stadium, track field, and the North Forest Independent School District's administration building.[51] Because Houston has been and continues to be highly segregated, few Houstonians are unaware of where the African American neighborhoods end and the white ones begin. In 1970, for example, more than 90 percent of the city's African American residents lived in mostly black areas. By 1980, 82 percent of Houston's African American population lived in mostly black areas.[52]

Houston is the only major U.S. city without zoning. In 1992, the city council voted to institute zoning, but the measure was defeated at the polls in 1993. The city's African American neighborhoods have paid a high price for the city's unrestrained growth and lack of a zoning policy. Black Houston was allowed to become the dumping ground for the city's garbage. In every case, the racial composition of Houston's African American neighborhoods had been established before the waste facilities were sited.[53]

From the early 1920s through the late 1970s, all five of the city-owned sanitary landfills and six out of eight of Houston's municipal solid-waste incinerators were located in mostly African American neighborhoods.[54] The other two incinerator sites were located in a Latino neighborhood and a white neighborhood. One of the oldest waste sites in Houston was located in Freedmen's Town, an African American neighborhood settled by former slaves in the 1860s. The site has been built over with a charity hospital and a low-income public housing project.

Private industry took its lead from the siting pattern established by the city government. From 1970 to 1978, three of the four privately owned landfills used to dispose of Houston's garbage were located in mostly African American neighborhoods. The fourth privately owned landfill, which was sited in 1971, was located in the mostly white Chattwood subdivision. A residential part, or "buffer zone," separates the white neighborhood from the landfill. Both government and industry responded to white neighborhood associations and their NIMBY (not in my backyard) organizations by siting LULUs according to the PIBBY (place in blacks backyards) strategy.[55]

The statistical evidence in *Bean v. Southwestern Waste* overwhelmingly supported the disproportionate impact argument. Overall, fourteen of the seventeen (82 percent) solid-waste facilities used to dispose of Houston's garbage were located in mostly African American neighborhoods. Considering that Houston's African American residents comprised only 28 percent of the city's total population, they clearly were forced to bear a disproportionate burden of the city's solid-waste facilities.[56] However, the federal judge ruled against the plaintiffs on the grounds that "purposeful discrimination" was not demonstrated.

Although the Northwood Manor residents lost their lawsuit, they did influence the way the Houston city government and the state of Texas addressed race and waste facility siting. Acting under intense pressure from the African American community, the Houston city council passed a resolution in 1980 that prohibited city-owned trucks from dumping at the controversial landfill. In 1981, the Houston city council passed an ordinance restricting the construction of solid-waste disposal sites near public facilities such as schools. And the Texas Department of Health updated its requirements of landfill permit applicants to include detailed land-use, economic, and sociodemographic data on areas where they proposed to site landfills. Black Houstonians had sent a clear signal to the Texas Department of Health, the city of Houston, and private disposal companies that they would fight any future attempts to place waste disposal facilities in their neighborhoods.

Since *Bean v. Southwestern Waste*, not a single landfill or incinerator has been sited in an African American neighborhood in Houston. Not until nearly a decade after that suit did environmental discrimination resurface in the courts. A number of recent cases have challenged siting decisions using the environmental discrimination argument: *East Bibb Twiggs Neighborhood Associaton v. Macon-Bibb County Planning and Zoning Commission* (1989), *Bordeaux Action Committee v. Metro Government of Nashville* (1990), *R.I.S.E. v. Kay* (1991), and *El Pueblo para El Aire y Agua Limpio v. County of Kings* (1991). Unfortunately, these legal challenges are also confronted with the test of demonstrating "purposeful" discrimination.

Redress Inequities

Disproportionate impacts must be redressed by targeting action and resources. Resources should be spent where environmental and health problems are greatest, as determined by some ranking scheme—but one not limited to risk assessment. The EPA already has geographic targeting that involves selecting a physical area, often a naturally defined area such as a watershed; assessing the condition of the natural resources and range of environmental threats, including risks to public health; formulating and implementing integrated, holistic strategies for restoring or protecting living resources and their habitats within that area; and evaluating the progress of those strategies toward their objectives.[57]

Relying solely on proof of a cause-and-effect relationship as defined by traditional epidemiology disguises the exploitative way the polluting industries have operated in some communities and condones a passive acceptance of the status quo.[58] Because it is difficult to establish causation, polluting industries have the upper hand. They can always hide behind "science" and demand "proof" that their activities are harmful to humans or the environment.

A 1992 EPA report, *Securing Our Legacy*, described the agency's geographic initiatives as "protecting what we love."[59] The strategy emphasized "pollution prevention, multimedia enforcement, research into causes and cures of environmental stress, stopping habitat loss, education, and constituency building."[60] Examples of geographic initiatives under way include the Chesapeake Bay, Great Lakes, Gulf of Mexico, and Mexican Border programs.

Such targeting should channel resources to the hot spots, communities that are burdened with more than their fair share of environmental problems. For example, EPA's Region VI has developed geographic information systems and comparative risk methodologies to evaluate environmental equity concerns in the region. The methodology combines susceptibility factors, such as age, pregnancy, race, income, preexisting disease, and lifestyle, with chemical release data from the Toxic Release inventory and monitoring information; state health department vital statistics data; and geographic and demographic data—especially from areas around hazardous waste sites—for its regional equity assessment.

Region VI's 1992 Gulf Coast Toxics Initiatives project is an outgrowth of its equity assessment. The project targets facilities on the Texas and Louisiana coast, a "sensitive . . . eco-region where most of the releases in the five-state region occur."[61] Inspectors will spend 38 percent of their time in this "multimedia enforcement effort."[62] It is not clear how this percentage was determined, but, for the project to move beyond the "first-step" phase and begin addressing real inequities, most of its resources (not just inspectors) must be channeled to the areas where most of the problems occur.

A 1993 EPA study of Toxic Release Inventory data from Louisiana's petrochemical corridor found that "populations within two miles of facilities releasing 90% of total industrial corridor air releases feature a higher proportion of minorities than the state average; facilities releasing 88% have a higher proportion than the Industrial Corridor parishes' average."[63]

To no one's surprise, communities in Corpus Christi, neighborhoods that run along the Houston Ship Channel and petrochemical corridor, and many unincorporated communities along the 85-mile stretch of the Mississippi River from Baton Rouge to New Orleans ranked at or near the top in terms of pollution discharges in EPA Region VI's Gulf Coast Toxics Initiatives equity assessment. It is very likely that similar rankings would be achieved using the environmental justice framework. However, the question that remains is one of resource allocation—the level of resources that Region VI will channel into solving the pollution problem in communities that have a disproportionately large share of poor people, working-class people, and people of color.

Health concerns raised by Louisiana's residents and grassroots activists in such communities as Alsen, St. Gabriel, Geismer, Morrisonville, and Lions—all of which are located in close proximity to polluting industries—have not been adequately addressed by local parish supervisors, state environmental and health officials, or the federal and regional offices of EPA.[64]

A few contaminated African American communities in southeast Louisiana have been bought out or are in the process of being bought out by industries under their "good neighbor" programs. Moving people away from the health threat is only a partial solution, however, as long as damage to the environment continues. For example, Dow Chemical, the state's largest chemical plant, is buying out residents of mostly African American Morrisonville.[65] The communities of Sun Rise and Reveilletown, which were founded by freed slaves, have already been bought out.

Many of the community buyout settlements are sealed. The secret nature of the agreements limits public scrutiny, community comparisons, and disclosure of harm or potential harm. Few of the recent settlement agreements allow for health monitoring or surveillance of affected residents once they are dispersed.[66] Some settlements have even required the "victims" to sign waivers that preclude them from bringing any further lawsuits against the polluting industry.

A Framework for Environmental Justice

The solution to unequal protection lies in the realm of environmental justice for all people. No community—rich or poor, black or white—should be allowed to become a "sacrifice zone." The lessons from the civil rights struggles around housing, employment, education, and public accommodations over the past four decades suggest that environmental justice requires a legislative foundation. It is not enough to demonstrate the existence of unjust and unfair conditions; the practices that cause the conditions must be made illegal.

The five principles already described—the right to protection, prevention of harm, shifting the burden of proof, obviating proof of intent to discriminate, and targeting resources to redress inequities—constitute a framework for environmental justice. The framework incorporates a legislative strategy, modeled after landmark civil rights mandates, that would make environmental discrimination illegal and costly.

Although enforcing current laws in a nondiscriminatory way would help, a new legislative initiative is needed. Unequal protection must be attacked via a federal "fair environmental protection act" that redefines protection as a right rather than a privilege. Legislative initiatives must also be directed at states because many of the decisions and problems lie with state actions.

Noxious facility siting and cleanup decisions involve very little science and a lot of politics. Institutional discrimination exists in every social arena, including environmental decision making. Burdens and benefits are not randomly distributed. Reliance solely on "objective" science for environmental decision making—in a world shaped largely by power politics and special interests—often masks institutional racism. For example, the assignment of "acceptable" risk and use of "averages" often results from value judgments that serve to legitimate existing inequities. A national environmental justice framework that incorporates the five principles presented above is needed to begin addressing environmental inequities that result from procedural, geographic, and societal imbalances.

The antidiscrimination and enforcement measures called for here are no more regressive than the initiatives undertaken to eliminate slavery and segregation in the United States. Opponents argued at the time that such actions would hurt the slaves by creating unemployment and destroying black institutions, such as businesses and schools. Similar arguments were made in opposition to sanctions against the racist system of apartheid in South Africa. But people of color who live in environmental "sacrifice zones"—from migrant farm workers who are exposed to deadly pesticides to the parents of inner-city children threatened by lead poisoning—will welcome any new approaches that will reduce environmental disparities and eliminate the threats to their families' health.

Notes

1. U.S. Environmental Protection Agency, *Environmental Equity: Reducing Risk for All Communities* (Washington, D.C., 1992); and K. Sexton and Y. Banks Anderson, eds., "Equity in Environmental Health: Research Issues and Needs," *Toxicology and Industrial Health* 9 (September/October 1993).

2. R. D. Bullard, "Solid Waste Sites and the Black Houston Community," *Sociological Inquiry* 53, nos. 2 and 3 (1983): 273–88; idem., *Invisible Houston: The Black Experience in Boom and Bust* (College Station, Tex.: Texas A&M University Press, 1987); idem., *Dumping in Dixie: Race, Class and Environmental Quality* (Boulder, Colo.: Westview Press, 1990); idem., *Confronting Environmental Racism: Voices from the Grassroots* (Boston, Mass.: South End Press, forthcoming); D. Russell, "Environmental Racism," *Anncas Journal* 11, no. 2 (1989): 22–32; M. Lavelle and M. Coyle, "Unequal Protection," *National Law Journal*, 21 September 1992, 1–2; R. Austin and M. Schill, "Black, Brown, Poor, and Poisoned: Minority Grassroots Environmentalism and the Quest for Eco-Justice," *Kansas Journal of Law and Public Policy* 1 (1991): 69–82; R. Godsil, "Remedying Environmental Racism," *Michigan Law Review* 90 (1991):394–427; and B. Bryant and P. Mohai, eds., *Race and the Incidence of Environmental Hazards: A Time for Discourse* (Boulder, Colo.: Westview Press, 1992).

3. R. B. Stewart, "Paradoxes of Liberty, Integrity, and Fraternity: The Collective Nature of Environmental Quality and Judicial Review of Administration Action," *Environmental Law* 7, no. 3 (1977): 474–76; M. A. Freeman, "The Distribution of Environmental Quality," in *Environmental Quality Analysis*, ed. by A. V. Kneese and B. T. Bower (Baltimore, Md.: Johns Hopkins University Press for Resources for the Future, 1972); W. J. Kruvant, "People, Energy, and Pollution," in *American Energy Consumer*, ed. by D. K. Newman and D. Day (Cambrige, Mass.: Ballinger, 1975), 125–67; and L. Gianessi, H. M. Peskin, and E. Wolff, "The Distributional Effects of Uniform Air Pollution Policy in the U.S.," *Quarterly Journal of Economics* 56, no. 1 (1979): 281–301.

4. Freeman, note 3 above; Kruvant, note 3 above; Bullard, 1983 and 1990, note 2 above; P. Asch and J. J. Seneca, "Some Evidence on the Distribution of Air Quality," *Land Economics* 54, no. 3 (1978): 278–97; United Church of Christ Commission for Racial Justice, *Toxic Wastes and Race in the United States: A National Study of the Racial and Socioeconomic Characteristics of Communities with Hazardous Waste Sites* (New York: United Church of Christ, 1987); Russell, note 2 above; R. D. Bullard and B. H. Wright, "Environmentalism and the Politics of Equity: Emergent Trends in the Black Community," *Mid-American Review of Sociology* 12, no. 2 (1987): 21–37; idem, "The Quest for Environmental Equity: Mobilizing the African American Community for Social Change," *Society and Natural Resources* 3, no. 4 (1990): 301–11; M. Gelobter, "The Distribution of Air Pollution by Income and Race" (paper presented at the Second Symposium on Social Science in Resource Management, Urbana, Ill., June 1988); R. D. Bullard and J. R. Reagin, "Rac-

ism and the City," in *Urban Life in Transition*, ed. by M. Gottdiener and C. V. Pickvance (Newbury Park, Calif.; Sage, 1991): 55–76; R. D. Bullard, "Urban Infrastructure: Social, Environmental, and Health Risks to African Americans," in *The State of Black America 1992*, ed. by B. J. Tidwell (New York: National Urban League, 1992): 183–96; P. Ong and E. Blumenberg, "Race and Environmentalism" (paper prepared for the Graduate School of Architecture and Urban Planning, University of California at Los Angeles, 14 March 1990); and B. H. Wright and R. D. Bullard, "Hazards in the Workplace and Black Health," *National Journal of Sociology* 4, no. 1 (1990): 45–62.

5. Freeman, note 3 above; Gianessi, Peskin, and Wolff, note 3 above; Gelobter, note 4 above; D. R. Wernette and L. A. Nieves, "Breathing Polluted Air," *EPA Journal* 18, no. 1 (1992): 16–17; Bullard, 1983, 1987, and 1990, note 2 above; R. D. Bullard, "Environmental Racism," *Environmental Protection* 2 (June 1991): 25–26; L. A. Nieves, "Not in Whose Backyard? Minority Population Concentrations and Noxious Facility Sites" (paper presented at the Annual Meeting of the American Association for the Advancement of Science, Chicago, 9 February 1992); United Church of Christ, note 4 above; Agency for Toxic Substances and Disease Registry, *The Nature and Extent of Lead Poisoning in Children in the United States: A Report to Congress* (Atlanta, Ga.: U.S. Department of Health and Human Services, 1988); K. Florini et al., *Legacy of Lead: America's Continuing Epidemic of Childhood Lead Poisoning* (Washington, D.C.: Environmental Defense Fund, 1990); and P. West, J. M. Fly, F. Larkin, and P. Marans, "Minority Anglers and Toxic Fish Consumption: Evidence of the State-Wide Survey of Michigan," in *The Proceedings of the Michigan Conference on Race and the Incidence of Environmental Hazards*, ed. by B. Bryant and P. Mohai (Ann Arbor, Mich.: University of Michigan School of Natural Resources, 1990): 108–22.

6. Gelobter, note 4 above; and M. Gelobter, "Toward a Model of Environmental Discrimination," in Bryant and Mohai, eds., note 5 above, 87–107.

7. B. Goldman, *Not Just Prosperity: Achieving Sustainability with Environmental Justice* (Washington, D.C.: National Wildlife Federation Corporate Conservation Council, 1994), 8.

8. Wernette and Nieves, note 5 above, 16–17.

9. H. P. Mak, P. Johnson, H. Abbey, and R. C. Talamo, "Prevalence of Asthma and Health Service Utilization of Asthmatic Children in an Inner City," *Journal of Allergy and Clinical Immunology* 70 (1982): 367–72; I. F. Goldstein and A. L. Weinstein, "Air Pollution and Asthma: Effects of Exposure to Short-Term Sulfur Dioxide Peaks," *Environmental Research* 40 (1986): 332–45; J. Schwartz et al., "Predictors of Asthma and Persistent Wheeze in a National Sample of Children in the United States," *American Review of Respiratory Disease* 142 (1990): 555–62; U.S. Environmental Protection Agency, note 1 above; and E. Mann, *L.A.'s Lethal Air: New Strategies for Policy, Organizing and Action* (Los Angeles: Labor/Community Strategy Center, 1991).

10. Lavelle and Coyle, note 2 above, 1–2.

11. Ibid., 2.

12. Bullard, 1983 and 1990, note 2 above; Gelobter, note 4 above; and United Church of Christ, note 4 above.

13. Bullard, 1983 and 1990, note 2 above; P. Costner and J. Thornton, *Playing with Fire* (Washington, D.C.: Greenpeace, 1990); and United Church of Christ, note 4 above.

14. Costner and Thornton, note 13 above.

15. M. H. Brown, *The Toxic Cloud: The Poisoning of America's Air* (New York: Harper and Row, 1987); and J. Summerhays, *Estimation and Evaluation of Cancer Risks Attributable to Air Pollution in Southeast Chicago* (Washington, D.C.: U.S. Environmental Protection Agency, 1989).

16. "Home Street, USA: Living with Pollution," *Greenpeace Magazine*, October/November/December 1991, 8–13.

17. Mann, note 9 above; and Ong and Blumenberg, note 4 above.

18. Mann, note 9 above; and J. Kay, "Fighting Toxic Racism: L.A.'s Minority Neighborhood Is the 'Dirtiest' in the State," *San Francisco Examiner*, 7 April 1991, Al.

19. Bullard, 1990, note 2 above.

20. K. C. Colquette and E. A. Henry Robertson, "Environmental Racism: The Causes, Consequences, and Commendations," *Tulane Environmental Law Journal 5*, no. 1 (1991): 153–207.

21. F. Ferrer, "Testimony by the Office of Bronx Borough President," in *Proceedings from the Public Hearing on Minorities and the Environment: An Exploration into the Effects of Environmental Policies, Practices, and Conditions on Minority and Low-Income Communities* (Bronx, N.Y.: Bronx Planning Office, 20 September 1991).

22. B. Angel, *The Toxic Threat to Indian Lands: A Greenpeace Report* (San Francisco. Calif.: Greenpeace, 1992); J. Kay, "Indian Lands Targeted for Waste Disposal Sites," *San Francisco Examiner*, 10 April 1991, Al.

23. M. Ambler, "The Lands the Feds Forgot," *Sierra*, May/June 1989, 44.

24. Angel, note 22 above; C. Beasley, "Of Poverty and Pollution: Deadly Threat on Native Lands," *Buzzworm 2*, no. 5 (1990): 39–45; and R. Tomsho, "Dumping Grounds: Indian Tribes Contend with Some of the Worst of America's Pollution," *Wall Street Journal*, 29 November 1990, A1.

25. Cerrell Associates, Inc., *Political Difficulties Facing Waste-to-Energy Conversion Plant Siting* (Los Angeles: California Waste Management Board, 1984).

26. L. Blumberg and R. Gottlieb, *War on Waste: Can America Win Its Battle with Garbage?* (Washington, D.C.: Island Press, 1989).

27. U.S. Commission on Civil Rights, *The Battle for Environmental Justice in Louisiana: Government, Industry and the People* (Kansas City, Mo., 1993).

28. Agency for Toxic Substances and Diseases Registry, note 5 above.

29. P. Reich, *The Hour of Lead* (Washington, D.C.: Environmental Defense Fund, 1992).

30. Agency for Toxic Substances and Disease Registry, note 5 above.

31. Florini et al., note 5 above.

32. P. J. Hilts, "White House Shuns Key Role in Lead Exposure," *New York Times*, 24 August 1991, 14.

33. Ibid.

34. Dallas Alliance Environmental Task Force, *Alliance Final Report* (Dallas, Tex.: Dallas Alliance, 1983).

35. J. Lash, K. Gillman, and D. Sheridan, *A Season of Spoils: The Reagan Administration's Attack on the Environment* (New York: Pantheon Books, 1984), 131–39.

36. D. W. Nauss, "EPA Official: Dallas Lead Study Misleading," *Dallas Times Herald*, 20 March 1983, 1; idem, "The People vs. the Lead Smelter," *Dallas Times Herald*, 17 July 1983, 18; B. Lodge, "EPA Official Faults Dallas Lead Smelter," *Dallas Morning News*, 20 March 1983, A1; and Lash, Gillman, and Sheridan, note 35 above.

37. U.S. Environmental Protection Agency Region VI, *Report of the Dallas Area Lead Assessment Study* (Dallas, Tex., 1993).

38. Lash, Gillman, and Sheridan, note 35 above.

39. Bullard, 1990, note 2 above.

40. S. Scott and R. L. Loftis, "Slag Sites' Health Risks Still Unclear," *Dallas Morning News*, 23 July 1991, A1.

41. Ibid.

42. B. L. Lee, "Environmental Litigation on Behalf of Poor, Minority Children: *Matthews v. Coye: A Case Study*" (paper presented at the Annual Meeting of the American Association for the Advancement of Science, Chicago, 9 February 1992).

43. Nuclear Regulatory Commission, *Draft Environmental Impact Statement for the Construction and Operation of Claiborne Enrichment Centre, Homer, Louisiana* (Washington, D.C., 1993), 3–108.

44. See U.S. Census Bureau, *1990 Census of Population General Population Characteristics-Louisiana* (Washington, D.C.: U.S. Government Printing Office, May 1992).

45. Nuclear Regulatory Commission, note 43 above, pages 4–38.

46. Citizens for a Better Environment, *Richmond at Risk* (San Francisco, Calif., 1992).

47. Bay Area Air Quality Management District, *General Chemical Incident of July 26, 1993* (San Francisco, Calif., 15 September 1993), 1.

48. R. Sanchez, "Health and Environmental Risks of the Maquiladora in Mexicali," *National Resources Journal 30* (Winter 1990): 163–86.

49. Center for Investigative Reporting, *Global Dumping Grounds: The International Traffic in Hazardous Waste* (Washington, D.C.: Seven Locks Press, 1989), 59.

50. Working Group on Canada-Mexico Free Trade, "Que Pasa? A Canada-Mexico 'Free' Trade Deal," *New Solutions: A Journal of Environmental and Occupational Health Policy 2* (1991): 10–25.

51. Bullard, 1983, note 2 above.

52. Bullard, 1987, note 2 above.

53. Bullard, 1983, 1987, and 1990, note 2 above. The unit of analysis for the Houston waste study was the neighborhood, not the census tract. The

concept of neighborhood predates census tract geography, which became available only in 1950. Neighborhood studies date back nearly a century. *Neighborhood* as used here is defined as "a social/spatial unit of social organization . . . larger than a household and smaller than a city." See A. Hunter, "Urban Neighborhoods: Its Analytical and Social Contexts," *Urban Affairs Quarterly 14* (1979): 270. The neighborhood is part of a city's geography, a place defined by specific physical boundaries and block groups. Similarly, the black neighborhood is a "highly diversified set of interrelated structures and aggregates of people who are held together by forces of white oppression and racism." See J. E. Blackwell, *The Black Community: Diversity and Unity* (New York: Harper & Row, 1985), xiii.

54. Bullard, 1983, 1987, and 1990, note 2 above.

55. Ibid.

56. Ibid.

57. U.S. Environmental Protection Agency, *Strategies and Framework for the Future: Final Report* (Washington, D.C., 1992), 12.

58. K. S. Shrader-Frechette, *Risk and Rationality: Philosophical Foundations for Populist Reform* (Berkeley, Calif.: University of California Press, 1992), 98.

59. U.S. Environmental Protection Agency, "Geographic Initiatives: Protecting What We Love," *Securing Our Legacy: An EPA Progress Report, 1989–1991* (Washington, D.C., 1992), 32.

60. Ibid.

61. U.S. Environmental Protection Agency, note 1 above, vol. 2, *Supporting Documents*, 60.

62. Ibid.

63. U.S. Environmental Protection Agency, *Toxic Release Inventory and Emission Reduction, 1987–1990, in the Lower Mississippi River Industrial Corridor* (Washington D.C., 1993), 25.

64. Bullard, 1990, note 2 above: C. Beasley, "Of Pollution and Poverty: Keeping Watch in Cancer Alley," *Buzzworm 2*, no. 4 (1990): 39–45; and S. Lewis, B. Keating, and D. Russell, *Inconclusive by Design: Waste, Fraud, and Abuse in Federal Environmental Health Research* (Boston, Mass.: National Toxics Campaign, 1992).

65. J. O'Byrne, "The Death of a Town," *Times Picayune*, 20 February 1991, A1.

66. Bullard, 1990, note 2 above; J. O'Byrne and M. Schleitstein, "Invisible Poisons," *Times Picayune*, 18 February 1991, A1; and Lewis, Keating, and Russell, note 64 above.

2

Environmental Justice: A National Priority

Clarice E. Gaylord
and Elizabeth Bell

Prior to 1990, environmental justice was not a priority at the U.S. Environmental Protection Agency (EPA) or any other federal agency or department. While actual accounts of different levels of environmental protection of underrepresented, underserved populations started appearing in the literature in the early 1970s, the EPA's position was that these were local issues requiring local intervention.[1] The general approach was that environmental policies, guidances, regulations, and laws developed around the "reference," average American were sufficient and protective of all people. Although there was some recognition of cultural population variances, for example, high pesticide exposure in farmworkers or high lead-paint exposure in poor African American children, these instances were viewed as deviations from the norm. The mentality that "one standard fits all" was widely accepted.

While EPA took this posture, there had been an abundance of evidence that people of color and low-income groups were subjected to a disproportionately large amount of pollution and environmental risks in their neighborhoods. Underrepresented residential areas were often adversely affected by unregulated growth, ineffective regulation of industrial toxins, and public policy decisions authorizing local land use that favored those communities with political and economic clout.[2] For instance, EPA had known for years that hazardous air pollution was primarily an urban phenomenon, where emission densities tended to be highest. A large proportion of African Americans and Hispanics, compared to whites, lived in air nonattainment areas for particulate matter, carbon monoxide, ozone, sulfur dioxide, and lead.[3] Health effects such as high asthma deaths, increased infant mortality, and high rates of all forms of cancer seem concentrated in these urban centers.[4]

But socioeconomic analyses were not given high priority by the young EPA of the seventies because of the need to establish the higher priority scientific expertise and regulatory posture of the agency. It was felt that more experienced agencies such as the U.S. Civil Rights Commission and other social agencies could deal more effectively with these types of problems.[5]

Native Americans—Unique Environmental Justice Problems

Tribal lands, like other impoverished areas, had been neglected in the nation's environmental protection efforts. Similarly, tribes, like other communities of color, struggled to find an equal voice in national decisions affecting their people and lands. But environmental justice for tribal communities and their lands had a unique twist.

Indian tribes are recognized in the Constitution and in opinions of the Supreme Court as unique entities with governments possessing attributes of sovereignty. Unfortunately, Indian sovereignty and the special rights it conveys in law have been largely ignored more than they have been honored. Having rights ignored was not new for people of color, but it had special frustrations for Native Americans who, after seeing their treaties broken, viewed their best hope for the future in the preservation of their homeland—and their right to govern that homeland.

For the first thirteen years of its existence, EPA devoted much of its energy to developing a national infrastructure of environmental programs in partnership with state governments. This was done despite tribal protests that state governments lacked authority over tribes and tribal lands and that the federal support of the states, without comparable support for tribes, was creating a power imbalance. Equally serious was the fact that the federal/state infrastructure left reservations and other tribal lands unprotected and vulnerable to many environmental threats such as middle-of-the-night dumping of toxic waste on Indian land. Nevertheless, EPA's attention was focused almost entirely on building relations with the states, and the tribal voice had little effect until 1984.

In 1984, EPA signed the Policy for the Administration of Environmental Programs on Indian Reservations. Adoption of this policy marked the beginning of a new era in which tribes were now recognized as appropriate governments to set and enforce environmental standards for tribal lands (including lands owned by non-Indians located within reservation boundaries).[6] This policy was universally hailed in Indian country as a good, even enlightened, beginning. As a practical matter, however, recognition of a formal policy (like earlier treaties and other laws) carries little real benefit for Indian people until Indian lands are protected and the 1984 policy is incorporated into the decisions of the agency's policies and the day-to-day conduct of the agency's business.

Today, ten years after adoption of the 1984 Indian policy, tribes have a high level of frustration. The EPA still has not established the tribal/federal infrastructure of regulatory programs needed to provide equal protection for tribal lands. The tribes judge EPA's performance in terms of the agency's progress in actually establishing programs to protect tribal environments and in providing resources to support them. Judged by this standard, EPA has established only a small percentage of the programs on reservations needed to provide equal protection.

The Rise of Environmental Justice At EPA

Environmental inequitable issues were formally brought to the attention of the EPA in 1990 by a group of social scientists, political activists, and biological investigators calling themselves the Michigan Coalition. They pressured the EPA, demanding that it focus more attention on the principles of environmental injustices.[7] William K. Reilly, the EPA administrator at the time, formed a work group to examine the agency's current and past practices and to determine whether the agency was negligent or insensitive to socioeconomic concerns as it developed and carried out it policies, rule making, enforcement, inspections, risk assessments, risk management, and risk communication. The work group's findings were reported in a two-volume report titled "Environmental Equity: Reducing Risk in All Communities" in June 1992.[8] In summary, the report found that

1. There are clear differences between racial groups in terms of disease and death rates; however, there is a general lack of data on environmental health effects by race and income. The notable exception is lead poisoning. A significantly higher percentage of Af-

rican American children, compared to white children, have unacceptably high levels of lead in their blood.

2. People of color and low-income populations experience higher than average exposures to selected air pollutants, hazardous waste facilities, contaminated fish, and farm pesticides in the workplace.

3. Data are not routinely collected on health risks posed by multiple industrial facilities, cumulative and synergistic effects, or multiple pathways of exposure.

4. American Indians are a unique ethnic group with a special relationship to the federal government and have distinct environmental problems. Tribes generally lack physical infrastructure, institutions, trained personnel, and resources necessary to protect their members.

As recommended by the work group, EPA created the Office of Environmental Equity (later changed to the Office of Environmental Justice) in November 1992 to coordinate the agency's efforts to develop and implement environmental justice initiatives. The office's responsibility was to serve as the point of contact for environmental justice outreach and educational activities, technical and financial assistance, and information dissemination. A separate senior executive committee, the Environmental Equity Cluster, was formed at the same time to develop the agency's national policies, guidances, and agenda for environmental justice. The office and the cluster worked in concert to frame the issues and develop broad directives.

While the EPA deliberated on whether to accept environmental injustice as a formal issue between 1990 and 1992, the movement gathered its strength and was fueled by grassroots organizations and community activists who viewed environmental injustices as a life and death struggle for the survival of their communities. These organizations held the First National People of Color Environmental Leadership Summit in Washington, D.C., in October 1991. More than 650 grassroots leaders adopted "Principles of Environmental Justice"—a platform calling for an end to the discriminatory poisoning of low-income communities and people of color world wide.[9]

The leaders of the environmental justice movement continued to hold the EPA accountable for its actions. These activists met four times with the EPA administrators (Reilly and then Carol Browner) and senior officials, constantly prodding for progress reports and requesting permission to review operating budget plans, procedures, guidances, policies, and agency reports. These same leaders worked on the Clinton Transition Team and were instrumental in drafting language for congressional legislation and the Executive Order on Environmental Justice signed by President Clinton on 11 February 1994.[10]

Promoting a National Environmental Justice Program

President Clinton's Executive Order 12898 established environmental justice as a national priority. The order, officially entitled "Federal Actions to Address Environmental Justice in Minority Populations and Low-Income Populations," focuses federal attention on the environmental and human health conditions in people of color and low-income populations with the goal of achieving equal environmental protection for all communities regardless of their race, income status, ethnicity, or culture. The order directs all federal agencies with a public health and environmental mission to make environmental justice an integral part of their missions; to develop strategies to ensure that federal programs, policies, and activities do not produce disproportionately high and adverse human effects on underrepresented communities; and to determine whether federal policies, regulations, or guidances adversely affect the poor or people of color. Agencies are also to ensure that states and other organizations receiving federal funding for environmental projects do not violate federal civil rights laws. Finally, federal officials must determine the extent to which environmental racism is a national problem.

One provision of Executive Order 12898 was the establishment of the Interagency Working Group on Environmental Justice with membership from the heads of agencies and departments like the Departments of Justice, Defense, Energy, Labor, Interior, Transportation, Agriculture, Housing and Urban Development, Commerce, Health and Human Services, and the EPA. The agencies are pooling resources and technical expertise to focus on a coordinated approach to address the factors that lead to environmental justice conditions. This collaboration and coordination is being concentrated in conducting expansive clinical studies in high-impact areas to determine if patterns of health effects can be determined by prolonged, disparate environmental exposures to toxins from different sources; interagency efforts to do targeted enforcement, inspections, and compliance monitoring in high-stress communities; combined projects to implement local community remediation, cleanup, and redevelopment efforts; collaborative efforts to enhance public participation and involvement in environmental decision making with public hearings, forums, and the formation of more citizen's advisory boards, and so on. The products of the interagency working group are still preliminary, but the cooperation of these agencies will go a long way toward advancing an environmental justice national program and keeping this issue as a national priority.

A major glaring problem in implementing an effective national program has been the absence of any specific legislation on environmental justice. Several bills were introduced on the congressional agenda between 1992 and 1994, but none were successful through the 103d Congress. Rep. John Lewis (D-GA) reintroduced H.R. 2105 cited as the Environmental Justice Act of 1993[11] (initially offered by then-senator Al Gore in 1992); Rep. John Conyers, Jr. (D-MI) introduced the Department of Environmental Protection Act [12] (also known as the EPA Elevation Act); and Rep. Cardiss Collins (D-IL) introduced H.R. 1924 called the Environmental Equal Rights Act of 1993.[13] Each of these proposed bills would have provided insight on the federal legislative agenda of the justice movement and provided opportunities for gauging the course of federal environmental justice directives.

The Environmental Justice Act of 1993 was designed "to establish a program to ensure nondiscriminatory compliance with environmental health and safety laws and to ensure equal protection of the public health." The bill included provisions for the identification and ranking of environmental high-impact areas, the reduction of toxic chemicals, and technical assistance grants for community groups. The Lewis bill also called for a moratorium on siting of facilities in high-impact areas and data collection on environmental health effects in impacted communities.

The Department of Environmental Protection Act of 1993 called for the elevation of EPA to cabinet status. Such high-level recognition of the EPA would clearly signify the commitment of the Clinton administration and Congress to environmental issues and would have enhanced EPA's ability to address environmental concerns more authoritatively. The proposal called for the creation of the Bureau of Environmental Statistics, the Office of Environmental Justice, and the Environmental Policy Commission. These three major divisions would have been required to compile and disseminate information concerning environmental conditions to address the disproportionate impact faced by people of color and low-income communities and to make recommendations for changes in management, organization, and priorities to the secretary.

The Environmental Equal Rights Act of 1993, an amendment to the Solid Waste Disposal Act, would have authorized petitions against the construction of specific waste facilities scheduled for low-income and people of color communities. The act would have granted "any citizen residing in a State in which a new facility for the management of solid or hazardous waste is proposed to be constructed in an environmentally disadvantaged community" the right to petition to prevent the issuance of an operating permit.

Unfortunately, all three bills along with most other environmental legislation introduced to the 103d Congress met with defeat. Some of the reasons for this tough environmental legislation resistance can be linked to risk-assessment requirements, unfunded mandates, cost benefit analysis, and industry's use of the Constitution's "takings" provisions. The science of risk assessment and analysis as currently being practiced has not been very helpful in proving that these communities are at risk. Previous risk assessments have been chemical specific and media specific and have not dealt with cumulative, synergistic effects of combined exposure. Thus risk analysis as it is currently being done has not been helpful in verifying specific risks to high-impact communities. Requiring environmental justice initiatives without authorizing specific funding to carry out these programs has led to charges that this effort is just another "unfunded mandate" by the government. The cost of initiating the provisions of environmental justice is being alleged to be prohibitive—the cost greatly outweighs any benefits to be gained. Restricting the development of new waste facilities or the expansion of existing ones via more stringent permitting or siting requirements is being viewed by industry and businesses as a "taking" of property without just compensation.

In lieu of federal legislation, several states have begun to address environmental justice concerns. Arkansas and Louisiana were the first to enact environmental justice laws. Virginia has passed a legislative resolution on environmental justice. California, Georgia, New York, North Carolina, and South Carolina have pending legislation to address inequities. Adopted and proposed laws include providing compensation to host communities, enhancing public notice and participation, improving risk assessment methodologies, creating state justice policy, and increasing public communication and information. In 1993, Texas created the Environmental Equity and Justice Taskforce, which was directed to investigate and identify factors contributing to inequitable environmental impacts and to recommend remedial and preventable actions to the Texas Natural Resource Conservation Commission.[14]

Environmental Justice and EPA

Although President Clinton's Executive Order made environmental justice a national priority for most federal agencies, EPA administrator Carol Browner made environmental justice an EPA priority when she assumed office in 1993. In an all-hands address, she stated that

Many people of color, low income and Native American communities have raised concerns that they suffer a disproportionate burden of health consequences due to the siting of industrial plants and waste dumps, and from exposure to pesticides or other toxic chemicals at home and on the job and that environmental programs do not adequately address these disproportionate exposures. . . . EPA is committed to address these concerns and is assuming a leadership role in environmental justice to enhance environmental quality for all residents of the United States. Incorporating environmental justice into "everyday" Agency activities and decisions will be a major undertaking. Fundamental reform will be needed in Agency operations.

With that she outlined a five-point strategy for agency action:[15]

1. Environmental justice must be integrated fully and consistently into the Agency's policies, programs and activities.

2. Additional research is needed to address human health and environmental risk to high risk populations, including the identification of multiple and cumulative exposures or synergistic effects.

3. Environmental data must be collected, analyzed and disseminated routinely. This is particularly true for data comparing environmental and human health risks to populations identified by national origin, income and race.

4. Compliance monitoring, inspections and enforcement actions must be targeted and have a multi-media focus.

5. There must be early involvement in the Agency's activities by all stakeholders and information on human health and the environment should be clear and readily accessible to all stakeholders.

To integrate environmental justice into EPA's policies, programs, and activities, the agency initiated a new internal infrastructure to work with a somewhat expanded Office of Environmental Justice. The structure established an executive steering committee comprised of the top management team from the media program offices (e.g., air, water, toxics, etc.) and the ten regional offices to provide agency leadership and direction on strategic planning to ensure that environmental justice is incorporated into agency operations. This committee has direct oversight of the agency's operating plans, budget needs, and research direction and yields tremendous influence on the overall commitment to environmental justice needs. The old environmental cluster was reconstituted as the Environmental Justice Policy Working Group to ensure that cross-media policy development and coordination occur at all levels. A third group called Environmental Justice Coordinators is responsible for education, training, and outreach efforts in all program and regional offices. This new structure establishes a clear commitment from senior management to integrate environmental justice issues into all programs and to move away from previously single-media orientation to a multimedia, holistic approach to protecting underserved communities.

Under the Browner administration, EPA has taken two important steps that may help turn the promise of the Indian policy into a reality. First, the Indian Office has been recently established to be headed by a Native American. This office will be responsible for coordinating establishment of the regulatory programs needed to provide equal protection for Indian lands. Second, the environmental justice movement has received unprecedented recognition and support by the Clinton administration and has generated a heightened awareness and willingness on the part of agency managers to listen to previously disenfranchised communities such as Native Americans. With a more focused tribal voice, in the form of the Indian Office, and a new willingness to listen, agency leadership may now act to establish much-needed regulatory programs for Indian lands.

In coordination with other federal agencies such as Health and Human Services, EPA is designing the environmental and human health research needed to support environmental justice programs. Studies are being conducted in urban and rural areas to identify risks to low-income communities and communities of color from aggregate exposures to toxic emissions. National human databases are being compiled and coordinated to address geographic and demographic analyses around environmental justice issues.

The EPA is investigating the use of currently available data systems to collect and analyze information that can support the needs of affected communities. Working with key outside organizations and other federal agencies, criteria are being developed to provide guidance on what to include in collecting information on demographic racial and national origin makeup of a community, income level, environmental health sensitivity, environmental exposures, past regulatory practices, and interactions with affected communities. Data issues, methodologies, analytic procedures, and other core issues are under development.

The EPA is giving prominent attention to environmental justice issues through compliance analysis and targeted data analysis of communities exposed to multiple environmental threats, enforcement initiatives, implementation of the nondiscrimination provisions of Title VI of the Civil Rights Act, and review and enforcement of other laws such as the National Environmental Policy Act. Specific activities will include an increase in the number of inspections and enforcement efforts in the most severely disadvantaged communities to protect their air, water, and land. The EPA is investigating the use of creative settlements for violations of federal environmental laws by targeting the use of supplemental environmental projects (SEPs) in these communities. The SEPs would allow violators to undertake projects that would provide greater long-term benefits to affected communities than would the payment of a penalty alone.

The EPA is enhancing its partnerships, outreach, training, and communications with all stakeholders including the affected communities, environmental organizations, nongovernment organizations, federal, state, tribal, and local governments, academic institutions, businesses, and industry. One way to reach stakeholders is through the new National Environmental Justice Advisory Council implemented in April 1994 to identify the needs of sensitive populations and to facilitate communication and outreach among affected stakeholders. The agency has formed partnerships with a number of community-based organizations and has provided financial assistance and outreach to people of color and low-income communities using more effective means of communication and education. One goal of EPA is to ensure that no segment of the population carry a disproportionate burden of pollution, especially not as a result of being uninformed of its rights and responsibilities under environmental laws. Program and regional offices have been devoting much effort to devising training programs, hosting conferences and workshops, providing user friendly, accessible materials, and building partnerships to focus on identifying environmental justice problems and determining possible solutions.

The EPA's ultimate goal is to ensure that all individuals and communities be treated equitably under environmental laws, policies, and regulations and that the benefits of environmental protection be shared by everyone.

Notes

This manuscript has not been subjected to review by the author's agency. The views expressed are solely those of the author and do not necessarily represent the views or policies of EPA.

1. Council on Environmental Quality, "Annual Report to Congress, 197:1" (Washington, D.C., 1971).

2. Robert D. Bullard, *Dumping in Dixie: Race, Class and Environmental Quality*, 2d ed. (Boulder, Colo.: Westview Press, 1994).

3. D. Wernette and L. Nieves, "Minorities and Air Pollution: A Prelim-

inary Geographic Analysis," presented at the Socio-economic Research Conference II, 27–28 June 1991.

4. National Center for Health Statistics (NCHS), "Health of Black and White Americans, 1985–87," Series 10. Data from the National Health Interview Survey, No. 171, U.S. Department of Health and Human Services, January 1990.

5. U.S. Commission on Civil Rights, Hearing held in Washington, D.C., "Testimony of William Ruckelshaus, Administrator of EPA," June 14–17, 1971.

6. U.S. Environmental Protection Agency, "Indian Policy" (Washington, D.C.: Office of Federal Activities), 1984.

7. Bunyan Bryant and Paul Mohai, *Race and the Incidence of Environmental Hazards* (Boulder, Colo: Westview Press, 1992).

8. U.S. Environmental Protection Agency, "Environmental Equity: Reducing Risk for All Communities," Vols. 1 and 2 (Washington, D.C.: June 1992).

9. United Church of Christ Commission for Racial Justice, "The First National People of Color Environmental Leadership Summit," New York, 1992.

10. Executive Order 12898, "Federal Actions to Address Environmental Justice in Minority Populations and Low-Income Populations," *Federal Register* 59, No. 32 (1994).

11. House of Representatives Report No. 2105, "Environmental Justice Act of 1993." 103d Congress, 1st Session, 1993.

12. House of Representatives Report No. 109, "Department of the Environment Act of 1993." 103d Congress, 1st Session, 1993.

13. House of Representatives Report No. 1924, "The Environmental Equal Rights Act of 1993, an Amendment to the Solid Waste Disposal Act." 103d Congress, 1st Session, 1993.

14. Center for Policy Alternatives, "Environmental Justice: Legislation in the States." Washington, D.C., 1994.

15. U.S. Environmental Protection Agency, "The New Generation of Environmental Protection: EPA's Five-Year Strategic Plan" (Washington, D.C.: Office of the Administrator, July 1994).

3

Living for the City: Urban United States and Environmental Justice

Bill Lawson

Living just enough, stop giving just enough for the City!

Stevie Wonder

Until recently, so-called classic environmentalists have given scant attention to the problems of the cities. Dale Jamieson notes this slight in 1984 and starts his insightful paper "The City Around Us" by stating, "It may seem odd to many people that a book devoted to environmental ethics includes an essay on the city. We often speak of the environment as if it is everywhere except where we live. The environment is Yellowstone, Estes Park, Cape Hatteras, and other vacation spots."[1] According to Jamieson, the environment in which most of us spend most of our time is the urban environment, and any deep understanding of our relationship to the environment cannot ignore this fact.[2]

Cities, Jamieson argues, are an important part of our American heritage and thus are worth preserving. His main point is that cities contain certain cultural landmarks that we should preserve. Jamieson gives an argument based on what he takes to be common wisdom why environmentalists should be concerned with preserving cities. Interestingly enough, Jamieson said nothing about the plight of poor people living in cities, what saving the urban landmarks would mean to them, or what viewing cities as landmarks would mean to urban residents.

While Jamieson was timely in his concerns, I want to raise what I take to be a concern for anyone working on the issue of environmental ethics. I contend that environmentalists have not given due consideration to negative attitudes about cities and how these attitudes

41

influence their environmental policies. I also want to contend that there are negative racial sentiments about black Americans. When negative attitudes about cities combine with certain racial attitudes, there is an adverse impact on the lives of the poor black people who live in cities. That is, if it is true that the overall conception of cities by most Americans is negative, environmentalists must consider what happens when those attitudes combine with negative views of racial groups who live there.

If these two attitudes do influence our conceptions of urban areas and African Americans, then theories of environmental justice, and indeed theories of justice overall, must take into account how theories of justice are applied.[3] There is now little disagreement that urban areas in the United States populated by racial minorities have been low on the environmental protection pecking order. Environmental pollution in large metropolitan areas has affected these areas adversely. Why is there more pollution in these areas? Though this question is complex, I want to suggest that negative conceptions of urban life and African Americans have to be factored into the answer.

Negative Views of United States Cities

From the earliest years of the American Republic, people have sought to expose the negative impact of cities not only on people, but also on democracy itself. While we have seen cities as centers of commercial activity, cities have also been seen as the enemy of virtue. Thomas Jefferson, for example, wrote: "I view great cities as pestilential to the morals, the health and the liberties of man."[4] Cities, according to Jefferson, were even a blockage to good government. He also commented:

> The mobs of great cities add just so much to the support of pure government, as sores do to the strength of the human body. It is the manner and spirit of a people which preserve a republic in vigour. A degeneracy in these is a canker which so eats to the heart of its laws and constitution.[5]

While Jefferson did not equate city life with any particular group, the French observer Alexis de Tocqueville (1805-1859) thought that American cities were already in crisis and pointed to the large number of blacks and European immigrants who lived there.

He wrote, in his classic *Democracy in America* published in 1835:

The lower ranks which inhabit these cities [Philadelphia and New York] constitute a rabble even more formidable than the populace of European towns. They consist of freed blacks in the first place, who are condemned by the laws and by public opinion to the hereditary state of misery and degradation. They also contain a multitude of Europeans who have been driven to the shores of the New World by their misfortunes or their conduct; and they bring to the United States all our greatest vices without any of those interests which counteract this baneful influence. As inhabitants of a country where they have no civil rights they are ready to turn all passions which agitate the community to their own advantage; thus, within the last few months serious riots have broken out in Philadelphia and New York.[6]

De Tocqueville went on to warn: "The size of certain American cities and especially . . . the nature of their population . . . [is] a real danger which threatens the future security of the democratic republics of the world."[7]

Cities, it seems, were hotbeds of crime, corruption, and moral decay. One would think that years later views of the cities and city life would have improved. This has not been the case.

In the early years of this century, cities became referred to as a wilderness. Life in cities was dangerous and untamed. Cities were populated by social predators. As Andrew Light notes in his discussion of the theme of urban wilderness, "the most famous attempt is surely Upton Sinclair's 1906 *The Jungle*, which documented the abuses of recent Eastern European immigrants in the meat packing industry." For this contribution, Sinclair may be thought of as in some respects the father of the urban wilderness theme.[8]

In recent times, however, both television and movies have shaped our conception of urban life and cities. Judith Martin, professor of urban studies at the University of Minnesota, notes how television shapes our conception of the city:

In the late 1950s and early 1960s, bus driver Ralph Cramden and sewer worker Ed Norton lived with their wives in their New York tenement; Ricky Ricardo, a Cuban bandleader, lived in a building where neighbors invade your private space at every opportunity. Both of these were high density/high intensity situations where laughter was a necessary antidote to inherent stress. Then there's the Ozzie Nelson family and the Anderson family whose father knew best, both properly ensconced in small city or suburban habitats. Lucy and Ricky, Alice and Ralph are funnier, but would you move into their apartments or choose them to be your neighbors?[9]

In the 1970s, she continues, we had different urban images:

> We had the hilarity of life in high-rise public housing on "Good Times"
> counterbalanced by the amusing reactionary Queens neighborhood of
> Archie Bunker. More recently, the darker urban verisimilitude of Stephen
> Bochco's "Blues" (Hill Street and NYPD) extended a cultural viewpoint
> already imprinted by decades of private eye/detective series. Such en-
> tertainment confirmed most Americans' notion that cities were/are threat-
> ening places filled with folks who are out to do you harm.[10]

I would add to this analysis movies like *Dirty Harry* and *Death Wish
1, 2, 3, 4,* and *5.* These movies and others of their genre have reinforced attitudes about urban life. We cannot minimize the impact of
popular culture on our views of cities and blacks. In the past five
years, films like *Menace II Society, Boyz in the Hood,* and *Strapped*
not only impact on views of urban life but also influence general attitudes about young African American males.

I do not think anyone can dispute that the general view of cities in
the United States has been bad. As I noted above from Jefferson to
the present, most Americans have viewed cities with disdain. Generally, social theorists have found cities alienating. Suggestions for overcoming urban alienation are found in the works of theorists like Louis
Wirth, Sigmund Freud, George Simmel, and Theodore Roszak. The
writings of these theorists push for extensive urban planning.[11]

Environmentalists might suggest that though we once viewed urban life in a negative manner, we do not view it so today. Look, for
example, at the large number of upper- and middle-class whites who
have returned to the cities.

While the movement of young affluent whites to urban centers like
San Francisco and Washington, D.C., have attracted attention, the
overall migration patterns have remained the same for the better part
of the twentieth century: as the poor enter the city, the more affluent
leave for the suburbs. In the past, more people migrated to the city
than from it; today more people are leaving the city than moving into
it. Those affluent whites who return to the cities often find what has
been called a "two cities phenomenon."[12] We now find in cities areas
that are marked off by the race and class of the inhabitants.[13]

Those whites who moved into the cities were thought to be moving into uncharted terrain. Consider for a moment the language used
to describe those persons who moved into the cities in the early 1970s.
The term used by many economists to describe them was "urban pio-
neers." A pioneer is one who travels uncharted (unexplored) terrain.
What does this language imply about the areas inhabited by blacks?
Cities are a form of wilderness. As Andrew Light notes, the metaphor

of "urban wilderness" carries with it certain impressions of the status of blacks who live in the cities.[14] Cities, no matter how bad they are, only become livable when whites are in the majority. Whites must move into urban areas and carve out a livable area. The white living area is seen as a haven in the wilds of the urban wilderness. Currently, many cities around the United States are trying to attract middle-class whites back to the cities.[15] These cities have been successful to varying degrees.

The movement of young suburban whites to the cities has most often helped certain sections of the city.[16] For example, a large Puerto Rican and African American community once populated the area around the art museum in Philadelphia. In the past ten years, there has been an influx of affluent whites. These whites have displaced the Puerto Ricans and African Americans in the process. The area is now a well-protected neighborhood well served by city services. We can contrast this area with sections of North Philadelphia populated by poor blacks. In certain sections of North Philadelphia, one gets the feeling of traveling through a Bantustan.[17]

Negative Attitudes and Blacks

Just as finding influential writers citing all the negatives of cities is not difficult, there is no shortage of negative tomes about black Americans. From the earliest days of the republic, white scholars have characterized persons of African descent in a negative light. One important aspect of this negative onslaught has been that persons of African descent are nearly always outside the moral circle. Because blacks were considered outside the moral sphere, whites felt they had the right to treat blacks in ways not permissible for treating whites. From the Dred Scot decision, to the Emancipation Proclamation, to Plessy, Brown, and the civil rights acts, blacks have had to fight negative social attitudes about their humanity and political status. We need not cite the various ways in which scholars and politicians have characterized blacks in a negative fashion.[18] Anyone with a scant knowledge of race relations in the United States can think of examples.[19]

Some might claim that blacks have not been viewed in a negative light, but such a claim is clearly unfounded and the characterization of young, black, urban males is a good example. Today, young black males are seen as the cause of most of society's ills. One would be hard pressed to find positive accounts of young urban blacks.[20] Even Rev. Jesse Jackson admitted being leery of young black males who approach him on the street.[21]

Cities as Sociological Entities

We can view cities in many ways. We will note only two here: cities as geographical entities and cities as sociological entities. Cities are of course located somewhere. They exist in a physical space. There are often physical attributes connected with cities. The views of San Francisco Bay and the New York skyline are only two examples. On the sociological side, cities have symbolic meaning. We often understand cities and our experience of them vicariously through the interpretations of symbolic representations.

Complex social interactions build upon these interpretations. In the United States, conceptions of race often color our interpretations of events, persons, and places. We often understand the meaning or nature of a place by reference to the race of the persons living there.

Michael Omi and Howard Winant discuss the connection between views of racial groups and our understanding of the social world.[22] They use the term *racialization* to signify the extension of racial meaning to a previously racially unclassified relationship, social practice, or group.[23] Cities, accordingly, should be to some extent race-neutral places, since members of various racial groups live in them.

However, racialization is the manner in which conceptions of racial standing enter into our understanding of social contexts and experiences. Thus, our understanding of certain social practices and experiences carries the various meanings associated with racial connotations at that time.[24]

The concept of race is an organizing principle of social relations that provides a description, a classification of racial phenomena in the United States, and also explains the continuity of these phenomena.[25]

In the United States, the category of "white" took on class meaning that early European immigrants readily bought into and supported. As chattel slavery evolved into the social fabric of America, Africans whose identity was Ibo, Yoruba, Fulani, and so on, were rendered black. Similarly, all Europeans were classified as white. These racial categories carried class distinctions. These racial distinctions were to transcend the ending of slavery and impact on the formation of the working class. Omi and Winant note that

> the very political organization of the working class was in important ways a racial project. The legacy of racial conflicts and arrangements shaped the definition of interests and in turn led to the consolidation of institutional patterns (e.g., segregated Unions, dual labor markets, exclusionary legislation) which perpetuated the color line within the working class.[26]

The Irish on the West Coast, for example, engaged in vicious anti-Chinese race-baiting and committed many pogrom-type assaults on Chinese in the course of consolidating the trade union movement in California.[27]

The development of both labor union policy and public policy involved notions of race. Labor unions refused to admit blacks as members and many skilled trades were nearly all white. In the public housing arena, politicians reinforced the notions of race as a defining factor in the life of a community. Politicians and realtors tightly enforced the laws and legal restrictions that prevented blacks from buying homes outside certain areas, producing the metropolitan color line. Such policies show the extent that the policy makers understand the negative meaning of race in our conceptions of both living and work space.

Thus, race is a fundamental organizing principle. The notion of race often works on two levels. It forms our conception of personal identity. Racial understanding informs the way we understand ourselves and interact with others, structuring our practical activity—in work and family. This understanding extends to our cultural practices. Historically, laws restricting interracial marriages can be seen as a way to structure racial standing in the United States, that is, to prevent the races from mixing.[28]

As citizens and as thinkers (or "philosophers") our attitudes are shaped by racial meanings and racial awareness.[29] For example, opinion poll after poll shows that blacks think O. J. Simpson is innocent, while most whites think that he is guilty.[30] Race also shapes our understanding of collective enterprises such as economic, political, and cultural structures. An example of how racial understanding can shape our understanding of a cultural artifact can be seen with the phrase "urban contemporary music." This type of music is readily identified with cities and blacks. Rap music and jazz are often cited as "black music."

Race also influences our understanding of how people fare in life. The current welfare debate has racial overtones. It is being claimed that poor black mothers are failing to do what is "socially correct" to provide for their children. These women, it is argued, have failed to play the social responsibility game as do poor white mothers. While there are more single white females with children on welfare, the face of poverty in the United States is a poor, inner-city, unmarried black woman with children.

In this regard, policy makers organize their understanding of certain events around their views about the race of the persons involved.

Our racial views influence our conceptions of events and carry public policy implications that are often not fully or readily appreciated. What happens when cities are seen as predominately populated by blacks? How do views about the behavior of blacks affect our views of cities? How are public policies formulated with racialized conceptions of cities? Have ethicists taken into account the impact of race on their theories of justice in general and of environmental justice in particular? These are important philosophical and public policy questions.

My claim is not that environmentalists are racists. Rather distributive justice requires treating equals equally and treating differently those who have relevant differences. If our culture influences us to perceive race and place negatively, these attributes will be considered relevant differences. These differences are factored into policy considerations. Environmentalists often fail to appreciate the manner in which conceptions of racial and spatial difference may hinder *just* urban environmental policies.

Racialization and the Cities

Claiming that a large number of blacks populate some American cities seems uncontroversial. The African American populations in Philadelphia, New York, Baltimore, Chicago, and Atlanta bear out this claim. However, because of the large black population these cities are often viewed as unsafe. These cities are seen as populated by welfare cheats and urban thugs, where many think that crime and mayhem are rampant.[31] Would you want to live in such a place? For most whites and many blacks the answer is no!

There is a tendency to view some cities as black enclaves. Suburbs are more likely than not viewed as white enclaves. In this way, urban and suburban space has become racialized. For many persons their understanding of the patterns of behavior associated with a racial group is connected with the space, giving meaning to the differences in lifestyles and standards of living based on a racial criterion.[32]

Racialization and Environmental Justice

As Peter Wenz correctly notes, environmental justice features those concerns within the environmental movement directed toward achieving equity and a fair sharing of environmental burdens and benefits.[33] Environmental burdens would include exposure to hazardous materi-

als and toxic wastes, pollution, health hazards, and resource depletion. Environmental benefits would include, but not be limited to, a
safe living space, a safe workplace, clean water and air, and the political power to influence environmental decisions.

When cities are seen as black homelands, urban residents claim that
policy makers minimize the impact of dumping and other hazardous
forms of pollution. Charles Lee, writing in the *Earth Island Journal,*
notes "People of color live in communities not only targeted for the
disposal of environmental toxins and hazardous waste but in fact live
in fully disposable communities to be thrown away when the population they hold have outlived their usefulness."[34]

Obviously we do not store waste in areas where there are people
like us; in this case white upper- and middle-class people are the people whom environmentalists must protect. Dumping waste in white
neighborhoods would not be the moral thing to do. Environmentalists,
it is claimed, often do not give the same moral weight to dumping
waste in poor black urban areas.

People sometimes ask the question: "Why should we care what happens to cities?" The blacks have taken them over. The main goal for
many whites has been to keep blacks out of white space. Justice has
come to mean protecting white space and not hurting white people.
This attitude is in some sense the colonial model of urban planning.
Why not put waste dumps in poor black neighborhoods? We are not
hurting anyone by dumping here. If we (the colonialists) put housing
and parks in these native neighborhoods, they will only destroy them.
The natives are different, morally and physically.

When we identify a group negatively, its members are unlike us
and often not deserving of the same treatment or respect. Accordingly, racial and spatial difference marks important differences that must
be given weight in our moral deliberations. That is, we treat all equals
the same unless there are some relevant differences that would warrant different treatment. Being black, poor, and living in the city can
seem, in the mind of many persons, a relevant difference for disparate treatment.

Environmentalists have a natural conception of pollution as a negative norm. If a place is thought to be already polluted by racial iden-
tifiers, we need to contain the pollution by keeping it in that area. If
the environment of blacks is negative, it does not seem likely that
their environmental interests will be given full consideration. Persons
in power will continue to consider the burden of environmental pol-
ices using a cost/benefit analysis. Greater weight will be given to those
policies that hurt whites the least. Because whites are wealthier, hurting them is usually a greater financial burden.

Environmentalists, in trying to do what is best for all, will have a slanted view of all, if they have not examined and considered their views about race and space in environmental policy. To this end the places where blacks live must be seen as places to protect environmentally, and blacks as persons must have a right to share in the benefits of environmental policies without undue burdens.

For some persons race-based policies connect the environmental justice movement to social justice. As Charles Lee notes, "Environmental issues afford us the opportunity to address many of the critical issues of the decade, including unemployment, community and urban development, energy and defense policy, resource exploitation, public health, and self determination."[35]

Environmental Justice and Race

While blacks often view the rush to dump as a continuation of the social injustices of the past, environmentalists want it known that environmentalism is compatible with social justice and by its very nature must include the cities. I agree that environmentalism is compatible with social justice. We should remember, however, that the claim is not that environmentalism is incompatible with social justice. What I am claiming is that environmentalists often fail to appreciate the manner in which racial categories impinge on their understanding of space. Do environmentalists connect any negative attributes associated with the group to the space? Clearly for many Americans, some cities are black homelands and cities as sources of pollution may reinforce negative images of blacks, for example, "Filthydelphia."[36]

Finally, it might be that liberal theories of distributive justice cannot adequately address the problem of racism in the distribution of social goods. Iris Young notes there is often a failure to appreciate that policies of distribution have a historical context and that this history often shapes views about who gets what and why.[37] Ideas of distributive justice cannot be separated from the institutional context that helps frame them.

People who write about justice in the distributive paradigm claim to be blocking out all the irrelevant differences that would cause a maldistribution of goods and benefits. On a theoretical level this claim works well, yet if my contentions about race and place are correct, attitudes about racialized space have to be addressed. We know that even behind the "veil of ignorance" persons must consider where they will be living. These persons will be thinking of living somewhere. How do these persons conceive of this space? It is a city or suburb? What is life like in this space?

Clearly, we have viewed racialized black space as a negative living habitat. This raises questions about the notion of the common good.

Some Final Thoughts

The notion of environmental justice is about place. Many environmentalists have a romanticized vision of place, a heightened concern for animals, and yet a seemingly perverse disdain for certain humans and their habitat. Environmentalism has been narrow concerning space. Many people have thought, until very recently, that the greatest concern of environmentalists was for those places with much water and trees. Environmentalists view this space as the wilderness that has to be protected. Urban areas have to be contained and/or the "urban wilderness" renewed.

Most environmentalists do not perceive themselves as having negative racial attitudes. These environmentalists think that their interests align with blacks around the issue of what is best for the overall environment. Many environmentalists are concerned with local issues, for example, pollution in the Delaware River, and so on. The stock phrase is "Act locally, think globally." Nevertheless, it must be admitted that few people can think globally. So far, the only truly "global" issues, that is, human induced influences that could affect the entire globe, are climate change and ozone depletion. It is very uncertain if climate change, or global warming, is occurring. All other environmental issues are local. Most environmental issues are local, and local interest and bias influence policy decisions. When environmental issues are local, they often do not allow for the interests of blacks.

Is the failure to consider the interests of poor urban blacks just an example of benign neglect? Is this neglect vicious? Clearly persons who are concerned with both the environment and social justice must realize that an ad hoc urban policy will not adequately address the problem of cities, and will consequently hurt the goals of the environmental movement. That is, if environmentalists are truly concerned with protecting urban resources, then protecting and respecting the places where poor people live must be a part of their environmental mandate. It is in this way urban areas can prosper. Thus environmentalists must address the question of what urban living means and what cities mean in the environmental movement.

Environmentalists cannot have the position that cities are sometimes a pleasant place to visit but they would not want to live there and in fact think that no one should live in cities. There is also a perception that many in the classical environmental movement think that urban residents, particularly blacks, deserve their plight. If African Americans were concerned about their welfare, they would not live in the city. This view is, of course, incompatible with the environmentalist's claims of concern for social justice and environmental protection, because environmentalists do not want cities dismantled and urban residents scattered into the pristine wilderness.

Environmentalists have often claimed that urban residents have not taken steps to ensure that they have protected their living space. This view assumes that it is the responsibility of each group to protect its space and that failure to protect one's space is one's own fault. This view takes social responsibility off the government and puts the weight solely on those groups that are usually unable to muster local or national support for their environmental interests. It also places the weight for urban environmental programs on the residents of urban America. If environmentalists take either of these positions, it signals a break between environmental issues and social concerns of justice.

Anyone concerned with the environment has a personal stake in the city. Cities are home to millions of United States residents and as such deserve the interest of those persons concerned with the environment. Many of these urban residents are pushing for a balance between their social justice interests and environmental interests. If the environmental movement is to succeed, it has to take the social justice interests of urban residents to heart. Social and political justice is a necessary condition for environmental justice. Yet, when we conceive of a space racially, attitudes about race may end up overriding theories of justice and fair social practice.[38] Environmentalists must be involved in urban planning with those persons most affected by urban pollution, poor persons of color. To paraphrase Karen Warren, "Any environmental ethic must be an urban ethic."[39]

Notes

1. Dale Jamieson, "The City around Us," in *Earthbound*, ed. by Tom Regan (Philadelphia: Temple University Press, 1984), 30.
2. Ibid.

3. David Goldberg, "'Polluting the Body Politic': Race and Urban Location," *Racist Culture* (Oxford: Blackwell, 1993), 185–205.

4. Thomas Jefferson, Letter to Benjamin Rush, *Works of Thomas Jefferson*, vol. 4, ed. P. Ford (New York: G. P. Putnam's, 1905), 146–47.

5. Thomas Jefferson, *Notes on the State of Virginia*, 1785 (Chapel Hill, N.C.: Published for the Institute of Early American History and Culture, Williamsburg, Virginia, by the University of North Carolina Press, 1955), 158.

6. Alexis de Tocqueville, *Democracy in America*, vol. 1, trans. P. Bradley (New York: Alfred A. Knopf, 1945), 289–90.

7. Ibid.

8. Andrew Light, "Urban Wilderness" in *Wild Ideas*, ed. by David Rothenberg (Minneapolis: University of Minn. Press, 1995).

9. Judith Martin, "A Nice Place to Visit, but . . . Two Centuries of American Ambivalence about Cities," *Utne Reader* (September/October 1994): 77–78.

10. Ibid., 77–78.

11. Michael P. Smith, *The City and Social Theory* (New York: St. Martin's Press, 1979).

12. Bryand D. Jones, *Governing Urban America* (Boston: Little, Brown, 1983), 82.

13. Alan Finder, "Majority in New York Poll Finds Quality of Life in City Is Eroding," *New York Times* vol. 143 (8 October 1993): A1, A18.

14. Light, 15.

15. Consider the following plea from the Twin Cities:

> Imagine a place to live in the Twin Cities so special that people move there from all over the country; a neighborhood in the heart of St. Paul that contains some of the area's most interesting and historic buildings; a beautiful, people-friendly park; a broad plaza and interesting byways; a smorgasbord of unique stores, theaters, art galleries, coffee shops, churches, restaurants, and entertainment choices; and active and stimulating arts, and cultural life; and friendly tree-lined streets that seem to have been made for walking, talking and relaxing.
>
> That place is Lowertown, the nation's first, and most successful, "urban village."
>
> Simultaneously charming and sophisticated, it is no wonder that Lowertown has become the Twin Cities' fastest growing neighborhood, combining big-city style and energy with the charm and friendliness of everyone's home town. (Lifestyles section, *Sun Country Airlines* [July/August 1994]: 34).

16. David Lampe, "The Role of Gentrification in Central City Revitalization," *National Civic Review* 82, no. 4 (Fall 1993): 363.

17. Years ago, when Kenneth Gibson was mayor, there was a sign on a wall as one entered Newark, New Jersey, stating, "Welcome to Gibsonwanna, a Dying Bantustan."

18. Tom W. Smith, *Ethnic Images*, GSS Topical Report No. 19 (National Opinion Research Center, University of Chicago, 1990), 8; Midge Decter,

"Looting and Liberal Racism," *Commentary* 64 (1977): 51; and Ronnie Dugger, *On Reagan, The Man and His Presidency* (New York: McGraw-Hill, 1983), 200–201.

19. George Frederickson, *The Black Image in the White Mind* (New York: Harper and Row, 1971).

20. See, for example, Michael Greenberg and Dona Schneider, "Violence in American Cities: Young Black Males Is the Answer, but What Is the Question?," *Social Science and Medicine* 39, no. 2 (15 July 1994): 179; and Kobena Mercer, "Fear of a Black Penis (White Male's Perception of Black Males)," *Artform* 32, no. 8 (April 1994): 80.

21. Bob Herbert, "Blacks Killing Blacks (Jesse Jackson Leading National Campaign against Violent Behavior by Young African Americans)," *New York Times* vol. 143 (20 October 1993): 15.

22. Michael Omi and Howard Winant, *Racial Formation in the United States* (New York: Routledge, 1986), 64.

23. Omi and Winant, 64.

24. Omi and Winant, 64.

25. Omi and Winant, 68.

26. Omi and Winant, 65.

27. Omi and Winant, 65.

28. See, for example, James Kenneth Lay, "Sexual Racism: A Legacy of Slavery," *National Black Law Journal* 13, no. 1–2 (Spring 1993): 165–83; and Ellis Cose, "Caught between Two Worlds: Why Simpson Can't Overcome the Barrier of Race," *Newsweek* 124 (11 July 1993): 28.

29. Omi and Winant, 67.

30. Andrew Blum, "Poll: More Lawyers See O. J. Walking: 70 Percent Now Say Simpson Will Go Free. Most Say Race Is a Factor," *National Law Journal* 17, no. 26 (27 February 1995): 1.

31. Joseph Sullivan, "Fearful Urban Neighbors Tell Bradley about Crime; Mugging Draws Senator to a Living Room," *New York Times* 143 (19 February 1994): 24L.

32. Howard McGary, "The Black Underclass and the Question of Values," in *The Underclass Question*, ed. by Bill E. Lawson (Philadelphia: Temple University Press, 1992).

33. Peter S. Wenz, *Environmental Justice* (Albany: State University of New York Press, 1988).

34. Charles Lee, "Urban Environmental Justice," *Earth Island Journal* (Spring 1993): 41.

35. Lee, 40.

36. I learned the term *Filthydelphia* from my colleague Nancy McCagney, who is involved with local environmental groups.

37. Iris Young, *Justice and the Politics of Difference* (Princeton: Princeton University Press, 1990).

38. While I have focused on views of the cities and race, environmentalist Robert D. Bullard writes that wherever blacks or other persons of color live, there is a flagrant disregard for the effects of environmental pollution in their neighborhoods. There is ample evidence to suggest a correlation between

race and where pollutants are dumped or stored. For example, the 1983 GAO study found a strong relationship between the location of off-site hazardous waste landfills and the race and socioeconomic status of the surrounding communities. The study identified four off-site hazardous waste landfills in eight states (Alabama, Florida, Georgia, Kentucky, Mississippi, North Carolina, South Carolina, and Tennessee) that constitute the EPA's Region IV.

African Americans made up the majority of the population in three of the four communities where off-site hazardous waste landfills were located. In 1983, African Americans were clearly overrepresented in communities with waste sites, since they made up only about one-fifth of the region's population, yet African American communities contained three-fourths of the off-site landfills. These ecological imbalances had not been reversed a decade later. In 1992, African Americans constituted about one-fifth of the population of Region IV. However, the two operating off-site hazardous waste landfills in the region were located in zip code regions where African Americans made up the majority of the population. See, for example, Benjamin A. Goldman, *The Truth about Where You Live: An Atlas for Action on Toxins and Mortality* (New York: Random House, 1991).

39. I want to thank Jim Anderson, Peter Wenz, Laura Westra, Bernard Boxhill, Laurence Kalkstein, Nancy McCagney, William Lance Lawson, and the Geography Department at the University of Delaware for their comments on this topic.

4

Just Garbage

Peter S. Wenz

Environmental racism is evident in practices that expose racial minorities in the United States, and people of color around the world, to disproportionate shares of environmental hazards.[1] These include toxic chemicals in factories, toxic herbicides and pesticides in agriculture, radiation from uranium mining, lead from paint on older buildings, toxic wastes illegally dumped, and toxic wastes legally stored. In this chapter, which concentrates on issues of toxic waste, both illegally dumped and legally stored, I will examine the justness of current practices as well as the arguments commonly given in their defense. I will then propose an alternative practice that is consistent with prevailing principles of justice.

A Defense of Current Practices

Defenders often claim that because economic, not racial, considerations account for disproportionate impacts on nonwhites, current practices are neither racist nor morally objectionable. Their reasoning recalls the Doctrine of Double Effect. According to that doctrine, an effect whose production is usually blameworthy becomes blameless when it is incidental to, although predictably conjoined with, the production of another effect whose production is morally justified. The classic case concerns a pregnant woman with uterine cancer. A common, acceptable treatment for uterine cancer is hysterectomy. This will predictably end the pregnancy, as would an abortion. However, Roman Catholic scholars who usually consider abortion blameworthy consider it blameless in this context because it is merely incidental to hysterectomy, which is morally justified to treat uterine cancer. The hysterectomy would be performed in the absence of pregnancy, so the abortion effect is produced neither as an end-in-itself, nor as a means to reach the desired end, which is the cure of cancer.

Defenders of practices that disproportionately disadvantage non-whites seem to claim, in keeping with the Doctrine of Double Effect, that racial effects are blameless because they are sought neither as ends-in-themselves nor as means to reach a desired goal. They are merely predictable side effects of economic and political practices that disproportionately expose poor people to toxic substances. The argument is that burial of toxic wastes, and other locally undesirable land uses (LULUs), lower property values. People who can afford to move elsewhere do so. They are replaced by buyers (or renters) who are predominantly poor and cannot afford housing in more desirable areas. Law professor Vicki Been puts it this way: "As long as the market allows the existing distribution of wealth to allocate goods and services, it would be surprising indeed if, over the long run, LULUs did not impose a disproportionate burden upon the poor." People of color are disproportionately burdened due primarily to poverty, not racism.[2] This defense against charges of racism is important in the American context because racial discrimination is illegal in the United States in circumstances where economic discrimination is permitted.[3] Thus, legal remedies to disproportionate exposure of nonwhites to toxic wastes are available if racism is the cause, but not if people of color are exposed merely because they are poor.

There is strong evidence against claims of racial neutrality. Professor Been acknowledges that even if there is no racism in the process of siting LULUs, racism plays at least some part in the disproportionate exposure of African Americans to them. She cites evidence that "racial discrimination in the sale and rental of housing relegates people of color (especially African Americans) to the least desirable neighborhoods, regardless of their income level."[4]

Without acknowledging for a moment, then, that racism plays no part in the disproportionate exposure of nonwhites to toxic waste, I will ignore this issue to display a weakness in the argument that justice is served when economic discrimination alone is influential. I claim that even if the only discrimination is economic, justice requires redress and significant alteration of current practices. Recourse to the Doctrine of Double Effect presupposes that the primary effect, with which a second effect is incidentally conjoined, is morally justifiable. In the classic case, abortion is justified only because hysterectomy is justified as treatment for uterine cancer. I argue that disproportionate impacts on poor people violate principles of distributive justice, and so are not morally justifiable in the first place. Thus, current practices disproportionately exposing nonwhites to toxic substances are not justifiable even if incidental to the exposure of poor people.

Alternate practices that comply with acceptable principles of distributive justice are suggested below. They would largely solve problems of environmental racism (disproportionate impacts on nonwhites) while ameliorating the injustice of disproportionately exposing poor people to toxic hazards. They would also discourage production of toxic substances, thereby reducing humanity's negative impact on the environment.

The Principle of Commensurate Burdens and Benefit

We usually assume that, other things being equal, those who derive benefits should sustain commensurate burdens. We typically associate the burden of work with the benefit of receiving money, and the burdens of monetary payment and tort liability with the benefits of ownership.

There are many exceptions. For example, people can inherit money without working, and be given ownership without purchase. Another exception, which dissociates the benefit of ownership from the burden of tort liability, is the use of tax money to protect the public from hazards associated with private property, as in Superfund legislation. Again, the benefit of money is dissociated from the burden of work when governments support people who are unemployed.

The fact that these exceptions require justification, however, indicates an abiding assumption that people who derive benefits should shoulder commensurate burdens. The ability to inherit without work is justified as a benefit owed to those who wish to bequeath their wealth (which someone in the line of inheritance is assumed to have shouldered burdens to acquire). The same reasoning applies to gifts.

Using tax money (public money) to protect the public from dangerous private property is justified as encouraging private industry and commerce, which are supposed to increase public wealth. The system also protects victims in case private owners become bankrupt as, for example, in Times Beach, Missouri, where the government bought homes made worthless due to dioxin pollution. The company responsible for the pollution was bankrupt.

Tax money is used to help people who are out of work to help them find a job, improve their credentials, or feed their children. This promotes economic growth and equal opportunity. These exceptions prove the rule by the fact that justification for any deviation from the commensuration of benefits and burdens is considered necessary.

Further indication of an abiding belief that benefits and burdens should be commensurate is grumbling that, for example, many professional athletes and corporate executives are overpaid. Although the athletes and executives shoulder the burden of work, the complaint is that their benefits are disproportionate to their burdens. People on welfare are sometimes criticized for receiving even modest amounts of taxpayer money without shouldering the burdens of work, hence recurrent calls for "welfare reform." Even though these calls are often justified as means to reducing government budget deficits, the moral issue is more basic than the economic. Welfare expenditures are minor compared to other programs, and alternatives that require poor people to work are often more expensive than welfare as we know it.

The principle of commensuration between benefits and burdens is not the only moral principle governing distributive justice, and may not be the most important, but it is basic. Practices can be justified by showing them to conform, all things considered, to this principle. Thus, there is no move to "reform" the receipt of moderate pay for ordinary work, because it exemplifies the principle. On the other hand, practices that do not conform are liable to attack and require alternate justification, as we have seen in the cases of inheritance, gifts, Superfund legislation, and welfare.

Applying the principle of commensuration between burdens and benefits to the issue at hand yields the following: In the absence of countervailing considerations, the burdens of ill health associated with toxic hazards should be related to benefits derived from processes and products that create these hazards.

Toxic Hazards and Consumerism

In order to assess, in light of the principle of commensuration between benefits and burdens, the justice of current distributions of toxic hazards, the benefits of their generation must be considered. Toxic wastes result from many manufacturing processes, including those for a host of common items and materials, such as paint, solvents, plastics, and most petrochemical-based materials. These materials surround us in the paint on our houses, in our refrigerator containers, in our clothing, in our plumbing, in our garbage pails, and elsewhere.

Toxins are released into the environment in greater quantities now than ever before because we now have a consumer-oriented society where the acquisition, use, and disposal of individually owned items is greatly desired. We associate the numerical dollar value of the items at our disposal with our "standard of living," and assume that a higher standard is conducive to, if not identical with, a better life. So toxic wastes needing disposal are produced as by-products of the general pursuit of what our society defines as valuable, that is, the consumption of material goods.

Our economy requires increasing consumer demand to keep people working (to produce what is demanded). This is why there is concern each Christmas season, for example, that shoppers may not buy enough. If demand is insufficient, people may be put out of work. Demand must increase, not merely hold steady, because commercial competition improves labor efficiency in manufacture (and now in the service sector as well), so fewer workers can produce desired items. More items must be desired to forestall labor efficiency-induced unemployment, which is grave in a society where people depend primarily on wages to secure life's necessities.

Demand is kept high largely by convincing people that their lives require improvement, which consumer purchases will effect. When improvements are seen as needed, not merely desired, people purchase more readily. So our culture encourages economic expansion by blurring the distinction between wants and needs.

One way the distinction is blurred is through promotion of worry. If one feels insecure without the desired item or service, and so worries about life without it, then its provision is easily seen as a need. Commercials, and other shapers of social expectations, keep people worried by adjusting downward toward the trivial what people are expected to worry about. People worry about the provision of food, clothing, and housing without much inducement. When these basic needs are satisfied, however, attention shifts to indoor plumbing, for example, then to stylish indoor plumbing. The process continues with needs for a second or third bathroom, a kitchen disposal, and a refrigerator attached to the plumbing so that ice is made automatically in the freezer, and cold water can be obtained without even opening the refrigerator door. The same kind of progression results in cars with CD players, cellular phones, and automatic readouts of average fuel consumption per mile.

Abraham Maslow was not accurately describing people in our society when he claimed that after physiological, safety, love, and (self-) esteem needs are met, people work toward self-actualization, becoming increasingly their own unique selves by fully developing their talents. Maslow's Hierarchy of Needs describes people in our society less than Wenz's Lowerarchy of Worry. When one source of worry is put to rest by an appropriate purchase, some matter less inherently or obviously worrisome takes its place as the focus of concern. Such worry-substitution must be amenable to indefinite repetition in order to motivate purchases needed to keep the economy growing without inherent limit. If commercial society is supported by consumer demand, it is worry all the way down. Toxic wastes are produced in this context.

People tend to worry about ill health and early death without much inducement. These concerns are heightened in a society dependent upon the production of worry, so expenditure on health care consumes an increasing percentage of the gross domestic product. As knowledge of health impairment due to toxic substances increases, people are decreasingly tolerant of risks associated with their proximity. Thus, the same mindset of worry that elicits production that generates toxic wastes, exacerbates reaction to their proximity. The result is a desire for their placement elsewhere, hence the NIMBY syndrome—Not In My Back Yard. On this account, NIMBYism is not aberrantly selfish behavior, but integral to the cultural value system required for great volumes of toxic waste to be generated in the first place.

Combined with the principle of Commensurate Burdens and Benefits, that value system indicates who should suffer the burden of proximity to toxic wastes. Other things being equal, those who benefit most from the production of waste should shoulder the greatest share of burdens associated with its disposal. In our society, consumption of goods is valued highly and constitutes the principal benefit associated with the generation of toxic wastes. Such consumption is generally correlated with income and wealth. So other things being equal, justice requires that people's proximity to toxic wastes be related positively to their income and wealth. This is exactly opposite to the predominant tendency in our society, where poor people are more proximate to toxic wastes dumped illegally and stored legally.

Rejected Theories of Justice

Proponents of some theories of distributive justice may claim that current practices are justified. In this section I will explore such claims.

A widely held view of justice is that all people deserve to have their interests given equal weight. John Rawls's popular thought experiment in which people choose principles of justice while ignorant of their personal identities dramatizes the importance of equal consideration of interests. Even selfish people behind the "veil of ignorance" in Rawls's "original position" would choose to accord equal consideration to everyone's interests because, they reason, they may themselves be the victims of any inequality. Equal consideration is a basic moral premise lacking serious challenge in our culture, so it is presupposed in what follows. Disagreement centers on application of the principle.

Libertarianism

Libertarians claim that each individual has an equal right to be free of interference from other people. All burdens imposed by other people are unjustified unless part of, or consequent upon, agreement by the party being burdened. So no individual who has not consented should be burdened by burial of toxic wastes (or the emission of air pollutants, or the use of agricultural pesticides, etc.) that may increase risks of disease, disablement, or death. Discussing the effects of air pollution, libertarian Murray Rothbard writes, "The remedy is simply to enjoin anyone from injecting pollutants into the air, and thereby invading the rights of persons and property. Period."[5] Libertarians John Hospers and Tibor R. Machan seem to endorse Rothbard's position.[6]

The problem is that implementation of this theory is impractical and unjust in the context of our civilization. Industrial life as we know it inevitably includes production of pollutants and toxic substances that threaten human life and health. It is impractical to secure the agreement of every individual to the placement, whether on land, in the air, or in water, of every chemical that may adversely affect the life or health of the individuals in question. After being duly informed of the hazard, someone potentially affected is bound to object, making the placement illegitimate by libertarian criteria.

In effect, libertarians give veto power to each individual over the continuation of industrial society. This seems a poor way to accord equal consideration to everyone's interests because the interest in physical safety of any one individual is allowed to override all other interests of all other individuals in the continuation of modern life. Whether or not such life is worth pursuing, it seems unjust to put the decision for everyone in the hands of any one person.

Utilitarianism

Utilitarians consider the interests of all individuals equally, and advocate pursuing courses of action that promise to produce results containing the greatest (net) sum of good. However, irrespective of how "good" is defined, problems with utilitarian accounts of justice are many and notorious.

Utilitarianism suffers in part because its direct interest is exclusively in the sum total of good, and in the future. Since the sum of good is all that counts in utilitarianism, there is no guarantee that the good of some will not be sacrificed for the greater good of others. Famous people could receive (justifiably according to utilitarians) particularly harsh sentences for criminal activity to effect general deterrence. Even when fame results from honest pursuits, a famous felon's sentence is likely to attract more attention than sentences in other cases of similar criminal activity. Because potential criminals are more likely to respond to sentences in such cases, harsh punishment is justified for utilitarian reasons on grounds that are unrelated to the crime.

Utilitarianism suffers in cases like this not only from its exclusive attention to the sum total of good, but also from its exclusive preoccupation with future consequences, which makes the relevance of past conduct indirect. This affects not only retribution, but also reciprocity and gratitude, which utilitarians endorse only to produce the greatest sum of future benefits. The direct relevance of past agreements and benefits, which common sense assumes, disappears in utilitarianism. So does direct application of the principle of Commensurate Burdens and Benefits.

The merits of the utilitarian rejection of common sense morality need not be assessed, however, because utilitarianism seems impossible to put into practice. Utilitarian support for any particular conclusion is undermined by the inability of anyone actually to perform the kinds of calculations that utilitarians profess to use. Whether the good is identified with happiness or preference-satisfaction, the two leading contenders at the moment, utilitarians announce the conclusions of their calculations without ever being able to show the calculation itself.

When I was in school, math teachers suspected that students who could never show their work were copying answers from other students. I suspect similarly that utilitarians, whose "calculations" often support conclusions that others reach by recourse to principles of gratitude, retributive justice, commensuration between burdens and benefits, and so forth, reach conclusions on grounds of intuitions influenced predominantly by these very principles.

Utilitarians may claim that, contrary to superficial appearances, these principles are themselves supported by utilitarian calculations. But, again, no one has produced a relevant calculation. Some principles seem *prima facie* opposed to utilitarianism, such as the one prescribing special solicitude of parents for their own children. It would seem that in cold climates more good would be produced if people bought winter coats for needy children, instead of special dress coats and ski attire for their own children. But utilitarians defend the principle of special parental concern. They declare this principle consistent with utilitarianism by appeal to entirely untested, unsubstantiated assumptions about counterfactuals. It is a kind of "Just So" story that explains how good is maximized by adherence to current standards. There is no calculation at all.

Another indication that utilitarians cannot perform the calculations they profess to rely upon concerns principles whose worth is in genuine dispute. Utilitarians offer no calculations that help to settle the matter. For example, many people wonder today whether or not patriotism is a worthy moral principle. Detailed utilitarian calculations play no part in the discussion.

These are some of the reasons why utilitarianism provides no help to those deciding whether or not disproportionate exposure of poor people to toxic wastes is just.

Free Market Approach

Toxic wastes, a burden, could be placed where residents accept them in return for monetary payment, a benefit. Since market transactions often satisfactorily commensurate burdens and benefits, this approach may seem to honor the principle of commensuration between burdens and benefits.

Unlike many market transactions, however, whole communities, acting as corporate bodies, would have to contract with those seeking to bury wastes. Otherwise, any single individual in the community could veto the transaction, resulting in the impasse attending libertarian approaches.[7] Communities could receive money to improve such public facilities as schools, parks, and hospitals, in addition to obtaining tax revenues and jobs that result ordinarily from business expansion.

The major problem with this free market approach is that it fails to accord equal consideration to everyone's interests. Where basic or vital goods and services are at issue, we usually think equal consideration of interests requires ameliorating inequalities of distribution that markets tend to produce. For example, one reason, although not the only reason, for public education is to provide every child with the basic intellectual tools necessary for success in our society. A purely free market approach, by contrast, would result in excellent education for children of wealthy parents and little or no education for children of the nation's poorest residents. Opportunities for children of poor parents would be so inferior that we would say the children's interests had not been given equal consideration.

The reasoning is similar where vital goods are concerned. The United States has the Medicaid program for poor people to supplement market transactions in health care precisely because equal consideration of interests requires that everyone be given access to health care. The 1994 health care debate in the United States was, ostensibly, about how to achieve universal coverage, not about whether or not justice required such coverage. With the exception of South Africa, every other industrialized country already has universal coverage for health care. Where vital needs are concerned, markets are supplemented or avoided in order to give equal consideration to everyone's interests.

Another example concerns military service in time of war. The United States employed conscription during the Civil War, both world wars, the Korean War, and the war in Vietnam. When the national interest requires placing many people in mortal danger, it is considered just that exposure be largely unrelated to income and market transactions.

The United States does not currently provide genuine equality in education or health care, nor did universal conscription (of males) put all men at equal risk in time of war. In all three areas, advantage accrues to those with greater income and wealth. (During the Civil War, paying for a substitute was legal in many cases.) Imperfection in practice, however, should not obscure general agreement in theory that justice requires equal consideration of interests, and that such equal consideration requires rejecting purely free market approaches where basic or vital needs are concerned.

Toxic substances affect basic and vital interests. Lead, arsenic, and cadmium in the vicinity of children's homes can result in mental retardation of the children.[8] Navaho teens exposed to radiation from uranium mine tailings have seventeen times the national average of reproductive organ cancer.[9] Environmental Protection Agency (EPA) officials estimate that toxic air pollution in areas of South Chicago increase cancer risks one hundred to one thousand times.[10] Pollution from Otis Air Force base in Massachusetts is associated with alarming increases in cancer rates.[11] Non-Hodgkin's Lymphoma is related to living near stone, clay, and glass industry facilities, and leukemia is related to living near chemical and petroleum plants.[12] In general, cancer rates are higher in the United States near industries that use toxic substances and discard them nearby.[13]

In sum, the placement of toxic wastes affects basic and vital interests just as do education, health care, and wartime military service. Exemption from market decisions is required to avoid unjust impositions on the poor, and to respect people's interests equally. A child dying of cancer receives little benefit from the community's new swimming pool.

Cost-Benefit Analysis (CBA)

CBA is an economist's version of utilitarianism, where the sum to be maximized is society's wealth, as measured in monetary units, instead of happiness or preference satisfaction. Society's wealth is computed by noting (and estimating where necessary) what people are willing to pay for goods and services. The more people are willing to pay for what exists in society, the better off society is, according to CBA.

CBA will characteristically require placement of toxic wastes near poor people. Such placement usually lowers land values (what people are willing to pay for property). Land that is already cheap, where poor people live, will not lose as much value as land that is currently expensive, where wealthier people live, so a smaller loss of social wealth attends placement of toxic wastes near poor people. This is just the opposite of what the Principle of Commensurate Burdens and Benefits requires.

The use of CBA also violates equal consideration of interests, operating much like free market approaches. Where a vital concern is at issue, equal consideration of interests requires that people be considered irrespective of income. The placement of toxic wastes affects vital interests. Yet CBA would have poor people exposed disproportionately to such wastes.[14]

In sum, libertarianism, utilitarianism, free market distribution, and cost-benefit analysis are inadequate principles and methodologies to guide the just distribution of toxic wastes.

LULU Points

An approach that avoids these difficulties assigns points to different types of locally undesirable land uses (LULUs) and requires that all communities earn LULU points.[15] In keeping with the Principle of Commensurate Benefits and Burdens, wealthy communities would be required to earn more LULU points than poorer ones. Communities would be identified by currently existing political divisions, such as villages, towns, city wards, cities, and counties.

Toxic waste dumps are only one kind of LULU. Others include prisons, half-way houses, municipal waste sites, low-income housing, and power plants, whether nuclear or coal fired. A large deposit of extremely toxic waste, for example, may be assigned twenty points when properly buried but fifty points when illegally dumped. A much smaller deposit of properly buried toxic waste may be assigned only ten points, as may a coal-fired power plant. A nuclear power plant may be assigned twenty-five points, while municipal waste sites are only five points, and one hundred units of low-income housing are eight points.

These numbers are only speculations. Points would be assigned by considering probable effects of different LULUs on basic needs, and responses to questionnaires investigating people's levels of discomfort with LULUs of various sorts. Once numbers are assigned, the total number of LULU points to be distributed in a given time period could be calculated by considering planned development and needs for prisons, power plants, low-income housing, and so on. One could also calculate points for a community's already existing LULUs. Communities could then be required to host LULUs in proportion to their income or wealth, with new allocation of LULUs (and associated points) correcting for currently existing deviations from the rule of proportionality.

Wherever significant differences of wealth or income exist between two areas, these areas should be considered part of different communities if there is any political division between them. Thus, a county with rich and poor areas would not be considered a single community for purposes of locating LULUs. Instead, villages or towns may be so considered. A city with rich and poor areas may similarly be reduced to its wards. The purpose of segregating areas of different income or wealth from one another is to permit the imposition of greater LULU burdens on wealthier communities. When wealthy and poor areas are considered as one larger community, there is the danger that the community will earn its LULU points by placing hazardous waste near its poorer members. This possibility is reduced when only relatively wealthy people live in a smaller community that must earn LULU points.

Practical Implications

Political strategy is beyond the scope of this chapter, so I will refrain from commenting on problems and prospects for securing passage and implementation of the foregoing proposal. I maintain that the proposal is just. In a society where injustice is common, it is no surprise that proposals for rectification meet stiff resistance.

Were the LULU points proposal implemented, environmental racism would be reduced enormously. To the extent that poor people exposed to environmental hazards are members of racial minorities, relieving the poor of disproportionate exposure would also relieve people of color.

This is not to say that environmental racism would be ended completely. Implementation of the proposal requires judgment in particular cases. Until racism is itself ended, such judgment will predictably be exercised at times to the disadvantage of minority populations. However, because most people of color currently burdened by environmental racism are relatively poor, implementing the proposal would remove 80 to 90 percent of the effects of environmental racism. While efforts to end racism at all levels should continue, reducing the burdens of racism is generally advantageous to people of color. Such reductions are especially worthy when integral to policies that improve distributive justice generally.

Besides improving distributive justice and reducing the burdens of environmental racism, implementing the LULU points proposal would benefit life on earth generally by reducing the generation of toxic hazards. When people of wealth, who exercise control of manufacturing processes, marketing campaigns, and media coverage, are themselves threatened disproportionately by toxic hazards, the culture will evolve quickly to find their production largely unnecessary. It will be discovered, for example, that many plastic items can be made of wood, just as it was discovered in the late 1980s that the production of many ozone-destroying chemicals is unnecessary. Similarly, necessity being the mother of invention, it was discovered during World War II that many women could work in factories. When certain interests are threatened, the impossible does not even take longer.

The above approach to environmental injustice should, of course, be applied internationally and intranationally within all countries. The same considerations of justice condemn universally, all other things being equal, exposing poor people to vital dangers whose generation predominantly benefits the rich. This implies that rich countries should not ship their toxic wastes to poor countries. Since many poorer countries, such as those in Africa, are inhabited primarily by nonwhites, prohibiting shipments of toxic wastes to them would reduce significantly worldwide environmental racism. A prohibition on such shipments would also discourage production of dangerous wastes, as it would require people in rich countries to live with whatever dangers they create. If the principle of LULU points were applied in all countries, including poor ones, elites in those countries would lose interest in earning foreign currency credits through importation of waste, as they would be disproportionately exposed to imported toxins.

In sum, we could reduce environmental injustice considerably through a general program of distributive justice concerning environmental hazards. Pollution would not thereby be eliminated, since to live is to pollute. But such a program would motivate significant reduction in the generation of toxic wastes, and help the poor, especially people of color, as well as the environment.

Notes

1. See the introduction to this volume for studies indicating the disproportionate burden of toxic wastes on people of color.

2. Vicki Been, "Market Forces, Not Racist Practices, May Affect the Siting of Locally Undesirable Land Uses," in *At Issue: Environmental Justice*, ed. by Jonathan Petrikin (San Diego, Calif.: Greenhaven Press, 1995), 41.

3. See *San Antonio Independent School District v. Rodriguez*, 411 R.S. 1 (1973) and *Village of Arlington Heights v. Metropolitan Housing Development Corporation*, 429 U.S. 252 (1977).

4. Been, 41.

5. Murray Rothbard, "The Great Ecology Issue," *The Individualist* 21, no. 2 (February 1970): 5.

6. See Peter S. Wenz, *Environmental Justice* (Albany, N.Y.: State University of New York Press, 1988), 65–67 and associated endnotes.

7. Christopher Boerner and Thomas Lambert, "Environmental Justice Can Be Achieved Through Negotiated Compensation," in *At Issue: Environmental Justice*.

8. F. Diaz-Barriga et al., "Arsenic and Cadmium Exposure in Children Living Near to Both Zinc and Copper Smelters," summarized in *Archives of Environmental Health* 46, no. 2 (March/April 1991): 119.

9. Dick Russell, "Environmental Racism," *Amicus Journal* (Spring 1989): 22–32, 24.

10. Marianne Lavelle, "The Minorities Equation," *National Law Journal* 21 (September 1992): 3.

11. Christopher Hallowell, "Water Crisis on the Cape," *Audubon* (July/August 1991): 65–74, especially 66 and 70.

12. Athena Linos et al., "Leukemia and Non-Hodgkin's Lymphoma and Residential Proximity to Industrial Plants," *Archives of Environmental Health* 46, no. 2 (March/April 1991): 70–74.

13. L. W. Pickle et al., *Atlas of Cancer Mortality among Whites: 1950–1980*, HHS publication # (NIH) 87-2900 (Washington, D.C.: U.S. Department of Health and Human Services, Government Printing Office: 1987).

14. Wenz, 216–18.

15. The idea of LULU points comes to me from Frank J. Popper, "LULUs and Their Blockage," in *Confronting Regional Challenges: Approaches to LULUs, Growth, and Other Vexing Governance Problems*, ed. by Joseph DiMento and Le Roy Graymer (Los Angeles, Calif.: Lincoln Institute of Land Policy, 1991), 13–27, especially 24.

Part Two

Racism in North America

5

Africville: Environmental Racism

Howard McCurdy

*(with special editorial and research
assistance from Richard Phillips)*

This case study will demonstrate that blacks in Africville, Nova Scotia,
Canada, lived under horrendous environmental conditions, and the reason for this was racism. It traverses Africville's history to reveal why
many have found themselves outlawed[1] within a society that has barred
their enfranchisement at almost every level. The legalistic ethic in
which this occurs can be considered through John Rawls's principle
of justice as fairness.[2] In the 1960s John Porter's *The Vertical Mosaic*
considered the claim that "one of the most persistent images that
Canadians have of their society is that it has no classes." For those
who held this belief, it was found that "this image becomes translated
into the assertion that Canadians are all relatively equal in their pos-
sessions, in the amount of money they earn, and in the opportunities
which they and their children have to get on in the world."[3] Donald
H. Clairmont and Dennis William Magill have investigated and revealed that this is not the case for blacks in Nova Scotia and particularly for blacks who once lived in Africville. They wrote:

> Throughout their settlement in Nova Scotia, blacks have had to carry a
> special burden, the burden of the white man's prejudice, discrimina-
> tion, and oppression. The result is that Nova Scotia's blacks became
> marginal people in a relatively depressed region. Marginality denotes
> here a lack of influence in societal decision making and a low degree
> of participation in the mainstream of political or economic life.[4]

Why did these conditions exist? The philosophical response is that
Nova Scotian society does not operate in a Rawlsian liberalist fash-

ion. It will be argued that the least advantaged are not usually considered. When the ruling group acts, it is often paternalistic, forcing minority residents in directions against their will or interest. The sociological response is that blacks are often cast as "outgroups." This relationship will now be examined.

The University of Windsor's sociology textbook displays as a quintessential "outgroup" the former community of Africville, Halifax, Nova Scotia. In the text, an ingroup is described as "a social group commanding a member's esteem and loyalty," and an outgroup as "a social group toward which one feels competition or opposition." Despite obvious problems with these definitions, the main contention here is that this text reveals some very serious divisions between a demoralized black community, which at the time of the writing of the text no longer existed, and the "we," which appears to be people of a higher order of humanity. The text says, "many Haligonians felt Africville was a 'blot on the face of Halifax.' The reality of race in Canada is that people of colour have often, and still do, find themselves cast in the role of 'outgroup.'"[5]

A white Haligonian businessman reflects on the political nature of racism in Nova Scotia: "I think perhaps the first thing, [Africville] wasn't regarded as part of the city of Halifax . . . and [the city] didn't regard, I suppose, the people as people, certainly not as citizens; and apathy, prejudice, fear and discrimination [existed]."[6] Hence, the politically powerful person is able to institutionalize his or her will, or the will of (his or her) respective "ingroup," in such a manner as to cause to be affected all persons, but more directly those who are powerless, within the social order.[7] These concepts and associations are purposefully developed through exploiting the cognitive faculties of every person within the polity. The goal is to establish a firm understanding of who, characteristically, is entitled to preferential treatment, and who, therefore, ought to be considered worthy to receive and control the abundance from the land.

Hence, an investigation as to whether racially based injustice is a part of the political infrastructure of a specific area in Canada is warranted. In more exact terms, it will be shown that "environmental racism" was a reality in Africville and is practiced in Nova Scotia, Canada.

The following section will provide a historic overview of Africville. The next subject area will provide the environmental impact and the relocation phenomenon. The third section will contrast demographic data from 1961 through thirty years of population movement and economic statistics in Nova Scotia and Halifax.

Africville

Bedford Basin, overlooking Halifax harbor, was one of the most picturesque locations in all of Nova Scotia. In the mid–nineteenth century it was settled by a population that was later described as "a community of intelligent young people and much is expected of them."[8] It is likely that the original settlers had equally high expectations of themselves but the racial climate of Nova Scotia dashed those hopes as it was to determine the name of this particular part of Halifax—Africville.

The history of blacks in Nova Scotia is as old as the history of the province itself. Until recent changes in Canadian immigration policies, which vastly increased the population of people of African descent throughout Canada, Nova Scotia had the largest African-Canadian population in the country.

In early days, the practice of slavery was common in Nova Scotia. Even before the American Revolutionary War, which produced massive population changes in the maritime provinces, there were some five hundred black slaves in various parts of Nova Scotia. References to their being auctioned in Halifax were common.[9] To add emphasis to this point, Clairmont and Magill provide evidence that from the nineteenth century when slavery was practiced, racial segregation in regards to the living conditions of blacks had not improved much. They write, "there was a parallel between governmental policy towards Africville, reinforced by everyday expectation, and its relative geographical isolation" that made sustenance extremely difficult.[10] We will now look back at the origins of this community.

The first large-scale immigration of blacks into Nova Scotia came with the Loyalist flight to the Maritimes following the American Revolutionary War. "Between 1782 and 1785, 2,300 black Loyalists,"[11] who had fought on the British side, were given land that was "unproductive, so most Blacks found making a living difficult."[12] Another 1,200 came as slaves of the approximately 30,000 white Loyalists.[13] According to Clairmont and Magill, "slavery was never instituted by statute in Nova Scotia yet slavery was practiced in Halifax a year after the city was founded and over the next five decades."[14] Although racism was not entrenched in the law, "'Jim Crow' practices and segregation even in many public services, including segregated schools, have been major obstacles to social and economic advancement of the black population."[15]

The black and white Loyalists were promised free land grants; however, in the hierarchical system of distribution that was applied, blacks finished last.[16] Fewer blacks received far less acreage of far lower quality agricultural land than their white counterparts and little of it was able to provide self-sufficiency.[17] Many blacks were relegated to poverty and forced off of the land by encroachment and appropriation instruments used by government. Because of their status as an out-group, their competition with white wage earners, members of the ingroup, bred conflict. Race riots occurred in several towns. Even when in possession of land, blacks were denied the vote as well as trial by jury for much of the nineteenth century. In relationship to the vote, the Royal Commission revealed that "many Blacks were said to have been deliberately denied the right to vote in municipal elections until 1965," a year after relocation.[18] But from the outset, they were excluded from white churches, schools, and cemeteries. When a white community expanded near a black school, the whites would force the black students to attend other schools, some great distances away, rather than risk racial contamination for their white children.[19] According to contemporary literature on the subject, little has changed since the eighteenth century.

The conditions in Halifax's north end were so bad that in 1792, 1,200, or half of all free blacks, including the most capable leaders, left for Sierra Leone. Virtually all of the black settlements (like Preston, Hammond Plains, and Birchtown) were decimated. Among those left, slaves, indentured laborers, and the ill and infirm were the dominant members.[20]

In 1796, some 550 Maroons were resettled in Halifax after ending their fierce resistance to the British in Jamaica. Greeted with both awe and some suspicion, they settled briefly in Preston, where they helped to construct the Citadel. Finally, dissatisfied both with the physical and social climate, they packed up and left for Sierra Leone. The second major immigration of blacks into Nova Scotia occurred after the War of 1812 when two thousand former slaves who had taken the British side appeared to claim the freedom and land promised them. Although treated more fairly in their land claims than the black Loyalists who preceded them, the land they received was just as barren and unproductive as before. Most settled in Preston and Hammond Plains.

The attitude toward blacks that was to characterize the next 150 years of their existence in Nova Scotia is reflected in a statement made in the Assembly at that time, which said that they were an inconvenience, they competed with white laborers, and they were a marked and separate people unfit for either the climate or association with whites.[21] Esmeralda Thornhill and her fellow consultants stated:

Racism exists as a demonstrable social factor in social relations in Canada and the justice system is not excepted. . . . A resolute political will must be adopted to acknowledge up front the existence of racism and to set about eliminating it by moving it onto the public policy agenda. Policy makers, legislators and government have a responsibility to create a climate which will be more inhospitable for racism [and racists]. [22]

As acknowledged here, racism plays a major part in the decision-making process of Canadian institutions, and this was evidenced, in Africville, from the difficulties that individuals had when they attempted to gain title to property that they were pledged.[23]

In Halifax, as a result of segregation—in schools, churches, communities, and even in cemeteries—blacks became a poorly educated, economically marginalized, and socially excluded subculture in Nova Scotian society that governments felt no obligation to respect. As the history of Africville illustrates *ipso facto,* they did not.

Evidence suggests that the first settlements on the Bedford Basin occurred during the 1840s. The first land deeds were registered in 1848 by former refugee residents of Hammond Plains and Preston where the rocky land, decimated wood lots, and distance from job opportunities made life difficult. The Bedford Basin location, being within Halifax, provided closer proximity to wage labor, more abundant wood lots, fishing in the basin, and at least some subsistence gardening.[24] However, "the pollution of Bedford Basin reduced the quality, quantity, and variety of available fish and made fishing for food less productive as the years went by."[25]

By 1851 there were some eighty residents in what was at that time called Richmond, or the Campbell Road settlement. A Baptist church was established in 1849. A petition was addressed, at that same time, to the provincial legislature for funding, but it was not until 1883 that school privileges were granted by the Halifax school board.[26] The school, which was always segregated, closed in 1957, and the students were diverted to Richmond where they faced considerable problems with racism.

Despite the inattention or worse of the municipal government, life in the early years was described by residents as almost idyllic and in comparison to other black settlements, it was. Its location within Halifax brought proximity to jobs so that for some there was work. Of the 394 residents of Africville in 1959, only 44 had "regular work."[27] Although there was a significant number of craftsmen, especially coopers and masons as well as several small contractors and haulers, most were laborers, domestics, and railway porters. The latter, as in many black communities in Canada, were the social and economic elite. Some residents raised farm animals to sustain their cartage operations or for family food consumption. Several piggeries, a specialization of blacks at the time, constituted the only farm market production. Fishing in the basin, while never commercially engaged in, was for nearly a century a significant activity.[28]

These activities were enough to sustain a sense of community self-sustainability and independence. For a while Africville thrived. Homes were sturdy and livable if not luxurious. In 1915, a city ordinance was passed that forbade raising pigs within the city limits. There was an irony in this: for such purposes Africville was within the municipal jurisdiction; however, when considering the deplorable social conditions that the community found itself in by the 1960s, it was not considered. The city, while not providing services as it would to any predominantly white community, poured its night-soil on Africville; at the same time the city took away what meager sustenance stock it had. Most livestock also disappeared. Garden produce would not grow, one reason being the significant toxification of the soil in Africville.[29] By the 1930s, there were two "penny stores," a post office, and a social club. The Seaview Baptist Church was the center of a vibrant social life that drew black people from the entire Halifax area for a variety of special activities.[30]

When and how the name "Africville" originated is not clear. Certainly among whites and even many blacks, it was intended to be derogatory and reflected the attitudes that doomed it to its subsequent fate. It was a segregated black community; therefore, it was regarded as an expendable nuisance standing in the way of commercial development rather than a desirable residential area.[31] A report by the city manager stated, "the area is not suited for residences but properly developed is ideal for industrial purposes. There is water frontage for piers, the railway for sidings, a road to be developed leading directly downtown and in the other direction to the provincial highway."[32] This was not a new developmental idea. It was also uncovered that "Africville, long a black mark against society, had been designated for future industrial and harbour development."[33]

The following provides insight into the social condition that prevailed: "Is there a different law for the poor and for the rich? For the minorities and the rich? Most minority groups are poor. They get it in the neck because they are poor. They get it in the neck because they are young. They get it in the neck because they are uneducated. They get it in the neck because they are racial minorities."[34] So we come to the reality that the behavior exhibited by the larger dominant society toward Africville's people was established upon two very potent factors: disenfranchisement of blacks and industrial development or greed, in that order.

The Environment and Relocation

Clairmont and Magill supply some graphic testimony about relocation:

> We had our land. We paid our taxes. And Jee-zus Kuh-rist, they got bothering us, and they finally got the place. Well, you come into this world with nothing and you go out with nothing. . . . We never had no peace anyway, so maybe it [the relocation] is all for the best. The City [was] tormenting us. And now they've got it [the Africville land]. . . . Still what can you do . . . getting yourself all messed up with insults.[35]

These words were spoken by a very old and matronly ex-resident of Africville. She was so accustomed to living with degradation and manipulation of her life affecting her welfare, that the loss of her home, her self-esteem, and her sense of autonomy was taken in stride. She had been so violated over the years that relocation and environmental assault were just two of the factors in a life history of powerlessness.[36]

The environmental attack on Africville began almost as soon as it was established.[37] By 1855, the pattern of railway construction through Africville, which was to continue intermittently over the next century, had begun. While it is true that the trains passing through provided transportation and some job opportunities, the dominant effect was to contribute to "blight, decay and the reduction of residential values,"[38] and to the attraction of other encroachments on the integrity of the village. Trains were also a menace, killing or injuring several inhabitants over the years. Clairmont and Magill cite noise pollution and "layers of soot" as health hazards that existed before the change to diesel fuel.[39] Thus, the immediate action of placing three railway lines through Africville was predicated on a choice that did not appear to consider the adverse environmental effects to the people living there. Africville became such an eyesore that the railway rerouted its passenger service west of the area.[40]

By the end of the nineteenth century, there were on the hills and shoreline surrounding Africville an oil plant/storage complex, a fertilizer plant, a rolling mill, two slaughter houses, a coal handling facility, a tar factory, a tannery, a shoe factory, several stone-crushing facilities, a foundry, and a fertilizer-producing plant. Some of these industries would close and be replaced by others such as a refinery, an oil plant complex, a cotton mill, and a huge hydro tower that dominated the landscape; but the basic picture of large-scale industrial encroachment remained the same. Despite the proximity of jobs, albeit "risky businesses," very few jobs were available for blacks, and these, as has already been shown, were at the most menial level.[41]

In 1855, under pressure from white citizens in south Halifax, human waste disposal pits were moved from that location to the edge of Africville.[42] In 1860, Rockhead Prison was built on a hill next to the town followed by the construction of the Infectious Disease Hospital in 1873 and the Trachoma Hospital in 1903. Raw sewage from these institutions emptied into a cesspool or the open waters of the Bedford Basin. Clairmont and Magill tell us that the "lack of water and sewage facilities had serious implications for the life and health of Africville residents. Contamination of wells was a constant problem."[43] This became a headline focus for the local, national, and international media. The wells were occasionally serviced by the city which periodically posted signs warning that the water should be boiled before use.[44] City officials could with impunity encourage the establishment in and around Africville of activities that would be deemed unacceptable elsewhere; this they did while denying even minimal services to that community. "In 1947 Halifax rezoned and the City Council approved designation of Africville as industrial land."[45] The coup de grace occurred in the 1950s when the City Council moved the open city dump to Africville because it was too much of a "health menace" to locate elsewhere.[46] To some, scavenging in the dump became a way of making ends meet and for the children this was their playground before, and remained so.[47]

Clairmont and Magill, Winks, and Pachai reveal that in spite of frequent protests and petitions from the leaders of Africville, many concerns are never recorded and action usually did not follow.[48] The Royal Commission wrote, "Blacks are still almost invisible in the institution operated by the majority White society in Nova Scotia."[49] In response to those who think the only method of retaining relevant social data is through the bureaucratic process, the experience of Alex Haley should be recalled. While in his search for his roots he was amazed at the capacity of native tribes to retain a genealogical history that was not written but was memorized by the elders and passed along orally to the young.[50] Although the city often neglected to record the voices of Africville, Africville remembered its struggle against generations of hegemonic relations with the white society.[51]

Serious outbreaks of disease were apparently rare. In the 1950s public health nurses, who are not qualified to diagnose illness, reported "many Africville children were thin and undernourished"; despite this they claimed that incidence of disease was low."[52] The question that arises is: How did access to health care affect the medical findings of such reports? This cannot be considered herein. Indeed, health officials seemed to find solace in the fact that while the children of Africville were often thin and malnourished, constant exposure to infectious agents had apparently made them more resistant than their white counterparts in the rest of the city! The *Mail-Star* featured an article, in 1964, that informed the public "that the contamination of wells in Africville is of long standing is shown by the fact that there have been no serious outbreaks of disease in the district. According to health authorities this indicates that, from infancy on, children have been exposed to water-borne disease germs. As a result they have built up a resistance."[53]

Garbage collection, law enforcement, and paved roads were all denied to Africville in spite of repeated requests. Lacking adequate means of drawing water, even from the basin, and with road access difficult, fires were an ever-present danger to the area's wooden homes. In 1923, 1930, 1937, and 1947, fires destroyed numbers of them.[54] In 1957, three children died in such a conflagration. Poverty, the commercial or municipal expropriation of homes, the construction of shelters on smaller and smaller lots subdivided from the original holdings, and the absence of any housing-standards enforcement had already produced slum conditions. The inability to replace uninsured homes destroyed by fire, and the presence of squatters on expropriated properties did not improve conditions.[55]

The physical decay was matched by social and economic degeneration as well as a well-justified sense of powerlessness even among the leaders of this segregated community. The small businesses and craftsmen had all but disappeared. The people were poorly trained, and the unskilled few had education levels below the grade-six level. By 1957, only 11 percent of the citizens of Africville had regular employment. Most of these were at the lowest levels of menial and domestic labor. It was therefore almost inevitable given the absence of any significant law enforcement, that there would be some who would seek incomes in such illegal activities as prostitution and bootlegging. By the fifties, Africville was the place to go for the kind of "good times" that were unavailable elsewhere for both blacks and whites. And although not a dominant part of the population, an increasing number of transients and undesirables began to contribute to the already negative reputation of the community.[56]

As already alluded to, by the 1960s Africville had become a national scandal. It was a blot on Canadian race relations, a segregated black slum that one national human rights worker described as "the worst and most degenerate area I have ever seen."[57] Dr. Albert Rose testified that "in a nutshell, my impression was . . . that, in the Canadian context, this was the worst urban appendage I had ever seen."[58]

The city's century-old plan to sacrifice Africville to industrial development was bolstered by a new priority set by the public, indeed, international outcry that finally something should be done about the horrible scab on race relations in Canada.[59] What had been a purely developmental ethic now gave way to a liberal/welfare model of urban renewal not just for industrial/commercial development but to solve the social problems of deprived classes as well. One of the conditions of environmental racism is that the relocatees had no say in or understanding of what was planned. The only information that they were privy to was how the plan developed under the auspices of development and social bureaucrats.[60] Thus, that Africville would be destroyed was a decision that was made by the City Council and concurred with by black and white advocates, who resided in the mainstream, and who paternalistically acted to protect the residents, despite their pleading for the preservation of their community. However, the cost of restoring housing and providing services was thought prohibitive compared to the cost of relocation. In addition, the integrationist thrust of the time made the preservation of a racially segregated community unacceptable.

This line of reasoning is predicated on a reactionary mindset and would be more effective if handled proactively. The prologue to a study entitled "Rebuilding the Idea of a Town" states the following causal relationship, which also applies to the injustice that brought about the demise of Africville: "The popular media describes the symptoms but doesn't, won't or can't identify the problem and so implies we have no power to act. . . . By virtue of our powerlessness we are made blameless. Lily-white. All is forgiven and the fantasy is complete, perhaps even entertaining. Remarkable." They continue with an attack on urban planners,

> Its also rubbish, [there is] a cynical manipulation and a complete mystification of the selfish and thoughtless roles we each play in the degradation of our environment. . . . Urban decay is our failure. . . . And it is we who out of meanness have consigned the weakest among us to our poorest schools and poorest housing.[61]

Africville's relocation was the solution chosen instead of providing public services and structural rebuilding. It was said that "the Development Officer of the City, when looking at any piece of real estate within the city of Halifax, looks at it through the eyes of a developer; that is a public developer. . . ."[62] Dr. Albert Rose, a professor of social work, who spent by his own admission a mere "two hours" in Africville wrote the condemning "Rose Report," which advocated the relocation.[63] His report appears to have been an indication of the prevailing political will. There is strong evidence that the conclusion he arrived at and the enclave's ultimate fate were reflective of the position held by the populace, including that of most blacks and residents of Africville.

So the people of Africville were relocated, with fair compensation. Many were unable to buy new homes elsewhere,[64] and when they obtained mortgages, for the first time, since in Africville their properties were usually unencumbered, employment discrimination often brought about defaults and loss of their homes. Others were relocated to a public tenement not of their choosing. The housing availability placed them in the north end of Halifax in which poor blacks were already a significant element. Soon after the relocation, some 80 percent of the residents were dissatisfied with the compensation, and even those who were satisfied—the marginal/transients—admitted that the oldliners got a bad deal.[65]

Contemporary Manifestation of Africville

An objection that must be anticipated here is that Africville was a phenomenon which was resolved, albeit poorly, over thirty years ago. Is the racial climate better in Nova Scotia now? One must remember that a contemporary sociology textbook uses Africville as a representation of an "outgroup." Also, settlements like Preston and Hammond Plains are still predominantly populated by blacks. This being the case, *ceteris paribus*, situations are better in Nova Scotia, but there is still much that is required to provide that the black is entitled to equal opportunity and unequal, that is concentrated, political regard.

The Royal Commission (1989) states, "although it is clear that while Blacks have made gains in Nova Scotia in recent decades they are still struggling in terms of income, employment and education."[66] We will examine educational and economic statistics that will assist in understanding the disparity that now exists and at the time just prior to relocation was manifest between blacks and whites in Nova Scotia.

Education is one consideration used to determine the potential to do well of any group within society. Some argue that it is the key determinant. Frances Henry conducted a study that in terms of education, concludes: "Our findings clearly indicate the Black people in Nova Scotia aspire to the same educational standards and share the same positive values about education as does the white middle class society in which they live. The motivation is there; the task is to provide opportunity for these people."[67]

A 1968 study shows the educational disparity that existed. It was reported that "in Nova Scotia only 24% of the boys and 27% of the girls had reached grade 12; whereas in British Columbia the proportions are 64% and 62% respectively."[68] Thus, social status, shortly after the destruction of Africville, in Nova Scotia appears to have been based on a population of undereducated people. The disparity for all Nova Scotians is eclipsed by the educational range of blacks, which spans as a modal frequency from grade five to grade eight."[69]

Population trends in Nova Scotia reveal an interesting pattern. The 1961 census, which preceded the Africville demise, recorded a population of 11,900 blacks in Nova Scotia; in 1991, the census found a black population of 10,185 blacks.[70] Of some interest is that in 1961 there were 5,905 blacks living in Halifax; and in 1991 there were 7,280.[71] The increase of the black population seems to be contrary to the provincial trend for blacks of 19 percent growth rate. This may be because blacks are likely to go where the best opportunities lie, in hope of acceptance. However, the population of Halifax in 1961 was 225,723, and in 1991 it was 317,630, an increase of 29 percent.[72] Therefore, the rate of increase of blacks is significantly less than that of the total population.

Henry's people found that "the entire province is an economically depressed area and that the Black population suffers doubly, both by being poor and by being located in one of the poorest provinces in Canada."[73] The Royal Commission reported the findings of a study conducted by the Black United Front (BUF), which is informative. Their survey (1978) revealed that "the median Black household income was $8,450 in 1978, which was roughly 57 percent of the median income for all Nova Scotia households in the same year which was $14,851."[74] These data add weight to the claim that the Afro-Canadian population in Nova Scotia is still, after Africville, victim of systemic racism.

Concluding Comments

It is interesting that the death of this community has caused it to receive much more concerned recognition, post mortem, than in its life history. Posthumously, "Africville" lives on as a reminder of what can happen to a people when their personhood is not respected by the dominant power structure. This prompts a query: it has been argued here that the reason Africville's people were so treated was a matter of environmental racism—but was this a case of classism instead? Admittedly, this is a difficult question, and one that will not be resolved here. However, there was much revealed in the case study, and there is work done from similar cases, of hazardous waste and toxic exposures that can assist in developing an opinion in regard to such cases.

Mark Sagoff states that the perspective taken "does not treat them [the persons exposed] as persons but only as locations at which affective states may be found."[75] Since the community that he was dealing with was a wealthy Caucasian community in Lewiston, New York, and these people were treated without regard for their personhood, as were the people at Africville, it is difficult to say that the racial component of the problem is relevant to the stands taken against them. However, the message that Sagoff conveys is, that the more victimized a person is considered to be, the more those whom the person must negotiate with perceive them as unable to "participate in the exercise of power."[76] From this reading it follows that the more the party is affected, the less that party is considered as a person, and the more that party is depicted as irrational.

This becomes clear when we consider that "some commentators argue that policies favoured by environmentalists . . . make consumer products more expensive and thus hurt the poor more than the rich."[77] Thus, the poorer the affected subjects, for these economists, the less right they have, as consumers, to expect environmental safety. On this note we can now turn back from classism to the issue of racism.

Marginal blacks can find themselves assaulted by hazardous substances that the mainstream society refuses to allow in its backyard—Africville was a victim of the NIMBY principle, which was practiced in many predominantly white urban and suburban communities in North America.[78] Robert Bullard helps us understand the Africville experience as representative of environmental racism. He cites the president of Houston's Northeast Community Action Group, as follows:

A silent war is being waged against our neighbourhoods. Slowly, we are being picked off by the industries that don't give a damn about polluting our neighbourhood, contaminating our water, fouling our air, clogging our streets with garbage, big trucks, and lowering our property values. It's hard enough for blacks to scrape and save enough money to buy a home, then you see your dream shattered by a garbage dump. That's a dirty trick. No amount can buy self respect.[79]

These words could just as easily have been spoken by a citizen of Africville.

The citizens of Lewiston were victimized by waste that was present at the time they purchased their property. Although they were not aware of the threat, it was a matter of *caveat emptor*. In the case of Africville, the environmental assault took place while they were occupying the land by the legal authority that they are bound as good citizens to abide by.

Clearly, what Africville became and its ultimate death were products of environmental racism. The pattern of exchange between its citizens and the city government was historically based on the devalued status of a black community that was economically marginalized and politically impotent. In the equation of the quality of life in white communities, of commercial interests, and the development priorities of the city and Africville, it was the latter that represented the line of least resistance. Therefore, Africville became the location for siting ecologically damaging facilities. No significant regard for the concerns of that community was ever evidenced and requests for the most ordinary environmental services were equally and routinely ignored.

While there are sociological studies to substantiate the social and economic deterioration of Africville, there are virtually no data to quantify the critical environmental assaults. But in addition to the noise, deteriorating housing stock, visual blight, and isolation, there must have been significant health effects from lead poisoning from burning batteries; toxic emissions from trains, factories, and the incinerator; sewage- and chemical-contaminated water; contaminated fish; and widespread rat and other vermin infestations.[80] This is in addition to the industrial effects already alluded to.

Special retraining, employment, income, and other support measures were never fully implemented. No account was ever taken of, nor any compensation paid for, the historic, fundamental, and racially motivated culpability of city government in creating the environment that caused Africville's social, economic, and physical decay in the first place.[81]

The industrial development plans for which Africville was sacrificed never came to fruition. There is a municipal park there now called Seaview, where former residents and their descendants come together each year to commemorate their lost community.[82] Indeed, the site now seems to be an excellent one for residential development. As it turned out, the cost of restoring Africville rather than destroying it would likely not have been greater than the cost of the relocation. Former residents know that as they seek to restore what relocation never took into account—Africville as a community with sufficiently strong community values that with a little help and a little respect would still have existed and could exist today.

For the black community of Nova Scotia, the relocation of Africville was a watershed. It is better organized now. The Black United Front and the Afro-Canadian Liberation movement were formed in the late sixties along with various community and professional organizations. There is a human rights commission that for many years was quite effective. Attitudes have changed sufficiently that even politicians involved in the relocation decision believe it was one that no one would consider appropriate now.[83]

Justice as fairness provides that, in all ways and at all times, those who are "least" in society must be considered first. If this had been the practice adopted by governmental agents, Africville would have thrived. The people would have retained their homes, their strong religious ties, and most importantly their health and dignity. Their community's death stands as an insult to all great black Loyalists.

Notes

The research for this study was supported by Social Sciences and Humanities Research Council Grant No. 806-93-0027 (Laura Westra).

1. Outlawed, in this way, does not indicate the fault of the person who is "outlawed." The meaning is connected to the lack of protection that the person receives from the functioning of the positive laws that he or she is a part of. See Bill Lawson, "Crime, Minorities, and the Social Contract" in *Criminal Justice Ethics* 9, no. 2 (Summer/Fall 1990).

2. John Rawls, *Political Liberalism* (New York, Chicago, Chichester, West Sussex: Columbia University Press, 1993).

3. John Porter, *The Vertical Mosaic—Analysis of Social Class and Power in Canada* (Toronto: University of Toronto Press, 1969), 3.

4. Donald H. Clairmont and Dennis Magill, *Africville—The Life and Death of a Canadian Black Community* (Toronto: Canadian Scholar's Press, 1987), 31.

5. John J. Macionis, Juanne Clarke, and Linda M. Gerber, *Sociology—*

Canadian Edition (Scarborough, Ontario: Prentice-Hall Canada Inc., 1994), 188.

6. Clairmont and Magill, 1987, 53.

7. James Baldwin, "Nobody Knows My Name," in *My Soul Looks Back 'Less I Forget—A Collection of Quotations by People of Colour,* ed. by Dorothy Winbush Riley (New York: Harper Collins Publishers, 1961).

8. P. E. MacKerrow, *A Brief History of the Coloured Baptists of Nova Scotia, 1832–1895* (Halifax: Nova Scotia Printing Co., 1895), 65.

9. Robin Winks, *The Blacks in Canada* (Montreal: McGill-Queen's University Press, 1971), 27–28.

10. Donald H. Clairmont and Dennis W. Magill, *Africville—The Life and Death of a Canadian Black Community* (Montreal: McClelland and Stewart, 1974), 61.

11. Paul A. Erikson, *Halifax's North End—An Anthropologist Looks at the City* (Hantsport, Nova Scotia: Lancelot Press, 1986), 66.

12. Ibid.

13. Bridglal Pachai, *Blacks—Peoples of the Maritimes* (Tantillon, N.S.: Four East Publications, 1987), 7–9.

14. Clairmont and Magill, 1974, 40.

15. Royal Commission Prosecution, *Discrimination against Blacks in Nova Scotia: The Criminal Justice System, A Research Study* (1989), vol. 4, 12.

16. Clairmont and Magill, 1974, 41.

17. Erikson, 65–67.

18. Ibid, 20.

19. Frances Henry, *Forgotten Canadians: The Blacks of Nova Scotia* (Canadian Social Problems Series-Longman Canada Limited, 1973), 74–75.

20. R. Winks, 42.

21. C. B. Ferguson, *A Documentary Study of the Establishment of Negroes in Nova Scotia between the War of 1812 and the Winning of Responsible Government* (Public Archives of Nova Scotia Bulletin No. 8, Bridglal Pachai 1987), 21.

22. Royal Commission on the Donald Marshall, Jr., Prosecution, vol. 1. 153, taken from Consultative Conference Proceedings, 7 (1989): 72.

23. Henry, 1973; Clairmont and Magill, 1974 and 1987.

24. Clairmont and Magill, 1974, 36–38.

25. Clairmont and Magill, 1987, 94.

26. Clairmont and Magill, 1974, 98.

27. Ibid., 61.

28. Ibid., 95.

29. Ibid., 94.

30. Ibid., 67.

31. Clairmont and Magill, 1974, 83.

32. Clairmont and Magill, 1987, 124, citing Report by the City Manager, 1.

33. Ibid., 11.

34. Royal Commission, vol. 1, 150, words cited from Dr. Wilson Head, vol. 4.

35. Clairmont and Magill, 1987, 100.

36. Ibid., 160.

37. Clairmont and Magill, 1974, 83.

38. Africville Genealogical Society, *The Spirit of Africville* (Halifax: Formac Publishing Company, 1992), 38.

39. Clairmont and Magill, 1974, 99.

40. Erikson, 1986, 68.

41. Elaine Draper [*Risky Business* (Cambridge: Cambridge University Press, 1991)] presents a poignant argument as to the adverse affects on employees and other persons who are outside of the manufacturing decision making circle.

42. Erikson, 1986, 68.

43. Ibid., 102.

44. Clairmont and Magill, 1987, front cover.

45. Ibid., 91.

46. Clairmont and Magill, 1974, 101.

47. Winks, 1971, 453.

48. Clairmont and Magill, 1987, 101.

49. Royal Commission, 1989, vol. 4, 152.

50. Alex Haley, *Roots* (Dell Book, 1977), 726.

51. Howard McGary and Bill E. Lawson, 1992. *Between Slavery and Freedom—Philosophy and American Slavery.* (Bloomington and Indianapolis: Indiana University Press).

52. Clairmont and Magill, 1987, 104.

53. *Halifax Mail Star*, "Works Department Undecided on How to Solve Problems," (Halifax, Nova Scotia) 1 Dec. 1964.

54. Clairmont and Magill, 1987, 106.

55. Ibid., 114.

56. Clairmont and Magill, 1974, 83.

57. Clairmont and Magill, 1987, 83.

58. Ibid., 141.

59. Susan Dexter, "The Black Ghetto that Fears Integration," *Maclean's Magazine* 78, no. 14: 36–38. *Detroit Free Press*: "Shocking Poverty in Nova Scotia," 1969.

60. Clairmont and Magill, 1987, 123.

61. Faculty of Architecture, *Rebuilding the Idea of a Town—Windsor, Nova Scotia* (Technical University of Nova Scotia), 7–8.

62. These words were spoken by a former senior and influential member of Halifax City Council, in Clairmont and Magill, 1987, 126.

63. Clairmont and Magill, 1987, 138–49.

64. Donald H. Clairmont and Dennis Magill, *Africville Relocation Report*, Supplement (Halifax, Canada: The Institute of Public Affairs), Dalhousie University, September 1973).

65. Ibid., 555–62.

66. Royal Commission, 1989, vol. 4, 15.

67. Henry, 1973, 70–75.

68. Ibid.

69. Ibid.

70. Royal Commission, 1989, vol. 4, 15; Statistics Canada, Cat. No. 93–315, Table 1A.

71. 1961 *Census of Canada—Series 1.2*, Table 37, in Henry, 32; Statistics Canada, Cat. No. 93–315, Table 1B.

72. 1961, *Census;* Statistics Canada, Table 1B.

73. Royal Commission, 1989, vol. 4, 77.

74. Royal Commission on the Donald Marshall, Jr., Prosecution, *Discrimination against Blacks in Nova Scotia: The Criminal Justice System—A Research Study, 1989* (Province of Nova Scotia), vol. 4, 14.

75. Mark Sagoff, *The Economy of the Earth—Philosophy, Law, and the Environment* (Cambridge: Cambridge University Press, 1988), Cambridge Studies in Philosophy and Public Policy, 46.

76. Ibid., 47.

77. Ibid., 39.

78. NIMBY stands for "not in my back yard."

79. Robert D. Bullard, *Dumping in Dixie* (Boulder, San Francisco, Oxford: Westview Press, 1994), 8.

80. Howard McCurdy is a retired biology professor and department head at the University of Windsor. He is also a politician who has been concerned about environmental quality of urban areas, particularly those where people live who are marginals. His postulating here, therefore, is not uninformed, although it is clearly not backed by empirical data.

81. Clairmont and Magill, 1974, 185–90.

82. The Africville Genealogical Society, 104.

83. Ibid., 101.

6

Evanston Community and Environmental Racism: A Case Study in Social Philosophy

Richard Phillips

Dora Dority and Edward Currie supplied the following abstract for the Issues in Science Sociology and the Urban Environment symposium.[1] Their presentation was entitled "Environmental Justice, Environmental Equity, Environmental Racism, Environmental Genocide in the Evanston Community, Cincinnati." Their presentation provided those in attendance with a first-hand account and an appropriate foundation for the defense of their charge of environmental racism. They testified

> We live in Cincinnati, Ohio in the community of Evanston. On July 19, 1990 at 2:30 pm EST, our community was devastated when the "BASF Inmont Division, Toxic and Hazardous (90-day) Treatment, Disposal and Storage" facility, *exploded.* This unleashed 164 different toxic chemicals and hazardous waste upon our community and surrounding areas. We were told there was nothing to worry about. The city administration said our fears were based on emotion despite the preponderance of evidence to the contrary found amongst government records.
>
> In August of 1990 a metal plating company called "Stamping Technologies" was investigated and from it were removed a 30 ft. deep pit of cadmium and 130 barrels of unspecified toxic waste. There are still three 4 ft. deep pits yet to be excavated of unknown contents, also the railroad tracks running behind the facility are known to be contaminated with creosote. Yet we are told there is nothing to worry about. The Hamilton County Prosecutors Office was able to forge two convictions out of a 16 count indictment with evidence to the contrary.
>
> After 20 years of lobbying, our community was granted a community centre which opened in February of 1992, not built on the original

site chosen, but on top of a toxic waste dump that was not remediated prior to its being built because the city administration felt the community would become "hostile." Despite methane gas build-up underneath the ground, and information contained within their own records in regards to high levels of contamination, we were told there is nothing to worry about.

In every case our rights under the U.S. Constitution and under every piece of environmental legislation ever passed including "The Right-to-Know and the Right-to-Know More," have been violated.

In every other environmental issue that has ever come before the City of Cincinnati involving a Caucasian community, the city has expressed its disgust and has acted accordingly to rectify and secure means to protect the health and the welfare of the residents. In none of the cases involving the community of Evanston, a community of color, have any of these actions (or sentiments) been expressed in our defense.[2]

Introduction

The following case study will concentrate primarily on the BASF incident; however, I believe, as did Dority and Currie, that BASF could not have accomplished the harm that it did and receive criminal impunity without the complicity of many levels of government. When a corporation is guilty of illicitly placing toxic materials into the community's ecosystem, as was the case with Stamping Technologies, BASF, and the city itself, it becomes apparent that something serious is afoot. This work will show that environmental practices of injustice and inequity are institutionally based. This provokes the charge that *facinus quos inquinat aequat* (villainy and guilt make all those whom they contaminate equal in character).

Dority and Currie provided us with three acts of environmental racism that some citizens of the Evanston community (population 8,300 with 95 percent people of color) have managed to survive. The community, whose roots go back to before the turn of the century, is engaged in an ongoing struggle, against toxification, to maintain good health—too many, however, have not been successful.

The state of Ohio responded to the BASF, Evanston explosion reactively, by convening a commission. Evanston and other minority communities were not effectively considered in the report. The report itself was revealing in that as a general state of affairs, any one of the many fatalities or toxic events in 1989 appeared "routine." Of the 4,500 discrete incidents reported, 156 were "likely to cause immediate harm to life, health or property."[3] How many of these events occurred in minority communities and whether there was a differential response will not be addressed here. The magnitude of the BASF explosion was significant enough to warrant the governor's attention and action. It is therefore our focus.

With this work I intend to answer the question, Should we agree that the citizens of Evanston are de facto victims of environmental racism? To respond to this question I will review events centered around the explosion in the following section. The essay will conclude with a perspective entitled, "Evanston Speaks."

The literature on this subject concentrates on justice and equity as being necessary in defining cases of environmental racism. It is held that if there is strong evidence of injustice and inequity in minority areas, then there is sufficient warrant for the charge of "environmental racism."[4] Evanston is such a community. However, there is the matter of conflicting rights.

According to the legal doctrine of eminent domain, BASF has a right to conduct business, as they see fit, on their property.[5] Mark Sagoff in citing Ellen Frankel Paul provides that "everyone who owns property has the duty, of course, to exercise his or her property rights in ways that respect the similar rights of others."[6] I submit that all duty is subject to Donald Scherer's upstream/downstream relationship as follows: (1) A central characteristic of upstream/downstream environments is that within them causation works, or is perceived as working, in only one direction. What happens upstream is perceived as working, in only one direction. What happens upstream is perceived to cause effects downstream, but not vice versa. Consequently, those who live upstream do not fear harms caused to them from downstream. In contrast, a fundamental reinforcer of human norms is "someday you may be in my position, and how would you like it if I. . . ." Thus, when one human community is upstream and another down, the two communities will typically not perceive *reciprocity* as constraining their relationship.[7] Scherer not only provides an understanding of the environmental relationship between the polluters and those who are contaminated, he also provides an essential element of environmental racism, "reciprocity."

A second factor that limits the corporate right to use its property for its own benefit is the concept of environmental racism which can be defined, according to the *Environmental Equity Handbook* (EEH), September 1993, as follows:

> Environmental racism is any environmental policy, practice, or directive that, intentionally or unintentionally, differentially impacts or disadvantages individuals, groups, or communities based on race, color, or ethnicity. It also refers to exclusionary and restive practices that limit

the participation by people of color on decision-making boards, commissions, and the staff of Government agencies with responsibilities in the areas of environmental policies, programs, and permits.[8]

Carol M. Browner of the U.S. Environmental Protection Agency confirms that a problem exists.

We now believe that the remedies we adopted to upgrade environmental quality during the past two decades have not benefited all communities. People of color and low-income communities have alleged that they have a higher level of environmental risk than the majority population, especially in hazardous waste exposure, disposal, and containment. In fact, some of these communities do bear a disproportionate share of the nation's air, water, and waste-contamination problems.[9]

To summarize the problem inherent when businesses manage to avoid their responsibility for the harmful effects of their hazardous enterprises, we must understand that those practicing risky business[10] may be within their legal rights, but these laws and standards are based on repressive power relationships and are *ipso facto* morally unjust. It is not possible to properly investigate all of the many manifestations that support a claim for environmental racism here; therefore, I have chosen to concentrate on one approach, from the perspective of the citizens of Evanston, Cincinnati, Ohio.

Evanston, Cincinnati, Ohio

There are two official accounts of the final cause that brought about the BASF (Dana) explosion on 19 July 1990.[11] According to the first report, the cause of the fire, as determined by the U.S. Department of Labor (USDL), Occupational Safety and Health Administration (OSHA), was unclear. Their spokesperson stated that, "an exact determination may not be possible because of the destruction at the site and the limited information available from witnesses to the explosion. However, the best evidence available thus far points to a gas fired therminol oil heater as the source of ignition."[12]

The report continues by pointing out dereliction of responsibility attributed to BASF Inmont: "There were no overpressure or high temperature alarms on the unit and no emergency interlocks to shut down the heat or relieve the pressure in case either exceeded desired levels."[13] From the same statement it was disclosed that the reactor required constant human monitoring. An operator was required to activate a shut-down rupture disc. "The reactor was equipped with a pressure relief system (rupture disc)."[14] According to the reports, then, it appears that a faulty, obsolete storage system and carelessly monitored equipment had a bearing on the explosion. The OEPA noted, "the employer did not take adequate measures to prevent a hazardous release of flammable materials."[15]

OSHA found BASF Inmont to be "willfully responsible" for the explosion and fire. OSHA defines a willful violation as "one in which the employer either knew that a condition constituted a violation or was aware that a hazardous condition existed and made no reasonable effort to correct it."[16] This is a very serious indictment. To further demonstrate the extent of the implications of this indictment OSHA further defined a willful violation as "one in which there is a substantial probability that death or serious physical harm could result from a hazardous condition, and that the employer knew or should have known of the hazard."[17] OSHA has certainly provided some important evidence, having charged BASF with 107 violations, making BASF de facto agents of harm through the practice of negligence. The fine paid was $1,061,000.

After the explosion, BASF was cited for such things as: oxygen and hydrogen cylinders stored together; flammable liquids in nonapproved containers; refuse contaminated with flammable solvent; improper labeling of containers; improper labeling of tanks that contained hazardous substances; and, the most relevant to the cause of explosions, the "employees were not trained in the hazards of chemicals."[18] The effects of improper training, misleading labels, defective, improperly labeled tanks, fires, and unauthorized spills were an environmental fact of life in Evanston.

The second account, conducted by the International Chemical Workers Union, is more detailed and useful. The investigators utilized a large number of interviews involving plant personnel during the month of July 1990. The main factors were established as follows: The accident occurred in Building #28 (resin production), reactor #6, a 2,000 gallon stainless steel reactor (process vessel) utilized to produce resin. At the time of the accident, the reactor was being washed out by refluxing flammable solvent to the condenser and back to the reactor. No chemical reaction was being performed. The accident resulted when several hundred gallons of flammable solvent were discharged from the vent containing the rupture disc on reactor #6. Normally this operation takes place at essentially atmospheric pressure, but in this instance pressure developed in the reactor to the extent that the rupture disc operated (blew). The boiling solvent then discharged through the vent line above the roof of the building. It rapidly vaporized and formed a large cloud of flammable gas. The vapors spread over a large area, some falling to the ground. After a considerable delay, as much as one to two minutes, the cloud encountered a source of ignition and the vapor cloud exploded. In addition to considerable blast damage, a serious fire was started that destroyed a major portion of the plant.[19]

Was this an accident? Why concentrate on BASF's Evanston operation? For BASF, an obvious defense can be offered—one major incident is not sufficient to allow for a claim of environmental racism. Furthermore, the authorities have labeled the explosion an accident. Why then should anyone accept any argument that this was something more then a mishap? It will be discovered that there is sufficient evidence to demonstrate that the plant (built in the 1940s) was operated in a manner that resulted in its neighbors being exposed to harms for many years before the accident.

One day after the fatal explosion, Scott Burgins of the *Cincinnati Enquirer* revealed that "in a few more months most of BASF's paint and coating plant in Evanston would have been out of town."[20] It is interesting that BASF, Evanston, had previously announced its decision to move the majority of its developmental and testing operations to its plant in Greenwood, Ohio.[21] The plant was slated to close altogether by the end of the year.[22] The age and size of the plant were cited by the company as reasons that they had planned to close the plant prior to the explosion.[23]

The spillover effects created by BASF and experienced by the community at large were the byproduct of "business as usual." The evidence considered provides some support that what occurred was not merely the direct result of "business as usual"—it was the result of the operation of a plant that was no longer valued. The plants infrastructure was in need of rebuilding at considerable expense.

In a report, Eric Mather found that five of the nineteen tanks failed inspection.[24] He provided the following historical information: "The tanks closed were reported to have been installed in 1941 (western) and 1961 (eastern). Corrosion pits were observed on some of the tanks when they were removed from the ground and soil contamination was noticeable in the tank pit."[25] The Ohio Environmental Protection Agency (OEPA) categorized those pits in this way: the "tanks were emptied and the tanks pulled, very strong odours produced in excavations, the Field Director observed that the tanks looked as if a shot gun blast had hit them."[26] The report continues: "the Field Director requested that we look into the situation because of liquid in the tank cavity."[27] Petro Environmental Technologies, a company retained by BASF, said "although no ground water was detected in the tank pit, an assessment of the ground water will be necessary."[28]

The presence of compounds ranging from arsenic to zinc was in fact discovered to be in the soil, sewers, and water tables.[29] The Fire Department claims that it did not, *nor did BASF*, have records of the full range of substances that were on site after the explosion. The Fire Department was reported to have no immediate access to BASF's records to assist it in combating the devastating fire and plant leakages.[30] Consequently, the authorities were unable to provide critical information on the potential risk to the citizens of Evanston.[31]

The Cincinnati fire chief, William Miller, presented testimony that denied allegations that the Fire Department was not aware of the chemicals that were involved with the explosion. He said, "the Cincinnati Fire Department knew what chemicals were stored on the site because of the Cincinnati Right-To-Know ordinance."[32] This only meant that they should have known. He also admits that there is an "inability of the Fire Department to inspect chemical processes for safety violations because of a lack of expertise within the department."[33] Even if they had the information they were not trained in the interpretation of the risk the local residents faced.

According to municipal and state regulations in Ohio, chemical-using operations were responsible for providing the OEPA and their local fire departments with a report of compounds that they, from time to time, were using. One purpose was to assist the authorities in informing firepersons and local citizens of possible health risks contained on site, in case of an emergency such as the one that did in fact occur. As already mentioned, the gravity of the dereliction of duty indicated in the BASF disaster, attributable to all authorities concerned, prompted the governor to commission a study into toxic waste.

The question has been raised as to whether BASF provided to the relevant authorities sufficient and current records of chemicals on site. The commission found that "in the case of the BASF explosion, all the combustion products of the basic solvents involved were unknown."[34] If BASF did not comply with regulations, and the fire department did not strictly enforce the municipal regulations, it is then correct to state that a case of "willful negligence" on the part of all parties is worthy of further exploration. The BASF plant itself was a toxic "hot spot" as indicated by a substantial number of reports. To demonstrate, in 1989 the presence of dangerous levels of VOCs were reported.[35] The preliminary findings report revealed the following:

> The analysis indicated that volatile organic chemicals [*sic*] were present in the concrete at concentrations of 50 to 70 parts per billion. Even at

this low concentration level off site disposal of the concrete may be difficult. The difficulty arises not from the concentration of the contaminant but the source. The products that leaked from the tanks were not characterized wastes but rather listed substances. Therefore anything that comes in contact with the waste takes on the status of that waste and must be handled accordingly, which in the case of some of the compounds is incineration.[36]

Of great weight is that all VOCs identified, after the disaster, were U.S. EPA[37] and/or OEPA-controlled substances.

Next, on 31 October 1989, ten months before the explosion, BASF had another fire; "the fire was caused by ignition of Heat Transfer Fluid 235."[38] There are abundant documents available as evidence that indicates licensed dumping and unlicensed spills were a regular event in the Evanston community's soil, sewers, and groundwater—fires were not uncommon. BASF, like so many other companies, employed unskilled labor, one factor in the numerous hazardous incidences it had brought about, and it continued to practice this during the cleanup.

OSHA was concerned about why the EPA did not take control of the site. In fact, OSHA warned BASF that they would take over the cleanup if BASF persisted in using a contractor (Heritage) who employed unskilled inspectors in the excavation area.[39] The U.S. EPA intervened, without apparent reason, to allow BASF to continue the cleaning despite the possibility of their contractors' incompetence. The attitude of the U.S. EPA is suspect in this case.

Lynne Weitzel, a law clerk to Deeohn Ferris, former director of the Lawyer's Committee for Civil Rights Under Law, states, "despite repeated requests, the information continues to be withheld by the EPA in the Washington, D.C., office."[40] It appears that there could be some reasons this information is being withheld. Weitzel added that "Mr. [Patrick] Cheng [of the U.S. EPA] also informed me that the information was being withheld under sections (b)(5) and (a)(4) of the Freedom of Information Act (FOIA)."[41] Given the potential and actual severity of the event this is strange and unsettling procedural behavior. This issue cannot be fully resolved here; however, it is rightly deserving of attention in a following study.

The citizens of Evanston have received only token acknowledgment of the toxic problems that plague their community. Dave Ortlieb, director of the International Chemical Workers Union Health and Safety Department, confirms that this is a problem for communities in general. He asserts that "industrial facilities and communities are unprepared to understand and respond to the consequences of chemical accidents."[42] The question that comes from this is if industry has not put in place safeguards, and they are the ones engaged in the risky business, who should provide the safety net? It is held that those who had the necessary information and were in a position of power to act in the citizens' interest did not immediately and preemptively do so. Therefore, this racial minority community is left with no choice but to inform, educate, and act for itself, fostering the appearance to those who are unfamiliar with federal, state, and local legislation and ordinances, of being reactionary.[43] Network Advocating Legislation Stopping Environmental Toxicity (NALSET) assumed the frustrating task of compelling the authorities to provide information about the possible risk that they had experienced.

The people of Evanston were victims of the authorities' failure to provide them with adequate protection against BASF, who could, would, and did harm them. What compounds this problem is that BASF was endowed with impunity and applauded for its economic strength.[44] It will be argued that BASF can be held accountable for *voluntary waste*,[45] and that it was in violation of its duty to notify the community of spills and excessive toxic risk. BASF has a history of polluting, and violating the Right-To-Know Act in minority communities.[46]

"On numerous occasions," write Dority and Currie, "the community prior to the explosion and after, has requested access to information, cooperation and communication." As earlier mentioned, the right to know is often not interpreted as such, but rather takes on the legal status of a privilege. According to a news report, resident Karl Price affirms that "we've had fumes from that plant (BASF) on a regular basis. All the time, we've complained, but nothing much was ever done."[47] Lillian Price makes some empirically based claims that are interesting: "The grass used to turn red," in her backyard, which was about one hundred yards from the plant. "It was a fine red dust or something. I'd have to close up the house. We never found out what it was."[48]

The BASF explosion at Inmont (Dana Avenue) had the potential of another Bhopal disaster.[49] There are a number of commentators who have argued that the BASF Dana plant explosion was a devastating phenomenon of environmental magnitude similar to the Bhopal experience.[50]

Groundwater Technologies, Inc., employed a map that shows that heavy concentrations of toluene and other toxic chemicals were found in the Evanston soil. The report of the governor's commission charted toxic soil contamination adjacent to the BASF plant encroaching on the residential community of Evanston. Only a very limited industrial zoned area in the Norwood community was in fact affected, and to

the east in Walnut Hills, another predominantly Caucasian community, there was no significant concentration of toxic waste substances.[51]

Joseph Curry of Walnut Hills, a community that fell within the
three-mile radius for the class action suit against BASF, stated, "I live
in adjacent East Walnut Hills where we were spared damage and where
BASF's peculiar response wouldn't be tolerated for a minute."[52] He
continues, "BASF can, and must do better. Few of us would be willing to eat what the Evanston community is being served."[53] Curry, a
public affairs officer, stated that for himself as well as many persons
involved in public affairs and the disaster contingency planning field,
"there must have been a second explosion at BASF, in their ethics
department."[54] As Curry stated, treatment like that forced on the Evanston community would not be and was not tolerated in the city of
Norwood or other predominantly white communities like Walnut Hills.

Geographically, the BASF chemical plant, Inmont (Dana Avenue),
was situated in Evanston, between two densely populated communities—of which, the city of Norwood has a predominantly Caucasian
population. Norwood had an industrial buffer between BASF and its
residential concentration. Further, Cincinnati's zoning department had
placed, on both the east and the west side of the plant, two of the
community's playgrounds. This was in keeping with Cincinnati's rec-
reational policy for the Evanston community. The city's choice of a
site for the Evanston Community Center establishes that the decision
process relative to location was manifestly unjust. Additionally, the
public school was positioned within two blocks of the BASF plant.[55]
A predominantly African American nursing/retirement complex was located kitty-corner from the plant, directly in line with the force of
the blast.

The Cincinnati Metropolitan Housing Authority operates a senior
high-rise residence across the street from the BASF facility.[56] Neil
Blunt, executive director of MHA, informed those in attendance that
there were no evacuation plans for the building. The senior high-rise
was built to Seismic 2 specifications, yet Blunt claimed to have no
knowledge of the risk that BASF posed. He also cited "a problem with
the Fireman's Automatic Control system. It impeded the evacuation
of elderly people from the building."[57] Even the elderly people living
in a municipal complex were not properly protected.

The Agency for Toxic Substances and Disease Registry, which is
part of the U.S. Department of Health and Human Services, stated that
"the study [they would be conducting] won't look at the health of
people in the Evanston area, although that might come later."[58] A lack
of concern for the citizens' health was still apparent two and a half

years after the explosion. BASF (Dana) at that time was still considered, according to a newspaper article, to be a hazardous site.[59] This gives credence to the assertion that even when investigation or inquiries are done, they are usually sketchy, or performed by unskilled, unqualified, or poorly equipped personnel. A headline in the *Cincinnati Post* of 30 July 1990 states "Toxicity a Guess at BASF—Inspections Done by Nose." This headline serves as a warrant for a claim of procedural negligence.[60]

The BASF Dana Avenue site had been investigated many times regarding its illicit toxic releases. The haphazard method employed by the OEPA of investigating citizen complaints is a further example of the disregard attributed earlier to BASF and the city of Cincinnati and the U.S. agencies. An inspector representing the OPEA ought to arrive at a potentially toxic cite with more tools than his nose.

It is a matter of public record that Norwood as a result of the explosion evacuated people in over one thousand homes, where Cincinnati allowed local residents to come in and out of Evanston. In testimony at the governor's commission, a resident claimed that "the Evanston community was concerned that during the incident there did not appear to be evacuation plans in place and that people were allowed to enter the community during the emergency."[61]

According to a BASF site cleanup progress report dated 13 August 1990, Norwood received immediate and ongoing remedial and compensatory and restitutive intervention by BASF.[62] Also, immediately after the explosion there were three areas with asbestos-containing debris that were in the process of being cleaned. The first two areas were on Norwood's side of the plant and the third was the employees' parking lot. The cleaning of the railroad track area was being planned; it was also on the Norwood side.

A report by the Hamilton County Local Emergency Planning Committee disclosed a lack of equitable consideration.[63] Fire Chief Klaene testified that in Norwood "a hotline was established for callers to get information."[64] Also, Norwood police were going door to door alerting residents to the incident. In the same report it was asked why the media hadn't published the emergency number and why the agencies hadn't given the emergency number to persons when they called, and why was the media not given accurate information.[65] When pressed, Klaene admits that all relevant information was not available.

Further, there is some confusion here, since Klaene stated, in a news report on the day of the accident, that the access to information was delayed because the reports were not immediately available and who specifically was in charge of the information was also in question. Chief Klaene, when asked if he knew what chemicals were involved said, "A variety of chemicals were kept in the area of the explosion."[66] This was a purely rhetorical response to the question. In answer to the question, Was there any contamination of the injured people? he stated, "no contamination was reported. Injuries of victims were being washed out."[67] If there was no contamination reported, it certainly was not because there was no contamination. They do not wash out "no contamination" or, in other words, nothing. The following summarizes the position taken here on the matter of equity. When asked if BASF had provided an evacuation plan, the response was, "Norwood has an emergency evacuation plan."[68] It follows that Evanston's population, those who had the most risk, was never planned for. As well it follows that BASF never provided emergency evacuation plans.

Those communities that were close to BASF—Norwood, Evanston, and Walnut Hills—according to the U.S. census, were working-class populations, and many in Evanston were unemployed. James O'Reilly wrote, in a limited objection to settlement to Judge Norman Murdock,[69] that the U.S. census tract indicates that the average economic condition in the radius area (Evanston, Norwood, and Walnut Hills) places the residents in similar financial circumstances. Thus, the choice of the target, Evanston, was not based solely on economic circumstances. The harm was directed toward Evanston and away from Norwood and Walnut Hills.

The BASF plant was licensed for "testing, storage, and development." Therefore, many adverse health-related effects from the variety of VOCs and/or other toxic substances were possibly present at any time. For chemical firms, like BASF, chemical hybridization is a particular nightmare, not to their principals, but to those who are forced to adjust to the daily struggle of surviving assaults from manmade exotic substances.[70]

For example, Dority and Currie say that despite many attempts over one year to find out what was wrong with a fifty-two-year-old woman, her doctor finally recognized the appropriateness of a "heavy metal analysis." Her doctor's examination revealed that she was suffering from intestinal hemorrhaging, numbness in her limbs, knee problems, two minor strokes at the base of her brain, chronic pressure in the top of her head, and an unexplained greying at the base of her brain. Her urine sample and other tests revealed that there was indeed a high concentration of heavy metal in her blood, which may have caused many of the ailments that she had experienced. The evidence was

provided by NALSET in an attempt to stop the uncontained soil rec-
lamation project that was being conducted by BASF at the site.[71]

From 1986 to 1990, the daily operations and the countless spills
and airborne emissions indicate that what occurred was not an accident: BASF, the city of Cincinnati, and the state of Ohio are each
responsible, because of negligence and willful disregard for the health
of minorities. Many must live with toxic emissions that were and still
are caused by the plant operations, the chemical fire, and the impact
of the chemically fueled explosions and the previous actions of willful violations of health standards and regulative codes.

Evanston Speaks

In sum, the Executive Summary of the Report of the Governor's Commission on the Storage and Use of Hazardous and Toxic Materials admits that "unfortunately, the BASF accident was not unique. As a major
industrial state Ohio has literally thousands of plants and businesses
that use hazardous and toxic substances on a regular basis."[72] Even if
it is conceded that industrial development must equal "risky business,"[73]
and it is not, it is a matter of fundamental justice that selection of
community targets ought not be based on arbitrary determinants such
as race, ethnicity, income, and so on. Those persons who are not status valued are placed, due to economic restrictions, in areas where
hazardous activity is practiced routinely and daily. Those who do the
harm, because of their income, are not forced to live in the midst of
their activities.

Concentric zoning, explained by the Chicago School, distances the
immediate consequences of these harmful effects from where the skilled
laborers, managers, directors, and executives live. By way of contrast,
menial labor employees and neighbors are subjected to the adverse
effects of the nocuous particles that come from the industrial site.[74]

This case study and abundant literature on the subject substantiate
the allegation of environmental racism stemming from industrial activity. Economics plays a major role in what amounts to a modern
form of "institutionalized environmental racism." The most violent
aspect of these phenomena can be seen in the idea presented by Rab-
bi Joachim Prinz. It is his position that the German Reich turned the
world into a ghetto by bringing about a state of "neighborlessness."
He recounts that "on the marketplace, in the street, in the public tav-
ern, everywhere is ghetto."[75] Remember the words of Martin Luther
King, Jr., who stated, "we cannot be satisfied as long as a Negro's
basic mobility is from a smaller ghetto to a larger one."[76]

Human enterprise must come to operationalize Scherer's upstream/downstream relationship as a global restraining objective. Any world ecological view must encompass the extent of all humans' ingenuity tempered by strict ethical deontological constraints.[77] What we must emphasize, and through further discussions demonstrate, is that we can employ our knowledge responsibly, overcoming our tendency toward unjust action toward the weak.

Can anything be done to reverse the present practice that allows corporations like BASF to continue to affect, initially and primarily, persons who are institutionally discriminated against or disempowered?[78] Can we understand that as W. E. B. DuBois states, "some have grown fat, some have grown rich by the aggression and destruction of others"?[79] It is little wonder that those who are adversely affected experience a form of status paralysis caused by the fear of death and are impeded in their efforts to deflect the institutionalized activity of large powerful bureaucracies and international corporations.[80]

In response to the questions just posed as to whether anything can be done, I admit that I am ill equipped to provide such an answer, but I believe that an ethical rule can direct all toward a better course. The ethical authority for this assertion can be summed up in these words, "social and economic inequalities are . . . to be to the greatest benefit of the least advantaged members of society."[81] Were the citizens of Evanston victims of environmental racism? I have endeavored to prove through this work that their belief that they were victimized is not based on emotion but on facts. They were treated unjustly and they were subjected to harsher treatment and greater disregard then any group should be treated in a fair, rule-based ethical and moral society—this has been established herein.

Notes

I would like to thank the cochairs of NALSET (Dora Dority and Ed Currie) and the citizens of Evanston whose courage is to be admired by all. NALSET is responsible for providing the majority of the research that has been utilized in this case study. Without them, there would be less depth to this investigation. My appreciation goes to Laura Westra and SSHRC Grant 806-93-0027, as well. Without her help and sponsorship I would not have had the resources to do this work.

1. Dora Dority and Edward Currie, cochairpersons: Network Advocating Legislation Stopping Environmental Toxicity (NALSET). Evanston, Cincinnati, Ohio U.S.A. NALSET is a nonfunded organization. Financial resources have come from Edward Currie and Dora Dority. Dority lives one and one-

half blocks from the BASF plant. The alliance formed as a result of the anguish they felt after years of pleas and fear for protection. Their apprehensions were finally manifested through the BASF explosion, yet their suffering remained a matter of little or no concern to the perpetrator. The aftermath of the BASF explosion yielded very little information about health or any risk. Thus, NALSET set out to compile as much data on the explosion's consequences as they could. Much of the material employed here was obtained as a result of their painstaking efforts. The expressions of frustration by the people of Evanston were the focus of *Issues in Science, Sociology and the Urban Environment* (I.S.S.U.E.), March 5, 1994: A symposium sponsored by the Association of Philosophical Thinkers, held at Assumption College, University of Windsor, Windsor, Ontario.

2. Sylvia Noble Tesh. *Hidden Arguments, Political Ideology, and Disease Prevention Policy* (New Brunswick and London: Rutgers University Press), 140. See also *Environmental Justice, Environmental Equity, Environmental Racism, Environmental Genocide in the Evanston Community, Cincinnati.* Abstract in *The I.S.S.U.E.* Program (University of Windsor) volume 4 (1994).

3. Report of the Governor's Commission on Storage and Use of Hazardous and Toxic Material. December 1990. Convened 13 August, 1990, I–1.

4. Robert D. Bullard, *Confronting Environmental Racism: Waste Trade and Agenda 21.* Conference, United Nations Program on Environment and Development, Agenda 21, 13–14 January 1994.

5. In British law and the laws of countries adopting the British jurisprudential model, "eminent domain" means that the queen has all rights to determine land use. "The crown" or the government are in fact surrogate agents of the queen. The authority vested in the queen's agency gives the absolute right to confiscate land for its use or purpose. By contrast, in the United States this term refers to natural law—the eminent domain of nature.

6. Mark Sagoff, "Takings, Just Compensation, and the Environment," in *Upstream/Downstream Issues in Environmental Ethics,* ed. by Donald Scherer (Philadelphia: Temple University Press, 1990), 148–79.

7. Donald Scherer, "The Molding of Norms and Environments," in *Upstream/Downstream,* 1990, 19–39.

8. Correspondence from Bob Knox, U.S. EPA, 4 January 1994.

9. U.S. Environmental Protection Agency, *Environmental Justice Initiatives* (Administration and Resources Management). EPA 200–R–93–001 (Washington, D.C.: Government Printing Office), February 1994.

10. Elaine Draper, *Risky Business* (Cambridge: Cambridge University Press, 1991). Laura Westra, "On Risky Business," in a review article for *Business Ethics Quarterly* 4, no. 1 (January 1994): 97–110.

11. Initially it is important to understand that the explosion was the result of the cumulative effects of the ongoing hazardous levels of toxification of the residential community of Evanston.

12. *Report of the Governor's Commission on Storage and Use of Hazardous and Toxic Materials,* Cincinnati Area Office, 29 October 1990, A–71.

13. Ibid.

14. Ibid.

15. Ohio Environmental Protection Agency (OEPA), *Fact Sheet Summary of BASF Corp. Citation and Proposed Penalties,* 1989.

16. News–USDL, 9 November 1990, U.S. Department of Labor Office of Information, Washington, D.C. Occupational Safety and Health Administration, Deborah Page Crawford; USDL 90–586.

17. Ibid.

18. U.S. Department of Labor, *Fact Sheet Summary of BASF Corp. and Proposed Penalties.*

19. Taken from the statement by Dave Ortlieb, director, Health and Safety Department, given on behalf of the International Chemical Workers Union, before the Ohio Governor's Commission on the Storage and Use of Hazardous and Toxic Waste Materials, at St. Marks Church, Evanston, Ohio, 20 September 1990.

20. Scott Burgins, " Safety Threats Plagued Plant," *Cincinnati Enquirer,* 20 July 1990.

21. This statement was provided to me by NALSET.

22. Nick Miller, "Safety concerns slow plant blast inquiry," *The Cincinnati Post* (*Post–Local News*), 3 July 1990.

23. This information was supplied by NALSET.

24. On 28 October 1989, Eric C. Mather of Petro Environmental Technologies (PET) submitted a report to BASF (PET Project No. 89–085).

25. Ibid., 32.

26. Ohio Environmental Protection Agency 1989; also OEPA 1982.

27. Ibid.

28. Eric Mather, *Preliminary Report of Findings for Closure of "59" Tank Pit Underground Storage Tanks* for BASF Corp., PET Project No. 89–085 (Norwood, Ohio, 1989); emphasis in brackets.

29. Table 5–10, *Summary of Tentatively Identified Compounds Detected in Soil Samples.* Number of VOCs, TICs: 1; Number of BNAs, TICs: 13. Primary compound groups: Aliphatic hydrocarbons and carborylic acids.

30. Hamilton County (Local Emergency Planning Committee) LEPC BASF–Response. As per Kim Burke—home office of BASF notified Cincinnati Communication Division at 1910 [Operator #14–SGT Collins (Supr.)]. Notification by Joe Stephenson.

31. Report of the Governor's Commission, A–7.

32. Report of the Governor's Commission, A–7.

33. Ibid.

34. *News—USDL,* 11–5.

35. Volatile organic compounds are different from volatile organic chemicals since the latter are known substances and the former are derivative substances composed of several chemicals.

36. Mather, *Preliminary Report of Findings for Closure.* It is interesting that the report refers to the plant's being in Norwood since geographically

this is not the case. Further I believe that this factual error is due to Norwood's influence in forcing BASF to clean up their act. Topographical maps show that a very small portion of the contamination from the plant is located in Norwood's jurisdiction. Whether this was the result of Norwood's ability to cause BASF to clean up could be the focus of another work.

37. U.S. Environmental Protection Act.

38. As noted in a letter from Valerie Thomas of BASF to John Trapp of the Metropolitan Sewer District of Greater Cincinnati, cc. to OEPA Emergency Response, Spill #10–31–4191.

39. An interoffice memorandum written on Weston Managers Designers Consultants letterhead 7 August 1990. Subject: OSHA activities at the BASF site.

40. A memorandum to Tom Henderson and Deeohn Ferris, IRE: Remaining questions to be explored concerning the BASF explosion 19 July 1990, dated 12 August 1993.

41. Ibid. When NALSET did in fact receive some of the information, there were words and sections that were blacked out.

42. Statement of Dave Ortlieb, director, Health and Safety Department, on behalf of the International Chemical Workers Union, before the Ohio Governor's Commission on the Storage and Use of Hazardous and Toxic Materials, at St. Mark's Church, Evanston, Ohio, 20 September 1990.

43. Dora Dority and Ed Currie, NALSET, 20 April 1993, *Review of BASF Case Study,* a letter addressed to Laura Westra. Mark Sagoff, *The Economy of the Earth—Philosophy, Law, and the Environment* (Cambridge: Cambridge University Press, 1988). He describes this as "affective states" which are ascribed to the person to discount the positive validity of their claims. Bill E. Lawson, "Crime, Minorities, and the Social Contract," *Criminal Justice Ethics* 9, no. 2 (Summer/Fall 1990): 14–24. Edited for effect.

44. Ibid., 16.

45. Generally, an act by one in rightful possession of land who has less than a renter's interest in the land, which decreases his or her property value, or in this case the value of their neighbor's property.

46. *BASF: A Report on the Company's Environmental Policies and Practices,* The Council of Economic Priorities, Corporate Environmental Data Clearinghouse, November 1991: (Council on Economic Priorities), 11.

47. Terry Flynn, "Fumes at BASF Plant Not New to Neighbors," *Cincinnati Enquirer,* 22 July 1990.

48. Ibid.

49. On 2 December 1984 two thousand residents of Bhopal, India, died and two hundred thousand others were seriously injured (and many are experiencing health problems still) from the Union Carbide pesticide plant explosion (Ibid., III–1). A report entitled *Profile—BASF Produces Transports and Disposes of Toxic Chemicals in Hundreds of Communities—Why You Should Be Concerned if BASF Is in Your Community* (Oil, Chemical, and Atomic Workers Union).

50. Report of the Governor's Commission.

51. Ibid., Drawings no. 5–22 through 5–29.

52. Randy Ludlow and Lisa Cardillo Rose, *Cincinnati Post*, 21 July 1990.

53. Ibid.

54. Ibid.

55. On 5 January 1987, a report done by student Frank Stoy, "Air Pollution Control," for Mrs. Cissell, St. Mark's School, complained of strong odors.

56. The Report of the Governor's Commission. *Cincinnati Hearing Notes,* A–8.

57. Ibid.

58. Linda Dono Reeves, "Neighbors Plead for Action on Health," *Cincinnati Enquirer*, 8 December 1993.

59. "City Sites Called Hazardous," *Cincinnati Enquirer*, 23 December 1992, D–2.

60. Lisa Popyk, "Toxicity a Guess at BASF—Inspections Done by Nose," *Cincinnati Post*, 30 July 1990.

61. The Report of the Governor's Commission, A–7.

62. Prepared and conducted by *Asbestos Compliance Technology Incorporated (ACT)*.

63. Hamilton County Local Emergency Planning Committee, 8 August 1990.

64. Ibid.

65. Ibid.

66. Ibid.

67. Ibid.

68. Ibid.

69. Cases A–90–075577 and A–90–07615, *Limited Objection to Settlement Terms by Class Member in Response to Notice of Class Certification* (Court of Common Pleas, Hamilton County, Ohio–Civil Division). O'Reilly is a professor of law at the University of Cincinnati College, and the author of sixteen law textbooks and more than eighty articles in environment and government regulation fields.

70. Elaine Draper, 1991; Laura Westra, "A Transgenic Dinner? Ethical and Social Issues in Biotechnology and Agriculture," *Journal of Social Philosophy* 24, no. 3 (Winter 1993): 215–32.

71. The information was taken from a cover letter sent to Agency for Toxic Substances and Disease Registry (ATSDR), Region 5, Ms. Muroya, RE: Resident Heavy Metal Urinalysis.

72. Ibid.

73. Westra, "On Risky Business."

74. Laura Westra, *Environmental Proposal for Ethics—The Principle of Integrity* (Lanham, Md.: Rowman & Littlefield, 1994).

75. Zygmunt Bauman, *Modernity and the Holocaust* (Ithaca, N.Y.: Cornell University Press, 1991), 123–24.

76. Martin Luther King, Jr., "I Have a Dream," speech given at the Lincoln Memorial, Washington, D.C.

77. This view is carefully articulated in the findings of the "Workshop on Prevention of Accidents Involving Hazardous Substances—Good Management

Practice" (Berlin, 22–25 May 1989); Westra, *Environmental Proposal for Ethics*, 96–101

78. Bauman, *Modernity and the Holocaust*; John Porter, *Vertical Mosaic—An Analysis of Social Class and Power in Canada* (University of Toronto Press, 1969); W. E. Burghhardt DuBois, *Black Reconstruction in America* (New York: S. A. Russell Company), 31; Robert D. Bullard, "Overcoming Racism in Environmental Decision Making," *Environment* 36, no. 4 (May 1994): 1–43.

79. DuBois, *Black Reconstruction*.

80. Ibid., 119.

81. John Rawls, *Political Liberalism* (New York: Columbia University Press, 1993), 6.

7

The Faces of Environmental Racism: Titusville, Alabama, and BFI

Laura Westra

BFI and Titusville, Alabama

In 1990 Browning-Ferris Industries (BFI) started to plan the siting for a "garbage transfer and recyclery" in Titusville, a predominantly black neighborhood in Birmingham, Alabama. The intent was to acquire a facility at which accumulated garbage and waste could be mechanically reduced, and recyclables could be separated for sale to other markets, while the rest could be transported to dumps in Walker and Lawrence Counties, about thirty miles away.

At first glance this plan does not appear to be problematic although even in this brief summary, questions arise. The main problem is the chosen location: a site in a predominantly black community. Further, a pattern seemed to be present since twenty-six of twenty-eight BFI Alabama operations were located in black neighborhoods.[1] Leaving this issue aside for the moment, we must consider some other problematic aspects of the case, before turning to a description of events.

The *goal* BFI was intent on achieving—that is, the siting of the facility, and linking it to a rural dump site—may reveal further difficulties, aside from the *means* BFI employed to achieve it. The proposed facility was to be placed on a lot owned by Golden Flake Co., a food manufacturer whose operation was on an adjacent lot. The area was zoned M-2 (Heavy Industry District), a designation that was restricted, under Section 2 (2), under Use Regulations as follows:[2]

> no building or occupancy permit shall be issued for any of the following uses until and unless the location of such use shall have been approved by the City Council after report by the Planning Commission in accordance with the procedure set forth in Article VII, Section 3:

a. Abattoir.
b. Acid manufacture.
c. Atomic power plant or reactor.
d. Explosive Manufacture or Storage.
e. Fat, grease, lard or tallow rendering or refining.
f. Glue or size manufacture.
g. Garbage, offal or dead animal reduction or dumping.
h. Petroleum refining.
i. Stockyard or slaughter of animals.
j. Junkyards, salvage yards.
k. Hazardous waste or toxic disposal.
l. Medical and infectious material disposal.

Item "g" appears to need clarification: does the proposed facility intend "garbage reduction" (prohibited explicitly) to refer to activities proposed by BFI, or does "reduction" only mean chemical, rather than mechanical treatment (as was later argued)? In other words, absent a special permit, is any handling of garbage implicitly prohibited by item g?

Another question is, what is the status of the dumping sites in Walker and Lawrence Counties, designated as final repositories of the waste, to which the trucks went daily, carrying 1,500 tons of garbage? About 30 percent of the city water in Birmingham is taken from Burnt Creek, Mulberry Fork, and the Warrior River, all of which are close enough to the Walker County landfill to raise serious concerns about hazardous seepage. Finally, the proposed siting of the BFI facility would add one more potential hazard to an area already containing heavy industry much too close to human habitation. Thus the "brown-fields" phenomenon would be perpetuated in a community already suffering from disproportionate environmental impacts. Brown-fields are geographic areas inhabited largely by people of color where polluting activities integral to industrial culture are concentrated to the detriment of human health and real estate values.

In sum, even aside from the means employed by BFI to achieve its goals, the goals were all questionable on various grounds. Regarding the means, or the practices and procedures employed by BFI, we will need to keep in mind several points: (1) issues related to freedom of consent; (2) secrecy, access to information, and due process; (3) the possibility of improper and illegal business practices; and (4) environmental racism, which is the main focus of this study.

BFI's own "Development Chronology for Birmingham Transfer Station" indicates that on 16 January 1991, BFI requested an opinion from Thomas Magee, chief planner at the Birmingham Department of Urban Planning, "as to whether BFI's proposed use of the subject property would require City Council approval under Section 2 (2) (g) of the M-2 Zoning Ordinance." On 23 January Magee confirmed the project's feasibility in accordance with the M-2 zoning, and in March, BFI retained BCM engineers to conduct environmental site assessment of the property. In April, the "Option Agreement" between BFI and Golden Flake Snack Foods, Inc., was executed for the purchase of the proposed site. In July, BFI submitted a subdivision application (which requires only notification of adjacent neighbors, that is, Golden Flake, of intent to subdivide), and a public hearing under Case No. S-73-91 was set up. They alone were deemed affected parties, as if others in the area had no legitimate interest in the matter. But even if the same notice *had* been sent to all property owners in the area either adjacent to or near the property in question, neither BFI's name nor its intended purpose appears anywhere on this document.[3]

Hence, when Thomas Magee, on 11 March 1992, signed the approval of the application on behalf of the State of Alabama, Jefferson County, and his office, only these officials appeared to be aware of the identity of the principals involved in the transaction and of their specific aims. The Public Hearing was set for the same date, 11 March 1992. On 3 June 1992, the Notice of Second Public Hearing was finally delivered to adjacent property owners, with a copy sent to a North Titusville neighborhood representative. This notice "specifically recites the proposed use of the property" as a "solid waste transfer and recyclery operation for Browning-Ferris Industries." The second public hearing took place in November 1992, at which time all permits/approvals were already long in place, conditional only to the "actual construction of the dedicated public street" as previously agreed upon.

In the interim, on 23 July at BFI's request, Magee issued a letter confirming that neither the subdivision application nor other documents of approval were subject to expiration. He confirmed these points once again on 10 August. In February 1993 the completion bond for the public street was posted, and in March of that year, the dedication of the public street was accepted by the City of Birmingham. The next day, BFI and Golden Flake Snack Foods closed the purchase and sale of the subject property. A foundation permit was issued to BFI on 29 April, and the final inspection of building plans took place on 14 May 1993. This chronology shows that BFI had indeed complied with the officials' interpretation of the letter of the law at that time, although later that interpretation was discredited by the courts. But the rash of news articles and short features appearing in the *Birmingham News* from May 1993 on indicates that the issue was by no means a simple bureaucratic decision with no implication beyond the parties involved.[4]

BFI's Proposed Goals and the
Means to Their Implementation

Once the citizens of Titusville became aware of the true nature of the transaction taking place and of the plans they had thought simply meant the expansion of the present snack food operation, the citizens' association retained an attorney, W. L. Williams. Citizens "flocked to the Council chambers" to attend all meetings,[5] to protest. Birmingham City Council member Eddie Blenkenship spoke strongly of his opposition to BFI's plans and of their attempt "to slip" the transfer station into the city. But he expressed his concern that, because of the care with which BFI had complied with all rules and regulations, even the strong opposition he anticipated might be frustrated.

In spite of his strong words ("I want you to know that no member of the council has anything to do with what is going on," and "whatever takes place, I stand with you one hundred percent") Blenkenship's commitment was later questioned. On 6 June 1993, the president of TAG (an association representing three Titusville neighborhoods), C. L. Danzey, suggested that Blenkenship was only attempting to "save face" in an election year. He should have been aware of BFI's plans all along, as his own son, Don Blenkenship, served as a lawyer for BFI in January 1991, when the company first approached urban planning for permission to build the transfer station.

Birmingham's black mayor, Richard Arrington, claimed he could not block BFI's plans or "instruct the Urban Planning Department to withhold these permits," without risking a multimillion dollar lawsuit from BFI. In June 1993, Michael Dobbins, director of urban planning, defended his approach, praising the fact that notices were duly executed but admitting that "notice procedures may have been too casual for a case of this sensitivity."[6] Dobbins said, "while I understand these are charged times politically, I would hope that we could find a path to allay the fears these people are harboring."

This move is typical of those who attempt to hide some private agenda from public scrutiny. Instead of fully accepting the blame for his complicity in the virtual secrecy surrounding the potentially hazardous project, for which no stakeholder consent had been obtained, Dobbins tried to cast the problem as one of faulty public relations, against public ignorance and unjustified fears. Instead, the primary concern should have been public safety and democratic process and consent. "Allaying fears" with whatever might be offered as a public pacifier,[7] instead of appropriate public policy, is grossly immoral. Citizens' anger over lack of consultation and free consent was well founded, as was their concern about the hazards facing them. As far as consultation is concerned, the initial steps taken by BFI were indeed shrouded in secrecy. This is evident from Dobbins' admission, as well as the wording of documents that bore no reference to BFI or to the plans for the property. What about risk exposure? The fact that, as Dobbins explains to Attorney W. L. Williams, "the nearest home is about 1,500 feet . . . away from the property line and about 2,000 feet away from the transfer building," is hardly reassuring.

In a somewhat similar case in Woburn, Massachusetts,[8] the required half-mile buffer zone, even when it was simply between industry and a residential area, proved insufficient, hence hazardous and even fatal in many cases. Thus, the BFI zoning, as it stood, was problematic. This in itself would constitute what I have elsewhere termed a problem of "risky business." No comfort is to be found in BFI's disingenuous assurance that "they would pledge to wash down the building's interior every day," when one realizes that the toxic water itself would not magically vanish from the area. It would simply add to the problems the residents already faced from the inappropriate concentration of businesses already allowed to operate too close to their homes. Further, although only "recyclables" would be expected to remain in the facility overnight, given the generally warm climate of the area, neither insects nor rodents could be excluded from consideration. The latter might present an extremely grave problem, as noted by the *Birmingham Press* in its discussion of a parallel facility in Marietta, Georgia. The recent Third World reemergence of pneumonic plague due to uncontrolled industrial waste in India should render one extremely cautious. An alternative would be to employ strong chemical pest/rodent controls, but these, too, carry their own health hazards. Finally, the intense heavy equipment traffic in the area would add yet another risk through increased street traffic and hazardous fumes.

The ultimate destination of the waste in Walker County was also problematic, considering BFI's questionable business practices in securing the exclusive control over the dump sites. Apparently, one of BFI's concerns was to put the facilities in place quickly, before new, more stringent laws governing garbage disposal would come into effect in October 1992. However, according to Alabama law, BFI's exclusive rights (or privilege rights) to operate dumps in Walker and Lawrence Counties constituted a form of "franchise," or monopoly. It should therefore have been open to bidding from other companies, but it was not. Hence Jimmy Evans, Alabama's attorney general, ruled to have BFI contracts in regard to the dumps declared invalid.

This case is primarily concerned with Titusville and BFI. But it is

important to note that tactics similar to those employed in the acquisition of the Titusville property were also employed in the related
proposed operation in Walker County. That case eventually came to
court on 24 June 1994, as Ralph Beavers and nine other residents of
Walker County sought "permanent injunctions to enjoin the defendants
(BFI) from constructing a sanitary solid waste landfill on 680 acres
in eastern Walker County." I cannot present all the details of the case
here; it suffices for our purpose to review the plaintiffs' appeal, since
they won against BFI:

> The plaintiffs have made many arguments on appeal: (1) that the lan-
> guage used in the contract entered by the authority, the Commission
> and BFI granted an exclusive franchise to BFI, and therefore, that the
> contract should have been competitively bid; (2) that all contracts en-
> tered into by local governments pursuant to the Solid Wastes Disposal
> Act are subject to Alabama's Competitive Bid Law requirements and,
> thus, must be competitively bid; (3) that a provision of the Solid Waste
> Disposal Authorities Act that they say it purports to exempt such au-
> thorities from the competitive Bid Law . . . ; and (5) that the October
> 19, 1990 agreement entered into by the Commission with BFI before
> BFI applied for local approval of the Bryan landfill site prevented the
> Commission from making the decision on local approval objectively and
> impartially and, thus, violated the plaintiffs' rights of due process in a
> fair hearing. Finally, the attorney general of Alabama has submitted
> amicus curiae briefs to this Court contending that the Authority and the
> Commission's agreement with BFI was an unconstitutional grant of
> exclusive franchise because it did not comply with the competitive Bid
> Law.[9]

Titusville citizens' concerns about their drinking water and their
rights to information and free consent were equally well founded, and
not simply unwarranted "fears," to be pacified through public relations campaigns. Before the Birmingham Zoning Board of Adjustments
voted against the citizens' appeal on 11 June 1993, a rare coalition of
mostly black citizens from the neighborhood, mostly white rural Walker
Countians, environmentalists, and UAB officials packed city council
chambers against BFI.[10] Four of the five zoning board members were
needed in order to approve the appeal; but the vote "was split along
racial lines." All three black members voted *in favor* of the appeal,
the two white members voted *against* it and defeated it. Lawyer
David Sullivan, representing the residents, appealed the decision primarily on the grounds that Tom Magee "misinterpreted the law" when
he equated M-2 zoning for heavy industry with any garbage-handling
facility, and failed to require a special permit for a garbage facility in

an area zoned for M-2 heavy industry. Further, the coalition lobbying against BFI protested on grounds of (1) environmental racism and (2) "sneakiness" on the part of BFI, or what I have termed the lack of democratic due process and of free, informed consent for all stakeholders.

Thus, both BFI's proposed facility and its link to improperly acquired landfills in rural counties outside Birmingham were open to moral and legal questions, as was the means by which they moved to implement their goals. Democratic procedures were not used, and since information was withheld from citizens, the residents could not be deemed to have freely consented to BFI's activities in their neighborhood, nor to those in Walker County, from which 30 percent of Birmingham's drinking water was drawn. In essence, their moral rights to be consulted and respected in regard to decisions expected to have a serious impact on their lives were not upheld, a position that conflicts with law, the U.S. Constitution (particularly Amendments 5 and 14), and morality.[11]

It can be argued that all stakeholders and potentially affected parties had an absolute right not to have grave health hazards imposed on them by any business operation.[12] But questions of unfair imposition of burdens, improper zoning, corporate irresponsibility, and lack of stakeholders' consent may unfortunately be imposed on all poor and powerless people regardless of color or ethnic origin. However, in the next section, I show specifically that the Titusville case is a blatant example of "environmental racism."

BFI's Project and Environmental Racism

The proposed site of the BFI facility was bordered by several industries, a highway, and railroad tracks, and the nearest residence was approximately half a mile from the property line of the proposed site, which, as already noted, was insufficient for safety. The practice of continuing to locate such operations in areas already used for "doubtful" enterprises, which amounts to the continued support of brown-fields in certain areas where minority and impoverished communities were also located, has decided racist overtones. If an area is already considered to be in a less valuable neighborhood, and if it has in it business enterprises that would not be tolerated in an affluent neighborhood, then the road has clearly been paved for the perpetuation of brown-fields, where fewer questions might be asked for the siting of similar, new facilities.[13]

This is in fact what happened in Titusville, according to the evidence of the chronology, which describes the events as they unfolded leading to conflict, disagreement, and eventually to violence. On 19 March 1991, we are told, "BFI hired BCM Engineers to conduct an environmental assessment of property [*sic*]." Two points are noteworthy in that regard: (1) the environmental assessment was of the property, and the connection between it and the environmental impact of BFI's operation was never assessed by either the EPA or any other institution or public body that could have funded an independent scientific study;[14] (2) the synergistic effects of the operation from a holistic point of view were never given scientific attention, a serious oversight since the proposed operation was already surrounded by other business operations. From a scientific standpoint, it is not sufficient to say "exposure to X is safe and can be allowed at level Y," unless *other* substance exposures are also factored into the toxicology or health assessment research.[15] It is clear that this recommendation is not usually followed by individual companies, who prefer to sponsor their own studies, without an independent scientific voice to counterbalance the inevitable bias of internally commissioned studies.

One can object at this point that the circumstances and hazards here described are not necessarily specific to one race or group. This, of course, is correct, as far as it goes; but what is left out is the original site choice for the various industrial operations, which predate the proposed BFI addition. This in turn shows and implies the deliberate perpetuation of brown-fields in the area of a community of color.

When assessing and analyzing the case, it helps to use the framework provided by Robert Bullard, the five "principles of environmental justice," including (1) rights to protection; (2) prevention of harm; (3) shifting the burden of proof to the polluters; (4) obviating the need for proof of intent to discriminate; and (5) redressing existing inequities.[16]

The EPA's Office of Civil Rights now investigates "charges of end environmental discrimination under Title VI of the 1964 Civil Rights Act" (including cases involving the siting of waste facilities in Michigan, Alabama, Mississippi, and Louisiana). The Environmental Equal Rights Act of 1993 (HR 1924) is intended to prevent waste facilities from being sited in environmentally disadvantaged communities.[17] Moreover, aside from race-specific legislation, the simple right to equal protection under the U.S. Constitution (Amendments 5 and 14) ought to be sufficient to guarantee these communities and individuals their rights to protection from harm. Yet it would take another act to clarify and codify the required protection for people and communities of color: that act was U.S. Executive Order No. 12898, The Environmental Justice Act, which was signed by President Bill Clinton on 11 February 1994. It states:

> each Federal agency shall make achieving environmental justice part of its mission identifying and addressing, as appropriate, disproportionately high and adverse human health or environmental effects of its programs, policies and activities on minorities and low income populations.[18]

What is at issue here is clearly a disproportionate burden placed on communities and neighborhoods of color in comparison to others and an unfair distribution of benefits. Hence, the prevention of harm becomes a focal point of consideration. Bullard says, "Prevention, the elimination of the threat before harm occurs, should be the preferred strategy of governments. For example, to solve the lead problem, the primary focus should be shifted from treating children who have been poisoned, to eliminating the threat by removing lead from houses."[19] The same point, that is, the need for prevention, also emphasizes the need to "shift the burden of proof" to polluters rather than waiting for an unavailable, chimeric proof that this or that substance/process/ activity is the clear-cut or sole cause of a specific harm, for which we also demand to see unequivocal results. This approach, as many have pointed out, is as flawed from the standpoint of justice as it is from that of logic. Substances and processes are not innocent until proven guilty, people are; and the idea of an unequivocal proof of harm clearly pointing the finger at one toxic substance is a logical and practical impossibility in the face of synergistic effects and multiple exposures. Hence, as I have argued in my discussion of risky business, it is up to the corporate bodies who produce, use, and eventually dispose of these hazardous substances to prove to us that their products will not be a threat to health and life from cradle to grave, *before* the inception of their activities, not after, when someone else may be unfairly burdened with the other side of their profitable operation.[20]

The fourth point Bullard advocates, "obviating proof of intent to discriminate," is particularly germane to the Titusville situation. There may not often be clear evidence of evil discriminatory intentions; most often, carelessness, negligence, and self-interest will be the main causes of environmental racism. Regarding the case at hand, some have claimed that racism played no part at all, since both public service and police were integrated, comprising both black and white individuals.[21] This is less than convincing. In Mussolini's Italy as in Hitler's

Germany, genocide was perpetrated by Italians and Germans on Italians and Germans for a host of reasons, including the quest for power and other benefits. Hence, even the fact that both the police and other officials and bureaucrats in the case were fully integrated does not suffice to disprove the existence of environmental racism.

Indeed this represents a dangerous assumption that is based neither on facts of the literature on the topic, nor on legal precedent.[22] In *Castaneda v. Partida*, Justice Thurgood Marshall concurs with Justice Blackmun's opinion for the Court in upholding a Court of Appeals ruling in regard to a denial of equal protection of the law in the grand jury selection process in a case involving Mexican Americans. Marshall's opinion was that even the political dominance and control by the Mexican American majority in Hidalgo County did not entitle one "to assume without any basis in the record that all Mexican Americans, indeed all members of all minority groups have an 'inclination to assure fairness' to other members of their group." Marshall's attack on the dissenting position of Justice Powell provides an important statement and legal precedent about this problem:

> In the first place, Mr. Justice Powell's assumptions about human nature, plausible as they may sound, fly in the face of a great deal of social science, theory and research. Social scientists agree that members of minority groups frequently respond to discrimination and prejudice by attempting to disassociate themselves from the group, even to the point of adopting the majority's negative attitude towards the minority.[23]

This phenomenon, the justice continues, is particularly applicable to those members of minority groups "who have achieved some measure of economic or political success and thereby have gained some acceptability among the dominant group."[24]

Finally, the need "to redress existing inequities" will be equally important, as any activity that perpetuates existing brown-fields must be considered *prima facie* suspect. The involvement of city planners was described in the previous section. What was almost totally lacking appeared to be a concern with the residents' health, safety, and basic welfare as well as their human and constitutional rights. Had the protection and support of citizens' lives been their main concern, appropriate research, including the background and practices of BFI as well as the scientific assessment of the proposed facility's impact, would have been part of the responsibility of those empowered to issue permits and licenses. We already noted that scientific assessment did not take place, so that any claim that the facility posed no environmental dangers was not based on fact, but on the unsupported preferences of public servants and others who might have benefited from the siting. Negligence is no excuse for hazardous activity.[25] When not preceded by a thorough search for impartial information, it can be termed culpable negligence, particularly in the case of those entrusted with the public interest.

Reliance on information supplied by BFI, in particular, is additional evidence of negligence, as BFI has a clear record of illegal, hazardous activities, much of which exposes minorities to risk. For instance, BFI was the target of a "confidential in-house report" conducted by the Ohio EPA.[26] We discover that 90 percent of the special investigation (in conjunction with the Bureau of Criminal Identification and Investigation) consisted of investigating illegal hazardous waste activities. The remaining 10 percent was divided among solid waste and other cases; their investigation in criminal convictions is 22 percent of cases investigated. BFI figures prominently in their 1989 records: In one case, because of "10 counts total failure to analyze, illegal disposal of hazardous waste, conspiracy, water pollution," the sentence for J. Stirnkorb (their employee) was "1 year imprisonment reduced to 60 days imprisonment, remainder in community service and $30,000.00 fine"; further, BFI also was forced to pay a $3.5 million fine in a civil case, involving "1 count failure to follow proper disposal process."

No information is available on the location of the facilities where the violations occurred, but Robert Bullard's work casts further light on BFI's activities. *Dumping in Dixie* documents numerous cases in which BFI's facilities are shown to have been repeatedly sited in and around black neighborhoods. Such communities as Emelle, Alabama, and West Dallas and Houston, Texas, have BFI landfills and waste sites. Charles Streadit, president of Houston's Northeast Community Action Group against the Whispering Pines landfill, says:

Sure Browning Ferris Industries (owner of Whispering Pines landfill) pays taxes, but so do we. We need all the money we can get to upgrade our school system. But we shouldn't have to be poisoned to get improvements for our children. A silent war is being waged against black communities. Slowly we are being picked off by industries that don't give a damn about polluting our neighborhoods, contaminating our water, fouling our air, clogging our streets with big garbage trucks, and lowering our property values. It's hard enough for blacks to scrape and save enough money to buy a home, then you see your dream shattered by a garbage dump. That's a dirty trick. No amount of money can buy self-respect.[27]

The project, one of many of BFI's infamous facilities sited in neighborhoods of color, was fought by organized local residents, the Northeast Community Action Group (NECAG), purposely convened "to halt the construction of the facility." We are told that "the residents thought they were getting a shopping center, or new homes in their subdivision when construction on the landfill site commenced."[28] Eventually a lawsuit was filed in 1979, and it went to trial in 1984. Bullard says, "residents were upset because the proposed site was not only near their homes but within 1400 feet of their high school. Smiley High School was not equipped with air conditioning—not an insignificant point in the hot and humid Houston climate. Windows are usually left open while school is in session."[29] Although the judge in the case eventually ruled against the citizens, several advantages were gained: (1) the city council passed an ordinance restricting the construction of solid waste facilities near schools; (2) a 1980 city resolution was also passed to prohibit trucks carrying solid waste to dump in the controversial landfill; (3) the department of health changed and made more stringent its requirements for landfill permit applicants; (4) the black residents sent a clear message to legislators, governments, and companies like BFI, that they were now organized and active on environmental issues.[30] Many other such examples can be adduced from BFI's record.

What conclusions can be drawn for our purpose? Elected officials are entrusted by the citizens with the defense of the public interest. Indeed, the public interest entails looking after the *economic* interests of all, but that is not its only or even its first priority. Surely the protection of health and safety as well as the respect for individual and community rights are both not only a part of the public "good" public servants are expected to uphold: they represent a clear priority in the concept of "public interest." Hence both common sense and a responsible approach would have demanded a serious and thorough investigation of BFI's record. Noting that residents had only BFI's commissioned study to ensure them of the environmental safety of the project, officials should have demanded, minimally, that their "engineers' study" be juxtaposed to some independent scientific data about possible impacts, in addition to seeking EPA's involvement, at least under the acts mentioned earlier, many of which were already in place at that time. To permit BFI with its lengthy record of problems, racism, and convictions for environmental infractions both criminal and civil to operate in a vulnerable community would appear to be the height of irresponsibility toward the citizens, whose good the public servants were sworn to protect.

The Aftermath of the BFI Conflict: Demonstrations and Violence in Birmingham and Ongoing Legal Actions

The final aspects of racist intervention on the part of the police and other public service officials took place from 16 to 22 January 1994, just a few weeks short of the signing of the Executive Order against environmental racism. On Saturday, 15 January, black activists initiated a march on city hall in Birmingham, Alabama, to protest the siting of the BFI facility. Apparently police attempted to contain the marchers, at least until they could ascertain whether they had a permit for their demonstration. When it was found they did not, police both black and white decided to disband the marchers by driving police vehicles directly at the group and using mace and sticks to disperse the melee that ensued, even though many of the participants were children or young teenagers. Newspaper articles from the *Birmingham News*, the *Birmingham Post Herald,* and the *Atlanta Journal and Constitution* (16 to 22 January 1994) described the melee, which was also taped with moderate success and shown to Mayor Richard Arrington after the fact; the latter records a confrontation that became acrimonious and finally violent. Arrington said "he (had) received some information that Saturday's melee between Birmingham police and young demonstrators might have been avoided, if officers had shown more discretion."[31]

The following Monday was Martin Luther King, Jr. Day, and the mayor expressed hope that the "unfortunate incident" would not "cast a great cloud" over the proposed celebration. The same hope was expressed by some of the young demonstrators, many of whom wore African dress and dreadlocks, and waved a liberation flag, as they belonged to activist groups, the Malcolm X grassroots movement, the Ujima Youth Organization, and the Southern Organizing Committee.

Some might say that the protest did not involve directly or exclusively the citizens of Titusville; nevertheless, it is clear that the marchers had direct information about the economic conflict and the citizens' qualms about the facility. I feel it is quite possible that a visible presence of Titusville residents might have resulted in some form of retaliation from public officials in Birmingham had they been too clearly active in the protest.[32]

Also, the way the protest was handled was quite different from the way similar protests might have been handled, had the marchers been white. For instance, people from all over Canada converged on Clayoquot Sound, B.C., to protest on principle a policy that was environmentally unsound (logging old growth forests, hence another environmental protest). Neither those demonstrators, nor any of the others I have seen protesting the toxic substances in the Great Lakes, were ever treated in a violent manner, although they disrupted activities and proceedings that were environmentally wrong but not in themselves illegal at the time. Hence, even if (and there is no evidence on this question) *all* the marchers had been blacks from another area, this fact would not be sufficient to permit us to dismiss or ignore the whole incident.[33]

As could be expected, the citizens sought legal remedy, and BFI was eventually found to have acted improperly, as had the City of Birmingham, in granting permits that were neither sought in accordance with proper procedure, nor found to conform to existing regulations. The judgment came down against BFI and the operation of the facility was not permitted. BFI, in turn, sued the city for not complying with its plans.

But Birmingham did not abide by the court ruling intended to stop BFI. Rather, it went on to cut a deal with the company, and agreed to pay it $6.75 million. Attorney David Sullivan, representing the Titusville community, is presently in litigation, taking the case to the Supreme Court of Alabama. His brief states:

> (the residents) correctly understood the comments of the elected public officials to mean that if the citizens continued to oppose the fraudulent, bad faith and illegal deal between the City of Birmingham and BFI as consummated by the Consent Decree, Birmingham officials would then refuse to protect the citizens and not stop BFI's plans to operate the garbage transfer plant in the Titusville Community. The message was clear, "Titusville and other citizens were to shut up or be forced to live with 1,500 daily tons of garbage."[34]

The case was still unsettled in late 1994, with no resolution in sight. Further, Sullivan and L. A. Williams, attorneys for the case, were denied attorney fees. According to American Rule, both winners and losers in a court case must pay their respective legal fees, whereas according to British Rule, losers pay all costs. There are only two exceptions to the American Rule: either the availability of a "common trust fund," or proof that the case was tried on behalf of the "common good."

They appealed the ruling to the Alabama Court of Civil Appeals and the case is presently in the courts.[35] The American Rule, according to which both winners and losers must pay their own legal costs, has exceptions. The most important exception here is that if the attorneys can demonstrate that their efforts resulted in "common benefit to the general public," then the American Rule can be set aside.

It has been the argument of this chapter that both public officials and the representatives of BFI acted in an immoral way, in flat disregard of the public good. The following section will summarize precisely the ways in which the Titusville case was a blatant case of environmental racism and also manifested a constant disregard for the public good.

Concluding Remarks

We have examined on these pages an example of environmental racism. But to present a case under this specific heading invites a further question. Is this a case of particular concern only to minorities? The answer is easily no, as the case clearly demonstrates the convergence of environmental racism with other attacks on the public interest and justice in four areas:

1. The public interest in general is under attack when powerful interests and even public officials, sworn to uphold the laws, ignore or seek to circumvent laws designed to be equally binding on all.

2. When justice is not sought and respected in a society, and those in power do not speak out against violations and do not try to redress the inequities that ensue, then all citizens lose.

3. The major public good lies in the defense of public safety and the prevention of harm (in the physical sense), that is, the protection of public health. But both BFI's antecedents, its previous practices and present goals,[36] raised grave doubts about the safety of its enterprise and its commitment to corporate responsibility in general. A further aspect of this problem is the presence of at least two major difficulties with environmental rules and regulations: (a) the question of the burden of proof and (b) the incommensurability of industry risks (that is, economic harms) and public risks (physical/health harms).

4. Harms are not only physical. When freedom of information, free consent, due process, and equal protection are all under attack, we are all losers.

Let us look at all four points in more detail.

1. In a democratic state, one assumes that laws are designed prima-

rily for the common good: their primary aim should be the citizens' safety and protection, and laws designed for that purpose gain their legitimacy from the citizens' support. In spite of the fact that at times laws may need to be fine-tuned or changed, respect for the law as such is a basic value for all in a democracy.

Titusville's case takes place against a background that includes the aftermath of segregation in Birmingham. In 1940, Birmingham's African American population reached 119,000 people, yet in spite of the U.S. Supreme Court decision that "barred both the exclusion of blacks from certain sections of the city, and covenants that restricted residential occupancy to certain preferred groups, usually white," few changes in race-based housing patterns occurred. In 1968, the Fair Housing Act banned racial discrimination in housing, but little changed.[37] However, Titusville was of the few areas where African Americans could buy property without fear of reprisals.

Hence, the area's heavy industrial zoning was imposed on an area that held captive specifically black citizens of Birmingham, not just the poor. The fair, just thing to do would have been to change the regulative patterns that were unfair to a specific minority group. Not to do so could demonstrate a lack of care and concern, even a dereliction of duty on the part of Birmingham's officials. Trying to circumvent the already unfair laws existing at this time further aggravated the situation and wronged all citizens. This is apparently a common concern in many of the U.S. southern states, as attested by Robert Bullard and others in this volume, by the EPA, and by the work of the World Council of Churches.[38]

2. In fact, laws are designed to uphold and implement one single concept that appears, more than any other, to symbolize the aspirations of all Americans, that of justice based on freedom. This aspiration, viewed by some as part of the American "vision"[39] and the basic national values of the country, is intended to be applied as universal fairness, or equal distribution of benefits and burdens in the community. As John Rawls says, "justice as fairness is framed to apply to . . . the basic structure of a modern constitutional democracy"; it indicates "a unified system of social cooperation."[40] His two principles of justice read as follows:

> 1. Each person has an equal right to a fully adequate scheme of equal basic rights and liberties, which scheme is compatible with a similar scheme for all.
> 2. Social and economic inequalities are to satisfy two conditions: first, they must be attached to offices and positions open to all under condi-

tions of fair equality of opportunity; and second, they must be to the greatest benefit of the least advantaged members of society.

Any attempt to subvert this foundational value (that is, justice as fairness) must represent an unacceptable attack on the public interest, whether one belongs to an "advantaged" or a "disadvantaged" group.

3. But the most basic common interest of all is surely the prevention of harm and the protection of public health. No government or public servant can ignore this mandate, which protects the most basic right of all citizens. Yet both BFI's antecedents, their previous practices, and their present goals could raise grave doubts about their concern for the general safety and their commitment to corporate responsibility.[41] Waste transfer stations and recyclers (the latter sometimes referred to as "material recovery facilities" in civil engineering textbooks) do not have a history long enough to permit the accumulation of scientific evidence sufficient to claim they are safe. In fact, recent literature supports our position, that is, that all available information indicates they are very hazardous and that there is an urgent need for studies and research to specify the hazards they present.[42]

A further serious question of public safety and health arises out of the complete lack of appropriate zoning, uniformly applied wherever hazardous products, processes and wastes exist.[43] When hazardous substances can be placed within a few miles of water supply sources, cultivated fields, homes and parks, then we have a problem that needs to be addressed urgently. Other complicating factors are the existing environmental rules and regulations, in which the burden of proof is normally taken to lie entirely on the side of the victims, or the affected lay people, in an inappropriate parody of criminal law practices. In criminal law the accused is deemed to be innocent until proven guilty beyond a reasonable doubt. But neither substances, activities, processes, nor corporations can possibly be identified with the "vulnerable accused." On the contrary, it is the stakeholders, or citizens at risk, who are vulnerable, not the former. Further, the incommensurability of industry risks (which are risks of economic harms) and that of public risks (risks to health and safety) is never openly confronted.[44] Finally, the fact that some risks are incompensable (for instance, those of incurable childhood cancers and other incurable diseases) is also not acknowledged.

In this case, the environmental racism that was aimed irresponsibly at North Titusville by BFI, and permitted by equally irresponsible public officials, was part of a plan that would have included Walker County dump sites and would have affected as much as one-third of Birmingham's drinking water.[45]

4. Finally, "harms" are not only physical. As the case unfolds, we see that democracy, civil rights, due process, and access to free information are all affected and denied to local citizens. These are clear violations of their rights, as well as the right to equal protection, and the universal right to free consent before the imposition of risks.[46] These aspects of the case were sufficiently discussed in the narrative, where several of BFI's actions and public officials' responses were isolated as examples of willful and malicious secrecy, attempts to thwart existing laws and regulations and the refusal to permit candid information to be available to the citizens involved. BFI repeatedly attempted to persuade citizens that the waste transfer station was "harmless," but scientific evidence existed to counter this claim. For a final example, a recent volume published by the National Institute of Public Health and Environmental Protection[47] discusses disposal of waste and the potential hazard of these activities. After listing production of goods and the consumption of goods as sources of waste, the authors say:

> The third category of waste products is the so-called cleaning up waste. This is produced during the processing of consumptive and productive waste towards a volume reduction of the flux (slag and fly-ash from incineration processes) or the prevention of emissions (electro-filter ash and sludge from sewage purification). It is characteristic that potentially contaminated substances are present in the process residue in more or less concentrated form.

In conclusion, Titusville and BFI's interaction is a clear case of environmental racism; moreover, precisely through that characteristic, it is equally a case in which the public interest or common good is attacked on several fronts. That is why it is important to make such a case public, in order to make people aware of these practices at scholarly and academic meetings, in classes at universities, and elsewhere. Cases and events where human rights are ignored, where citizens are disempowered, and good and respectable laws and regulations intended for their protection are disregarded are reasons for serious concern for everyone, regardless of race, gender, or ethnic background.

When this happens in a modern, wealthy country that prides itself on freedom and democracy, we are all affected and must share a common blame if we do not speak out against such abuses. As Abraham Lincoln once said, "Silence makes men cowards."

Although no great disaster or immediate tragedy occurred, the principles of sound environmental policy and fairness, justice, and respect for all races were not followed, so that the charge of environmental racism can fairly be leveled at the administrators and officials who dealt with the BFI project, and also at the police and others who reacted to the subsequent protest and demonstrations. This is precisely the sort of situation, I believe, which the new executive order and the office of Environmental Justice is intended to prevent and correct.

Notes

For information about this case I am indebted to Clarice Gaylord, David Sullivan, L. A. Williams, Whitlynn Battle, and Jackie Ward. Many thanks for your help.

1. "True or False," handout by TAG, Total Awareness Group, Titusville Neighborhood Association.

2. Section 2 (2), under Use Regulations. All information taken from Jefferson County Circuit Court Case No. CV–93–6975; Supreme Court Case 1931248.

3. Sullivan. The Notice of Public Hearing only lists Walter Schoel Engineering Co. and Golden Flake Snack Foods; no mention is made of BFI.

4. BFI, "Development Chronology for Birmingham Transfer Station," *Birmingham News* (May–June 1993).

5. *Birmingham News*, 5 May and 12 May 1993.

6. *Birmingham News*, 6 June 1993.

7. Kristin Shrader-Frechette, *Risk and Rationality* (Berkeley: University of California Press, 1991), 14–35.

8. G. Letowski, "The Case in Woburn, Massachusetts," a presentation to the American Association for the Advancement of Science, Boston, Massachusetts, 1993; cp. Laura Westra, *An Environmental Proposal for Ethics: The Principle of Integrity* (Lanham, Md.: Rowman & Littlefield, 1994), 216-19.

9. *Ralph Beavers et al., 192187 v. County of Walker, Alabama et al.*; Supreme Court of Alabama, 24 June 1994.

10. *Birmingham News*, 11 June 1993.

11. Shrader-Frechette, 72–74, 86–88, 140; Westra, 97–110.

12. A. Gewirth, *Human Rights* (Chicago, Ill.: University of Chicago Press, 1982), 181–96.

13. Robert D. Bullard and Beverly H. Wright, "Environmental Justice for All: Community Perspectives on Health and Research Needs," *Toxicology and Industrial Health* 9, no. 5 (1993): 821.

14. Confirmed by Dr. Clarice Gaylord, private communication.

15. Shrader-Frechette, 22–26; 70–72.

16. Robert D. Bullard, "Overcoming Racism in Environmental Decision-making," originally published in *Environment* 36, no. 4 (May 1994): 11–44, reprinted as chapter 1 of this volume.

17. Robert D. Bullard, *Dumping in Dixie* (Boulder, Colo.: Westview, 1994), 5–11.

18. Bullard, "Overcoming Racism."

19. Ibid.

20. Laura Westra, "Corporate Responsibility and Hazardous Products," *Business Ethics Quarterly* 4, no. 1 (January 1994): 97–110.

21. S. Kimerling, "The Public Ethics Compromised: The Politics of Environmental Racism? And the Subversion of Public Employee," paper presented at a seminar on Priorities in Public Service and the Environment in the Conference on Ethics in the Public Service, Stockholm, Sweden, June 16, 1994.

22. *Castaneda v. Partida* (975 t. 1272 (1977) 430 US 501.

23. Gordon W. Allport, *The Nature of Prejudice: Unabridged* (Reading, Mass.: Addison-Wesley, 1954); A. M. Rose, *The Negro's Morale: Group Identification and Protest* (Minneapolis: University of Minnesota Press, 1949); George Simpson, *Racial and Cultural Minorities: An Analysis of Prejudice and Discrimination* (New York: Plenum, 1985).

24. Aram Kardiner, *The Mark of Oppression: A Psychological Study of the American Negro* (New York: Norton, 1951).

25. Westra, *Environmental Proposal for Ethics*, 110–16.

26. Ohio EPA special investigation section, 1989.

27. Bullard, *Dumping in Dixie,* 88.

28. Ibid., 88–89.

29. Ibid.

30. Ibid., 89–95.

31. *Birmingham News*, 18 January 1994.

32. Whitlynn Battle, personal communication, November 1994.

33. S. Kimerling, "The Public Ethics Compromised."

34. Jefferson County Circuit Court Case No. CV-93-6975; Supreme Court Case 1931248.

35. Alabama Court of Civil Appeals AV 93000104, *Wm. F. Horn et al. v. City of Birmingham et al.*, Jefferson Circuit Court CV-93-50132, 14 October 1994.

36. B. Lipset, 1990; *Fort Lauderdale News/Sentinel*, 1987; cp. discussion of BFI's practices in section 2 of this chapter.

37. J. H. Franklin and Alfred Moss, Jr., *From Freedom to Slavery,* 7th ed. (New York: McGraw-Hill, 1994).

38. Bullard, *Dumping in Dixie*; C. Lee, 1993; Commission for Racial Justice, United Church of Christ, 1987.

39. Mark Sagoff, *The Economy of the Earth* (New York: Cambridge University Press, 1988), 124–45.

40. J. Rawls, "Justice as Fairness: Political Not Metaphysical," in *Justice and Economic Distribution*, 2d. ed., ed. by J. Arthur and W. B. Shaw (Englewood Cliffs, N.J.: Prentice-Hall, 1991), 320–39.

41. Citizens' Clearinghouse for Hazardous Wastes, 1993; Fort Lauderdale *News/Sun Sentinel*, 6–10 December 1987.

42. George Tchobanoglous and Hillary Theisen et al., *Integrated Solid Waste Management* (New York: McGraw Hill, 1993).

43. Laura Westra, "The Foundational Value of the Wild: Ecosystem Integrity and Sustainability," in *Ethical and Scientific Perspectives on Integri-*

ty, ed. by Laura Westra and J. Lemons (Dordrecht, The Netherlands: Kluwer Academic Publications, 1995); Westra, *Environmental Proposal for Ethics*; Westra, "Corporate Responsibility and Hazardous Products," 97–110.

44. Shrader-Frechette, 131–36.

45. Carl F. Cranor, *Regulating Toxic Substances: A Philosophy of Science and the Law* (New York: Oxford University Press, 1993); Benedetto Terracini, "Cancer Hazard Identification and Risk Assessment," paper presented to the WHO/ISEE International Workshop on Ethical and Philosophical Issues in Environmental Epidemiology, Research Triangle Park, N.C., Sept. 16–18, 1994; Stevens Coughlin, "Environmental Justice: Reflections on the Role of Epidemiologists in Protecting Unempowered Communities from Environmental Hazards," paper presented to the WHO/ISEE International Workshop on Ethical and Philosophical Issues in Environmental Epidemiology, Research Triangle Park, N.C., Sept. 16–18, 1994; Greenpeace, 1994, "Wasting the World," a video about toxic-hazardous dumping (total running time: 13:00).

46. Shrader-Frechette, 72–74, 86–88. Gewirth, 181–96.

47. RIVM Research for Man and Environment. *Concern for Tomorrow: A National Environmental Survey 1985–2010* (Bilthoven, The Netherlands: 1986).

8

Consent, Equity, and Environmental Justice: A Lousiana Case Study

Daniel C. Wigley and
Kristin Shrader-Frechette

Near Homer, Louisiana, there are two small African American settlements: Center Springs and Forest Grove. They are laced with loblolly pines, cottontails, dirt roads, and unpainted outhouses. Once the homes of freed slaves, they are quiet and proud communities. They are towns of rural hospitality and warmth, towns of kin and cornbread, towns where children learn to catch crawfish by night and catfish by day. Although these settlements are nestled in a lush, almost pristine, natural environment, they are among the poorest communities in the United States. Per capita earnings are only about $5,800 per year. Unemployment and school dropout rates are 50 percent. Center Springs and Forest Grove have recently become the target site for a uranium enrichment plant that would increase the radioactive pollution borne by local residents. Although NIMBY ("not in my backyard") would be the typical response of an affluent white town, the corporation siting the facility expects acceptance from the communities.

Introduction

Evidence indicates that the Center Springs/Forest Grove situation is typical—that minorities in the United States (eg., African Americans, Pacific Islanders, Hispanics, and Native Americans) who are disadvantaged in terms of education, income, and occupation bear a disproportionate share of environmental risks.[1] For example, studies consistently show that socioeconomically deprived groups are more

135

likely than affluent whites to live near polluting facilities, eat contaminated fish, and be employed at risky occupations.[2] Because minorities are statistically more likely to be economically disadvantaged, some researchers assert that "environmental racism" is the central cause of these disparities in the risks they face.[3] Indeed, some social scientists have found that race is an independent factor, not reducible to socioeconomic status, in predicting the distribution of air pollution, contaminated fish consumption, the siting of municipal landfills and incinerators, the location of abandoned toxic waste dumps, and lead poisoning in children.[4]

Because there is growing national recognition that disparities in environmental health risks are related to race and socioeconomic status, environmental justice is now a top priority on the public health agenda of the United States.[5] Environmental justice, according all people equal protection and equal opportunity in matters of pollution and resource consumption—regardless of their race, ethnicity, class, age, or gender—is currently an explicit goal of U.S. environmental policy. A widespread, grassroots, environmental justice movement has caused problems facing disadvantaged, nonwhite communities to become prominent national issues during the 1990s. As a result, Congress members have introduced legislation dealing with environmental justice,[6] and the federal Environmental Protection Agency (EPA) has finally begun to address the disproportionately high levels of environmental risks borne by people of color and members of low-income communities.[7] A 1992 EPA report found significant evidence that low-income, nonwhite communities are disproportionately exposed to lead, air pollution, hazardous-waste facilities, contaminated fish tissue, and pesticides, and recommended a higher priority for problems of environmental equity and justice.[8] In September of the same year, a report by the *National Law Journal* showed that environmental laws were not enforced equally by the EPA.[9] By November of 1992, the EPA established the Office of Environmental Equity (OEE) to deal with issues of environmental justice, and in December the General Accounting Office (GAO) began an ongoing study to examine EPA's activities relating to environmental equity.[10] The Clinton administration likewise demonstrated its priorities for the EPA when it selected a prominent leader of the environmental justice movement, Professor Robert D. Bullard, to serve on the Clinton-Gore Transition Team.[11] On Earth Day 1993, the president announced a commitment to pursue a federal action plan to achieve environmental justice for all Americans. On 11 February 1994, he signed an executive order that directs each federal agency to develop an environmental justice strategy for "identifying and addressing . . . disproportionately high and adverse human health or environmental effects of its programs, policies, and activities on minority . . . and low-income populations."[12] As these developments indicate, environmental justice has become an important and ongoing national priority.

In this chapter we give a brief analysis of the concept of environmental justice and argue that resource- and pollution-related decision making—resulting in inequitable treatment of individuals on the basis of race and socioeconomic status—is prima facie wrong. Second, we survey the history of the doctrine of free informed consent and argue that the consent of those affected is necessary for ensuring the fairness of decision making used for siting hazardous facilities. We also point out that equal opportunity to environmental protection and free informed consent are important American rights. Third, we present a case study on the proposed uranium enrichment facility near Homer, Louisiana, and argue that siting the plant there would violate norms of distributive equity and free informed consent. We conclude that the attempted siting of the Louisiana installation is ethically unjustified and likely a case of environmental racism or classism. Finally, we answer possible objections to our conclusion.

Environmental Justice

Environmental justice is mainly concerned with distributive equity and is based on the principle of equal treatment for equal beings—giving equal consideration to everyone's interests in pollution- and resource-related decision making. The principle of equal treatment requires that we treat people equally when they are the same in all ethically relevant respects and that we treat them unequally when they differ in ethically relevant respects. That is, treatment should be proportional to individual differences.[13] We meet the requirements of justice when we can justify unequal treatment by reference to relevant differences and when we can justify equal treatment by reference to relevant similarities. Of course, absolutely equal treatment is impossible, so ethical theorists often claim that relevant similarities justify equal consideration of interests and that relevant differences justify unequal consideration of interests. This does not mean that such differences may justify ignoring someone's interests, but rather differences may be grounds for giving one person's interests priority over another's. For example, in certain circumstances, protecting the president of the United States from physical harm may outweigh protecting a particular citizen.[14] If we accept a principle of equal rights and equal treatment under the law, then we have a prima facie obligation to provide equal protection to all people in these ethically relevant respects. If we do not protect people equally, then we must have ethically relevant grounds for not doing so. Otherwise we treat them unjustly.

Environmental justice forms an important part of normative theory. It specifies prima facie duties regarding the distribution of benefits and burdens produced by environment-related decisions and actions. Whenever our behavior has consequences affecting the welfare of others, we have a prima facie obligation to fairness. Although all of our prima facie duties, including that of justice, may presuppose this prima facie principle, our obligation to fairness does not tell us how we are to distribute benefits and burdens. In order to establish our prima facie duties regarding the distribution of environmental benefits and burdens, we need principles of environmental justice. Thus, environmental justice is an important part of our normative theory of obligation.

It is a truism that we have a prima facie obligation not to discriminate on the basis of race or class in our environment-related decisions. Differences such as race/ethnicity, social rank, or wealth are morally irrelevant grounds for treating people unequally in matters of distributive justice.[15] We use the terms "environmental racism" and "environmental classism," respectively, to characterize environment-related discrimination on the basis of race and socioeconomic class. To use race in this way is especially groundless because it is, as William Frankena puts it, "to treat people differently in ways that profoundly affect their lives because of differences for which they have no responsibility."[16] Differences can be ethically relevant for matters of distributive justice only if individuals can be responsible for them, and no one can be responsible for their race. Moreover, because it is arguable that, on the basis of fairness and equal opportunity, we should give the interests of the least-advantaged members of society highest priority,[17] discrimination against individuals of lower socioeconomic status is especially groundless.

Environmental justice is also defensible on the grounds of our accepting a prima facie principle of equal protection for all. If everyone has an equal right to life, and therefore an equal right to bodily security, then to allow one group of people to bear a disproportionate environmental risk, without morally relevant reasons, amounts to a violation of their rights. Because of equal rights to bodily security, all Americans deserve equal protection from environmental risks, regardless of differences such as race and socioeconomic status. This ethical belief is embodied, for example, in U.S. environmental law. The Senate held that the major provisions of the National Environmental Policy Act of 1969 (NEPA) protected everyone's fundamental human right to a safe environment.[18] NEPA aims to establish national environmental policy and goals that "assure for all Americans a safe, healthful, productive, and aesthetically and culturally pleasing environment."[19] Recent environmental legislation also calls for nondiscriminatory compliance with environmental, health, and safety laws and for equal protection of public health.

The doctrine of free informed consent, an important part of the traditional American value system, likewise provides a foundation for environmental justice. This concept rose to importance during the late 1950s when legal cases brought the concept to the attention of physicians who were defendants in malpractice suits. However, the concept began to receive serious ethical analysis only around 1972.[20] In the 1970s a new interdisciplinary "biomedical ethics" helped emphasize the ethical dimensions of consent.[21] Wider societal concerns about individual liberties and social equality, heightened interest in the legal right of self-determination, increased philosophical concern for autonomy, and wider recognition of civil rights, women's rights, consumer rights, and prisoners' rights, all influenced interest in the concept of informed consent.[22] Most of the discussion concerning the concept, to date, has centered around issues in medical ethics, not technological or environmental ethics. Over the past two decades, two principles— protection of individual human autonomy and protection from harm— have emerged as the main grounds for justifying rights to free informed consent.[23] In recognition of this justification, virtually all medical, legal, and professional codes of ethics require physicians and other professionals to obtain the free informed consent of employees, patients, and subjects before putting them at risk.[24] There is currently consensus that, in order to satisfy conditions necessary for free informed consent, at least four criteria must be satisfied: the risk imposers must disclose full information about the threat; potential victims must be competent to evaluate it; they must understand the danger; and they must voluntarily accept it.[25]

To the degree that medical ethics is analogous to technological and environmental ethics,[26] decision makers have a prima facie obligation to respect norms of free informed consent. For example, they have a duty to respect the consent of communities that are potential hosts for hazardous facilities. And communities have a right to refuse environmental hazards that may be imposed on them, especially if the risks are inequitable or uncompensated.[27] The following case study on the proposed siting of a uranium enrichment facility near Homer, Louisiana, illustrates how principles of environmental justice—and the related concepts of equity and free informed consent—can be applied to cases of environmental decision making.

Case Study on Homer, Louisiana

Louisiana Energy Services (LES) recently applied for a license to build and operate a uranium enrichment facility, the Claiborne Enrichment Center (CEC), near Homer, Louisiana. In accord with the requirements of the National Environmental Policy Act of 1969 (NEPA), the Nuclear Regulatory Commission (NRC) prepared an Environmental Impact Statement (EIS). The EIS analyzed the potential environmental impacts associated with the construction, operation, decontamination, and decommissioning of the facility. Other issues covered by the EIS include the purpose and need for the facility and the site-selection process. According to the EIS, the primary function of the proposed CEC installation is to produce various grades of enriched uranium for use in commercial nuclear power generating stations in the United States. During its thirty-year operational life, the plant is expected to have an annual production capacity of about 866 tonnes of enriched uranium.

The EIS explains the need for the facility.[28] According to LES, as of 1990, the Department of Energy (DOE) supplied approximately 89 percent of the national purchases of enriched uranium. By 1996, LES projects that 60 percent of the U.S. demand for enrichment services will be uncommitted to DOE suppliers and that, by the year 2000, this percentage will grow to 70.[29] Owners of LES believe that the growing uncommitted demand provides an opportunity for a competing company to successfully enter the enrichment market. The EIS argues that the LES facility is likely to be an effective competitor because the proposed plant will utilize the gas centrifuge technology, which uses about fifty times less electrical energy than the DOE's old gas diffusion technology.[30] LES owners claim that the CEC will (1) pressure other U.S. enrichment suppliers to maintain competitive positions in the world enrichment market, (2) reduce U.S. dependence on foreign suppliers, and (3) provide an opportunity to replace the older gas diffusion process with an energy-efficient one.[31]

LES followed a three-phase screening process to identify a suitable site for the proposed enrichment facility.[32] Investigators at each phase used a set of economic, technical, social, and environmental criteria. The first phase identified geographical areas within the United States suitable for locating the plant. This coarse screening process led to the selection of the northern Louisiana region. Some of the socioeconomic criteria used for this first phase included siting the facility in a location where it would (1) "be considered an asset to the community"; (2) "promote local community acceptance"; and (3) have "a favorable business climate exemplified by the presence of communities with large labor pools available and states having right-to-work laws."[33]

The second and third screening processes for the proposed plant consisted of phases that focused on the selection of a final site in northern Louisiana. LES canvassed community leaders "for their interest in being the host site for a new manufacturing facility" and requested that they "nominate potential sites" using LES's "criteria." After receiving twenty-one offers from solicited groups, LES eliminated some nominated locations through the use of additional criteria, such as the need for the community to have a "strong manufacturing mentality." LES then used a decision-making methodology of "musts" and "wants" to further narrow the list of potential sites. "Musts" had to be satisfied; for example, the site had to meet certain geologic and soil requirements. On the other hand, LES assigned a weighting factor to each "want." According to LES, among the most desirable "wants" were local citizen support for the facility. Investigators at this scoring phase of the second screening process selected Homer, a town in Claiborne Parish, Louisiana. In the final phase, researchers ranked potential sites around Homer and emphasized their "want" for community leadership. They finally selected a location near Center Springs and Forest Grove, five miles from Homer, Louisiana.[34]

According to the EIS, the site selected is in Claiborne Parish, an economically depressed area with a high percentage of minority residents. The racial/ethnic composition is 53.43 percent white, 46.09 percent black, 0.16 percent American Indian, 0.07 percent Asian, and 0.23 percent Hispanic.[35] The host communities for the facility, Center Springs and Forest Grove, are almost entirely African American.[36] As the EIS explains,

> Employment in Claiborne Parish . . . is generally low-wage and low-skill. Per capita earnings for the residents is about $5,800 per year. . . . The average for the broadly defined LES labor market is only about $8,500 per year compared to the national average of almost $12,800. These figures, in particular the Claiborne Parish figures, make it one of the poorest regions in the United States as measured by per capita earnings.[37]

In terms of total per capita personal income, Louisiana is ranked 45th in the United States, and Claiborne Parish is ranked in the bottom third of Louisiana parishes. Unemployment in Claiborne Parish is 8 percent, with "minority unemployment" being "minimally 50 percent greater than white unemployment." The high school dropout rate in Claiborne Parish is 47 percent.[38]

Despite the economically depressed conditions of Claiborne Parish, the NRC concluded that licensing LES for the construction and operation of the proposed enrichment facility would not result in a significant impact to the environment. The NRC also stated that, "On balance, CEC should be a major socioeconomic asset to Homer, Claiborne Parish, and neighboring parishes. The negative impacts of CEC are likely to be similar to those of any relatively large-scale socioeconomic development in a small, rural area. . . . [T]he costs of CEC to the local population and municipalities should be minimal."[39]

The CEC Siting Is Not Ethically Justified

Based on the information in the Environmental Impact Statement (EIS) and the associated documents, we argue that the ethical assumptions used to justify siting the CEC are seriously flawed in at least three respects. (1) Selection of the Louisiana site likely would violate prima facie norms for free informed consent. (2) LES's community solicitation procedures have violated actual norms for free informed consent. (3) Socioeconomic and environmental impacts at the site will almost certainly violate norms of distributive equity. These three ethical failures revealed in the EIS show that, contrary to the NEPA requirement to give "appropriate consideration" to "values," the EIS has undercut traditional American values of equity and free informed consent.

To see why members of the communities hosting the LES facility likely are unable to give free informed consent, one needs to understand the requirements (already mentioned in section 2) for obtaining free informed consent. Scholars who have studied the concept claim that it is best analyzed as "autonomous authorization" and that it may be broken down in terms of four analytical components: (1) disclosure, which requires professionals to pass on risk information to potential victims and decision makers; (2) understanding, which requires professionals to help persons overcome factors (e.g., irrationality, immaturity, distorted information) that can limit their comprehension of a situation to which they have a right to give or withhold consent; (3) voluntariness, which requires that subjects be free of manipulation and coercion; and (4) competence, which requires subjects to have the ability to give autonomous authorization to some act.[40] Competence usually includes having the ability to make a decision based on rational grounds. Traditionally, these four requirements or norms must be met before one can obtain subjects' free informed consent.

There are certain types of cases in which, prima facie, risk imposers cannot meet the requirements for free informed consent of subjects. For example, because prisons provide a very coercive context for decision making, inmates who expect early release in exchange for being subjects in risky medical experimentation very likely are unable to give free informed consent to the risk.[41] Requirements for free informed consent cannot be met in such cases because the situations provide coercive contexts that, prima facie, prevent the voluntariness criterion from being satisfied. In other instances, it is doubtful, prima facie, that the understanding and competence requirements can be met, as in the case of a fourteen-year-old girl consenting to a risky medical procedure in order to help her mother.[42] Likewise, a community's depressed economy, high unemployment rate, and low level of education constitute conditions that, prima facie, can jeopardize its ability to meet the four standard requirements for free informed consent. Low levels of education can prevent the understanding condition from being satisfied, and a depressed economic situation can provide a coercive context that does not allow the voluntariness condition to be met. Very attractive offers (such as risky jobs promising large salaries) can leave persons who live within difficult socioeconomic conditions without any alternative but to accept the questionable offers.[43] If communities hosting the LES facility suffer from low levels of education and disadvantaged socioeconomic conditions, then this may keep them from meeting the requirements for free informed consent.

One main ethical problem with the EIS is its failure to take account of the fact that the communities hosting the proposed CEC site suffer from severely depressed socioeconomic conditions and that this situation, prima facie, prevents the members of these communities from meeting the requirements for free informed consent. If they are socially or economically disenfranchised, then this situation, prima facie, militates against their citizens' having the freedom to accept or reject the LES facility, especially because it promises badly needed jobs (but few for the lowest and poorest groups), high salaries, and attractive secondary economic effects.[44] For instance, the EIS states, "Regional benefits are primarily in the form of high-paying construction and operations jobs (averaging $37,000 and $44,000, respectively) in an area with average earnings about half those levels and high unemployment and underemployment."[45] If educational levels in the community surrounding the proposed site are low, then this situation likewise militates against residents' having adequate understanding to give or withhold free informed consent. Furthermore, if unemployment for minorities in Claiborne Parish is high—twice what it is for whites— then this situation militates against their having the freedom to accept or reject a risky CEC facility that might employ some of them. Therefore, depressed socioeconomic conditions have created a situation in which, prima facie, it is likely that neither the voluntariness nor the understanding criterion for free informed consent can be met for the communities hosting the facility. Because it is unlikely that the prima facie norms for free informed consent can be satisfied for such communities, it is doubtful, prima facie, that any additional imposition of serious societal risks on these groups can be ethically justified.

LES Violation of Free Informed Consent in Solicitation Procedures

Claiming that it is prima facie questionable to impose additional risks on disenfranchised communities, however, does not tell us what our actual duty will be in a particular case. Such norms tell us our actual duty only if all other things are equal. Particular circumstances may require us to override a given prima facie norm in favor of other ethical requirements. For example, we recognize a prima facie obligation to tell the truth, but a particular situation may require us to override this duty if we face circumstances in which lying is necessary to save an individual's life. If so, then our actual obligation will be to save the person's life, despite our prima facie duty to tell the truth. Although we may have different and conflicting prima facie obligations, the particular circumstances of the case under consideration may determine what our actual duties will be.

An ethical problem with the EIS is that LES's actual procedures for community solicitation, in the CEC case, violate norms for free informed consent. Norms for free informed consent apply to the site-selection process when the LES solicited communities to determine their alleged preferences about the proposed CEC facility. As mentioned earlier, the LES canvassed communities in northern Louisiana for "their interest in being the host site for a new manufacturing facility." The company requested communities to use LES's "criteria" and "to nominate potential sites for a proposed chemical facility."[46] CEC nominations and solicitations violated community rights to free informed consent, however, in at least seven ways. First, the procedure presupposed that some chemical facility would be built somewhere, and only the location needed to be determined. In begging the question regarding whether (and what kind of) a facility would be built, the procedure undercut the freedom of respondents and was coercive.

Second, in its solicitations the LES avoided disclosure of certain criteria that it judged to be necessary for siting the facility. For example, LES solicitors did not tell communities that potential sites had to be within the Louisiana Power & Light (LP&L) service area. They also did not disclose that the site should avoid flood-prone areas, nor did they explain how such factors might affect plant risks. Nevertheless, LES used these two criteria and others, not given to the communities, to eliminate nominated sites.[47] Withholding criteria for site selection not only violated disclosure norms for free informed consent but it also indicates that LES begged the question regarding the rejection of sites. For instance, LES solicitors begged the question concerning which sites to remove from consideration because they canvassed communities outside of the LP&L service area and then rejected their nominated sites on grounds that the locations lay outside of the LP&L service area. LES eliminated four proposed sites in this way.[48] Moreover, because LES did not tell communities to avoid flood-prone locations, residents in or near such areas were much more likely to select unacceptable sites than those who were not near such areas. Because the failure to disclose these site requirements begged the question regarding the rejection of sites, LES in effect coerced some communities to choose sites that would be rejected. Hence, LES violated the voluntariness norm for free informed consent.

Third, LES has not shown that it fully informed solicited communities about the precise nature of the proposed facility. The EIS states that LES officials canvassed communities for their interest in being the host site for a "new manufacturing facility" and asked them to nominate sites for "a proposed chemical facility."[49] Although the terms "manufacturing facility" and "chemical facility" may have helped laypersons understand some of the functions of the proposed LES plant, they ignore or misrepresent the significant radiological risk posed by virtue of the fact that the installation would be a chemical plant manufacturing enriched uranium for use in nuclear reactors. Obviously, LES solicitors should have conveyed accurately such information if they were to avoid violating individuals' rights to free informed consent. In the absence of evidence that LES fully informed communities about the precise nature of the proposed facility, LES canvassing appears to have violated important societal rights to free informed consent.

Fourth, even if the precise nature of the facility was accurately conveyed to solicited communities (and this has not been shown in the EIS), citizens could not have understood the real nature and magnitude of the accident and health hazards associated with the plant, because CEC representatives could not have disclosed properly such risks, costs, and benefits to them. Because there is neither a probabilistic risk assessment (PRA) for the proposed facility, nor a quantitative determination of many of its hazardous impacts and costs (e.g., increased crime), it is impossible to know, reliably, the actual risks associated with the plant.[50] LES officials could not have properly disclosed risk and cost information that they did not have. Thus, community decision makers could not have understood these threats and could not have given free informed consent to them.

Fifth, because EIS assessors based their conclusions concerning hazards of the facility on old data, omissions, and largely subjective judgments formulated in purely qualitative language, it is likely that any risk information that might have been given to solicited communities was biased and greatly underestimated the risks involved with the proposed plant. For example, the EIS used a ten-year-old study of facilities that differ "significantly from the CEC" to identify potential accident scenarios. Also, some events that could produce the "largest potential release to the atmosphere for accidents inside the Separations Building" were "not analyzed in detail." In addition, other potential failures in the sampling and blending systems that could result in "large" releases were "not evaluated in the accident analysis." The EIS assessors ignored some catastrophic accident scenarios (and assumed they would never occur) merely on the grounds that they had "never occurred" in thirty-two years of enrichment-facility experience or on the grounds that there were "redundant protection controls." Even redundant protections, however, often fall victim to human and operator error, and 60 to 90 percent of serious technological accidents (according to the U.S. Office of Technology Assessment) typically involve human error. Also, an alleged accident rate of 0 in 32 (years) is not necessarily low but is consistent with a rate as high as 1 in 10 or 20 years, for example. Because the U.S. government typically regulates risks larger than 1 in 1,000,000, the possible enrichment-facility accident rate of 1 in 10 or 20 appears quite high. Moreover, the NRC assessors used subjective and qualitative judgments, rather than probabilistic assessments in their evaluation of accident releases. They claim, for example, that operator errors (associated with inadequate degassing of the lines) could result in dangerous "releases of relatively small magnitude," yet they give no probabilities for such accidents and no justification for the predicted range of possible quantities of materials that could be released. Thus, even if LES gave some information to solicited communities concerning the risks of the facility (and this has not been shown in the EIS), it appears likely that this information would have underestimated the actual risks. Thus, LES representatives appear to have violated the criterion regarding understanding (for free informed consent).[51]

Sixth, the site solicitation process and scoring or evaluation procedures did not involve the host communities, Center Springs and Forest Grove, which are located approximately 0.25 miles and 1.25 miles, respectively, from the proposed CEC. Instead, LES solicited the opinion of leaders from Homer (located 5 miles from the chosen site) and did not use the views of community leaders from Center Springs and Forest Grove for determining site-selection scores.[52] As previously explained, the company's most important "wants" for evaluating potential sites included local citizens' acceptance and leadership; LES desired a location where the facility "would be considered an asset to the community" and "would promote local community acceptance." Because the scoring process did not take into consideration the opinions of the communities that would actually host the proposed CEC, the site-selection process prevented these communities from voluntarily giving or withholding consent to the facility. For this reason, the site-selection process was coercive and violated the voluntariness requirement for free informed consent.

Seventh, the LES screening process did not fully inform decision makers and affected parties regarding alternatives to the proposed site. Although the third and final part of the siting process allegedly identified "alternative" sites, the EIS admits that "alternative sites considered by LES are not alternatives available to the NRC, and are therefore not alternatives for the purpose of this EIS."[53] Because the screening process limited consideration of alternatives and therefore disclosure to persons who ought to consent to the site, it is arguable that the CEC activities violated community rights to free informed consent.

Violations of Regional Equity

Another reason the CEC siting likely violates environmental justice is that the socioeconomic and environmental impacts on the host communities threaten geographical or regional equity. In this section, we argue that having the facility, without adequately compensating communities for the regional inequities imposed on them, is unjustified. Impacts resulting from CEC operations include increased housing and land prices, loss of land use, crime, higher taxes, and public exposure to radioactive material.[54] These and other consequences, we argue, unjustifiably impose inequities among groups within Claiborne Parish and between the communities surrounding the CEC and other areas of the United States. The uncompensated imposition of such regional inequities is contrary to NEPA guarantees of safeguarding the environmental welfare of "all Americans" and its demands for consideration of values and distributive equity.[55] Because the EIS ignores regional inequities, it has not provided an adequate ethical justification for the CEC. Moreover, because the inequities imposed by the proposed enrichment facility would harm poor, nonwhite people the most, the EIS is arguably guilty of "environmental racism" or "environmental classism."

In addition to regional inequities, impacts resulting from the CEC also impose inequities among groups in Claiborne Parish. The EIS provides no adequate evaluation of the distributive impacts of the CEC but admits that those lower on the economic scale will carry the burden of the social costs of the facility, while those better off will enjoy the benefits. The EIS states that "the distribution of benefits is likely to be concentrated in the middle-income groups," not the lower-income groups, and that "higher-income households benefit most from the income generation process." Higher-income people benefit most because low-income households spend a higher percentage of their money on goods and services supplied by higher-income households than vice versa. The Draft EIS concluded that "the income benefit to the unemployed or very low-income people . . . will be less than might be expected." The EIS also admitted that, if local residents are employed, they are likely to work in the lowest paying jobs. For example, high-paying "radiological and specialized chemical or nuclear-related jobs are unlikely to be filled by local residents," and "construction jobs, especially high skilled construction jobs, are more likely to attract temporary workers from outside the area." In addition to receiving fewer benefits (like jobs) from the CEC, lower-income groups will also carry a disproportionate burden of the costs of the facility. For example, because of the influx of additional residents and increased economic activity, the LES expects an increase in crime, which will impact largely on lower-income groups. Furthermore, in part because of increased demand arising from the influx of facility workers, the plant is likely to raise both housing and land prices. However, since higher property prices will increase rental and home purchase prices, people who do not own property are more likely to suffer from the increase, while those who own real estate are more likely to benefit. On the other hand, violent crime and drug-related property crimes are likely to decrease property values in low-income areas. There also will be an extremely inequitable risk imposition (from radiological hazards) on infants and children from the facility. For example, because there is a greater potential for them to consume contaminated cow milk, the EIS estimates that potential radioactive doses from liquid releases will be two to ten times higher for children and infants than it is for adults. For these reasons, it is likely that the siting of the CEC will actually exacerbate inequities among groups within the Claiborne Parish area.[56]

The siting of the CEC will also impose regional inequities between Louisiana residents who must bear the costs of the facility and other people nationwide and worldwide who receive the benefits. Benefits enjoyed nationwide include promotion of technology, economic expansion, increased production, and cheaper enriched uranium. Private profits will accrue to people worldwide from the facility, because Urenco Investments, the general partner that will have "majority operating control of the CEC," is a "wholly owned subsidiary of Urenco Ltd., which in turn is owned by the United Kingdom, the Netherlands, and West Germany."[57] Because significant profits resulting from the facility will go to foreign investors, nationwide economic benefits that could reach Louisiana communities may be significantly less than they would be if all private income remained in the United States. The inequity arises because the communities who must bear all of the risks of the facility will not share in its various economic benefits. Although Louisiana residents may enjoy some of the nationwide benefits, people living near the plant—especially those in the poorest groups—must bear all of the costs of the facility. In addition, the depressed socioeconomic situation of the host communities suggests that they will not enjoy the nationwide economic benefits of the CEC, because the poor are usually "isolated from economic growth."[58] In the United States, for example, in the last four decades, although there has been an absolute increase in the standard of living, the poorest 20 percent continues to receive 5 percent of the wealth, while the richest 20 percent now holds well over 40 percent; the shares of the middle three quintiles have remained just as constant.[59] Because the Center Springs/ Forest Grove area is one of the poorest in the United States, it is likely that the siting of the plant will exacerbate the socioeconomic inequalities that exist between these communities and other areas of the country.

Despite such inequities arising from the proposed facility, the EIS does not provide a justification for the imposition of negative geographical and socioeconomic impacts. In its section on environmental justice, the EIS argues that because the proposed facility "will not cause any significant adverse impacts on nearby residents or anybody else," it follows that "there will be no significant disproportionate adverse impact" on low-income minorities.[60] The NRC staff concluded that "the proposed LES facility is not an example of environmental injustice."[61] This argument is unsound for at least two reasons: (1) because of consequences already discussed, it is very questionable that there will be no significant negative impacts; and (2) inequitable distributions of benefits can result in environmental racism or other injustice. First, the EIS allegation that there is no significant threat to public health and safety from the CEC is highly questionable and likely underestimates the real accident risk because, as previously explained, assessors performed no PRA. They based their conclusions on largely subjective judgments formulated in purely qualitative language. They used old empirical studies to draw their conclusions, and they did not analyze in detail worst-case accidents. Without correcting these inadequacies, it is impossible to know, reliably, that there will be no adverse impacts from the plant. Second, although there are recognized costs associated with the facility (e.g., increased crime and higher radiation exposure), an inequitable distribution of benefits can result in environmental injustice. As argued earlier, alleged benefits from the plant (e.g., economic expansion, promotion of technology, and private profits) do not serve the overall interests of everyone in an equal way; the poor—especially minorities—who bear the costs of the facility will enjoy a disproportionately low share of the benefits, if at all. Such inequities may be unjust because they may amount to treating one set of persons merely as means to the socioeconomic ends of others.[62] If we accept that all humans have equal rights and equal dignity, then using some people as means to the ends of others, without justification, is ethically wrong.[63] For these reasons, the EIS has not shown that the proposed siting of the CEC is consistent with norms of environmental justice.

Objections and Replies

One objection to our claim (that the attempted siting of the CEC is unethical) is that the plant has to be located somewhere, and it is better to put it where it will help the economy. There are two problems, however, with this response: (1) it assumes that the plant is needed; and (2) it assumes that the facility will help the economy. Both of these assumptions are questionable.

First, there are good reasons to think that the installation is not needed. As previously discussed, LES officials argue that there is a need for the facility.[64] But although they claim that their plant will be a complementary supplier of enriched uranium, the CEC may be inconsistent with the U.S. government's response to current enrichment problems.[65] For example, both the DOE and American taxpayers currently face the enormous costs of future decontamination and decommissioning of old enrichment facilities, environmental restoration of plant sites, and new technology deployment related to uranium enrichment.[66] The EIS states that the facility will be in direct competition with DOE suppliers.[67] It is questionable whether such domestic competition will help the United States solve its enrichment problems because competition from the LES facility would take customers away from the DOE and this could hinder the DOE's ability to handle future expenses related to U.S. enrichment needs.

Furthermore, the current U.S. enrichment strategy, which includes privatizing the United States Enrichment Corporation and developing more cost-efficient technology, may eliminate the need for the LES facility.[68] The DOE is committed to the Uranium-Atomic Vapor Laser Isotope Separation (U-AVLIS) process, a means of enriching uranium at a cost that is 50 percent lower than any other enrichment process, including the centrifuge technology that is to be used at the proposed CEC.[69] Although the U.S. government has not yet proceeded with the commercialization of the U-AVLIS process, experts have indicated that the new technology can be put in operation shortly after the year 2000 and in facilities whose production will be much greater than the proposed CEC.[70] Moreover, according to the EIS, "in 1993, the U.S. and Russia reached an agreement which provides for the U.S. to buy Russian uranium."[71] The uranium from dismantled Russian nuclear weapons will supply more than "50 percent of projected U.S. demand" during the first fifteen years of CEC operation.[72] Given these U.S. strategies for addressing current enrichment problems, it is very uncertain whether there is a need for the CEC facility.

Moreover, the EIS does not show that there is a need for the LES plant because it adequately discusses neither the status of the U.S. nuclear power industry nor U.S. policy regarding the industry. The justification for building any enrichment facility seems to depend in part on the existence of a healthy nuclear industry. According to the

EIS, LES has projected that U.S. requirements for enrichment services will begin to increase significantly in the year 2000.[73] However, this projected increase is doubtful because the nuclear industry in the United States has been in a state of severe decline since the 1970s.[74] The cessation and eventual cancellation of all orders for new commercial reactors marked the collapse of the nuclear industry. Although utilities ordered 231 fission plants through 1974, only 15 reactors were ordered after 1974, and all of the latter, including over 100 other nuclear plants, were canceled or indefinitely deferred, even though many were already under construction.[75] Furthermore, no utility has ordered a new nuclear plant since 1978, and all but a handful of the approximately 120 commercial reactors now existing (or under construction) in the U.S. will have ended their thirty- to forty-year lifetime by the year 2004—before the proposed LES facility is expected to be fully operational.

It is arguable that the present collapsed state of the commercial nuclear industry will continue for the foreseeable future because many of the problems that precipitated the nuclear decline remain and show no real signs of being solved. Some of the reasons for this collapse include (1) a sharp downturn in expected electricity demand; (2) increased costs, brought about by inflation, construction time extensions, and unanticipated new regulatory requirements; (3) public opposition; and (4) instances of poor management.[76] Another important factor that currently hinders the revival of the nuclear industry is the DOE's uncertain progress in siting a permanent repository for high-level nuclear waste.[77] Utility officials believe that many of the difficulties that led to the problems besetting the nuclear industry will persist, at least until after the beginning of the next century.[78] In a 1990 report, the GAO interviewed no utility officials who were willing even to consider purchasing a new nuclear reactor before the beginning of the next century.[79] In addition, reluctance to consider fission-generated electricity, primarily because of strong public opposition and high financial risks for utilities, is likely to continue.[80] Because of the continued collapse of the U.S. nuclear industry, it is questionable whether there is a real need in the United States for the LES enrichment facility, especially given the strategy of the U.S. government for revitalizing the nation's enrichment services.

A second set of problems with the objection that the plant has to be sited somewhere, and it is better to put it where it will help the economy, is that many of the claimed primary economic benefits allegedly deriving from the proposed facility are highly questionable. For example, the Draft EIS asserts (without evidence and without any quantification) that "for CEC most goods and services (excluding the centrifuges and related extremely specialized equipment) can probably be procured within the state."[81] If builders of the facility guaranteed that particular amounts of specific kinds of goods and services will be obtained within the state, then it would be reasonable to claim these goods and services as part of the benefits of the plant. Otherwise, such benefits are purely hypothetical, particularly in the light of the educational, social, financial, and industrial problems of the region and the state, problems that could undercut their provision of goods and services. Also, the EIS assumes that benefits will flow to communities during the entire life of the facility even though, as already discussed, the U.S. commercial nuclear program actually came to a standstill in the middle 1970s. If most U.S. reactors will have ended their useful life by the time that the proposed CEC facility opens, then it is questionable whether many U.S. economic benefits will flow from the plant, especially in light of socioeconomic problems (mentioned below) created in the region because of the plant.

Apart from alleged primary economic consequences, many of the claimed secondary economic benefits allegedly deriving from the proposed facility are questionable. For instance, the EIS claims that many secondary economic effects will arise from the wages and construction associated with the plant, as a result of more money being pumped into the nearby Louisiana region. Such multiplication of secondary economic benefits may be invalid, however, because most of the facility-related benefits will go to the middle and not lower economic classes, because crime will increase as a result of the plant, because drug trafficking will increase, and because property values will increase, but not in areas affected by drugs and crime. If the economic benefits of the LES facility cause greater social inequities, more drug trafficking, and greater crime, however, then the "hidden economy" of the underworld may divert potential secondary benefits of the plant into crime-related activities rather than into strengthening the economy. In other words, if the regional economic infrastructure cannot utilize the secondary economic *benefits* associated with new construction and higher employment from the CEC, then criminal networks could divert these monies to create secondary economic *burdens*. Meanwhile the plant will exacerbate problems that will require explicit and increased government expenditures. Because the EIS never quantified and costed the additional and serious costs of drug trafficking, increased crime, exacerbated inequities, and so on, it is clear that it has underestimated the social costs associated with the facility and overestimated alleged secondary economic benefits. Indeed, there may be an excess of secondary economic burdens. The presence of such extreme social costs as a result of the proposed plant suggests that one ought not use standard multipliers for secondary economic benefits, as authors of the EIS have done. Indeed, use of such multipliers (for economic consequences), in the CEC case, may err because facility impacts may actually require use of divisors for secondary economic benefits.[82]

A second objection to our claim (that the proposed CEC siting is unethical) is that the greater good requires some people to bear greater burdens than others. In other words, the objection is that perfect egalitarianism is impossible. This response, of course, assumes that one can justify inequalities whenever they are necessary for achieving the greatest good overall. But justifications for unequal treatment must be based on morally relevant considerations. If we accept that all humans have equal rights and equal dignity, then we must respect their moral autonomy, which means treating them as ends in themselves and never merely as means to the ends of others. To impose uncompensated, avoidable inequalities on people, even though the imposition does not result in greater equality among people, at least in the long run, is to treat some individuals merely as means to the ends of others.[83] Thus, one can justify such inequalities only if one can show that they eventually lead to greater equality. Hence, the objection is wrong in presupposing that inequalities always are acceptable whenever their proponents appeal to "the greater good."

Allegedly maximizing the good will not justify the inequalities resulting from the proposed LES facility because it is unlikely that they eventually would lead to greater equality. As we have explained, members of the communities hosting the facility would bear a disproportionate share of the socioeconomic and environmental burdens. Because the plant would exacerbate inequalities and because the poor, unlike higher-income groups, do not enjoy the benefits of economic growth, the proposed siting of the CEC is not likely to promote greater equality. Therefore, allegedly maximizing the overall good cannot justify the uncompensated, avoidable inequalities resulting from the LES plant.

Conclusion

The Louisiana Energy Services (LES) recently has selected two African American communities, Center Springs and Forest Grove, to host the Claiborne Enrichment Center (CEC), a uranium enrichment facility that would increase local radioactive pollution. We have argued that the ethical assumptions underlying the Nuclear Regulatory Commission's (NRC's) Environmental Impact Statement (EIS) are seriously flawed in several respects: (1) the selection of the Center Springs/Forest Grove site would violate prima facie norms for free informed consent, (2) LES's procedures of community solicitation violated actual norms for free informed consent, and (3) socioeconomic and environmental impacts at the site will almost certainly violate principles of distributive equity. Because the proposed siting would violate norms of distributive equity and free informed consent, we have argued that it is unethical. Because poor, nonwhite members of the community would bear a disproportionate share of the burdens resulting from the CEC, we have suggested that the proposed siting is likely a case of environmental racism or classism.

We also answered possible objections to our conclusion that the proposed siting is unethical. One objection is that the plant has to be sited somewhere, and it is better to put it where it will help the economy. We reject this response because it makes two questionable assumptions: (1) the plant is needed; (2) the plant will help the economy. A second objection is that the greater good requires that some people must bear greater burdens than others, because perfect egalitarianism is impossible. We rejected this response because it assumes that inequalities are justified whenever they are alleged necessary for achieving the greatest good overall. But inequalities are not ethically justifiable when they are avoidable, uncompensated, and treat people merely as means to the ends of others, even if they appear necessary for promoting the greatest good overall.

Notes

1. R. D. Bullard, *Dumping in Dixie: Race, Class, and Environmental Quality* (Boulder, Colo.: Westview Press, 1990, hereafter cited as Bullard, *Dumping*; R. D. Bullard, ed., *Confronting Environmental Racism: Voices from the Grassroots* (Boston, Mass.: South End Press, 1993), hereafter cited as Bullard, *Racism*; R. D. Bullard, ed., *Unequal Protection: Environmental Justice and Communities of Color* (San Francisco, Calif.: Sierra Club Books, 1994), hereafter cited as Bullard, *Unequal Protection*; U.S. Environmental Protection Agency (U.S. EPA), *Environmental Equity: Reducing Risks for All Communities*, EPA–230–R–92–008 (Washington, D.C., 1992); hereafter cited as U.S. EPA, *Equity*; United Church of Christ (UCC), Commission for Racial Justice, *Toxic Wastes and Race in the United States: A National Report on the Racial and Socioeconomic Characteristics of Communities with Hazardous Waste Sites* (New York: UCC, 1987), hereafter cited as UCC, *Toxic Wastes*.

2. Regarding living near polluting facilities see J. Gould, *Quality of Life*

156   *Daniel C. Wigley and Kristin Shrader-Frechette*

in American Neighborhoods: Levels of Affluence, Toxic Waste, and Cancer Mortality in Residential Zip Code Areas (Boulder, Colo.: Westview Press, 1986); UCC, *Toxic Wastes*; Bullard, *Dumping*; B. A. Goldman, *The Truth about Where You Live: An Atlas for Action on Toxins and Mortality* (New York: Times Books, 1991).

Regarding consumption of contaminated foods see B. Bryant and P. Mohai, eds., *Race and the Incidence of Environmental Hazards: A Time for Discourse* (Boulder, Colo.: Westview Press, 1992); R. L. Calderon et al., "Health Risks from Contaminated Water: Do Class and Race Matter?" *Toxicology and Industrial Health* 9, no. 5 (1993): 879–900.

Regarding employment at risky occupations, see U.S. EPA, *Equity*; M. Moses et al., "Environmental Equity and Pesticide Exposure," *Toxicology and Industrial Health* 9, no. 5 (1993): 913–59; K. Sexton et al., "'Environmental Justice': The Central Role of Research in Establishing a Credible Scientific Foundation for Informed Decision Making," *Toxicology and Industrial Health* 9, no. 5 (1993): 686; hereafter cited as: Sexton, "Environmental Justice."

3. R. D. Bullard, "Environmental Racism in America?" *Environmental Protection* 206 (1991): 25–26; R. D. Bullard and B. H. Wright, "The Politics of Pollution: Implications for the Black Community," *Phylon* 47 (1986): 71–78; R. D. Bullard and B. H. Wright, "Environmentalism and the Politics of Equity: Emergent Trends in the Black Community," *Mid-American Review of Sociology* 12 (1987): 21–38; D. Russell, "Environmental Racism: Minority Communities and Their Battle against Toxics," *Amicus Journal*, Spring 1989: 22–23.

4. See R. D. Bullard, "Anatomy of Environmental Racism and the Environmental Justice Movement," in Bullard, *Racism*, 21.

5. See U.S. EPA, *Equity*; S. C. Jones, "EPA Targets 'Environmental Racism,'" *National Law Journal* 15, no. 49 (9 August 1993): 28; P. Cotton, "Pollution and Poverty Overlap Becomes Issue, Administration Promises Action," *Journal of the American Medical Association* 271, no. 13 (6 April 1994): 967–69; J. H. Cushman, Jr., "Clinton to Order Effort to Make Pollution Fairer," *New York Times,* 10 February 1994, A1; M. Lavelle, "EPA Responds to Concerns of Minorities on Cleanups," *National Law Journal* 16, no. 36 (9 May 1994): A11; B. Ward, "Environmental Racism Becomes Key Clinton EPA Focus," *Safety and Health* 149, no. 3 (March 1994): 183–86.

6. See R. D. Bullard, "Overcoming Racism in Environmental Decision-making," *Environment* 36, no. 4 (May 1994): 15; hereafter cited as Bullard, "Overcoming Racism."

7. See U.S. EPA, *Equity*. See also Bullard, *Racism*, ch. 12.

8. U.S. EPA, *Equity*.

9. *National Law Journal* (Special issue: "Unequal Protection: The Racial Divide in Environmental Law") 15, no. 3 (21 September 1992).

10. See Sexton, "Environmental Justice," 688–92.

11. D. Ferris, "A Call for Justice and Equal Environmental Protection," in Bullard, *Unequal Protection*, 298-320.

12. Executive Order No. 12898, Sec. 1–101. For a reprint of the order, see *Environment* 36, no. 4 (May 1994): 16–19.

13. J. Feinberg, *Social Philosophy* (Englewood Cliffs, N.J.: Prentice-Hall, 1973), 98–119, hereafter cited as: Feinberg, SP; W. Frankena, *Ethics* (Englewood Cliffs, NJ: Prentice-Hall, 1963), 39; hereafter cited as Frankena, *Ethics*; P. S. Wenz, *Environmental Justice* (New York: SUNY, 1988), 22–24, hereafter cited as Wenz, EJ.

14. See K. S. Shrader-Frechette, *Science Policy, Ethics, and Economic Methodology* (Reidel: Dordrecht, 1985), 221–22; hereafter cited as: Shrader-Frechette, SPEEM.

15. Frankena, *Ethics*, 40.

16. W. Frankena, "Some Beliefs about Justice," *The Lindley Lecture*. Department of Philosophy Pamphlet (Lawrence: University of Kansas, 1966), 10; see also Feinberg, SP, 98–119.

17. J. Rawls, *A Theory of Justice* (Cambridge, Mass.: Harvard University Press, 1971).

18. Wenz, EJ, 106.

19. *National Environmental Policy Act of 1969* (NEPA), P.L. 91–190, Sec. 101 (b)(2); hereafter cited as NEPA; see also U.S. Nuclear Regulatory Commission (NRC), *Final Environmental Impact Statement for the Construction and Operation of Claiborne Enrichment Center, Homer, Louisiana*, NUREG–1484 (Washington, D.C: U.S. NRC, Office of Nuclear Material Safety and Safeguards, August 1994), vol. 1, 6–1: hereafter cited as EIS.

20. R. R. Faden and T. L. Beauchamp, *A History and Theory of Informed Consent* (New York: Oxford University Press, 1986), 86–91; hereafter cited as: Faden and Beauchamp, *Consent*; T. L. Beauchamp and J. F. Childress, *Principles of Biomedical Ethics*, 3rd ed. (New York: Oxford University Press, 1989), 74; hereafter cited as Beauchamp and Childress, PBE.

21. Faden and Beauchamp, *Consent*, 91–93.

22. Ibid., 87.

23. Beauchamp and Childress, PBE, 74ff.

24. Ibid., 74.

25. See previous notes and K. S. Shrader-Frechette, *Burying Uncertainty: Risk and the Case against Geological Disposal of Nuclear Waste* (Berkeley: University of California Press, 1993), 195–207; hereafter cited as Shrader-Frechette, BU.

26. K. S. Shrader-Frechette, *Risk and Rationality* (Berkeley: University of California Press, 1991), 73, 86; hereafter cited as: Shrader-Frechette, RR.

27. Shrader-Frechette, RR, 86–87.

28. EIS, 1–5 through 1–9.

29. EIS, 1–5.

30. Ibid.

31. EIS, 4–77.

32. EIS, 2–3 through 2–19.

33. EIS, 2–3 through 2–8.

34. EIS, 2–11 to 2–13, 2–15, and 2–18.

35. EIS, 3–103.

36. EIS, xxvi.

37. EIS, 3–109.

38. EIS, 3–110 to 3–112. See also U.S. Nuclear Regulatory Commission (NRC), *Draft Environmental Impact Statement for the Construction and Operation of Claiborne Enrichment Center, Homer, Louisiana,* NUREG–1484 (Washington, D.C.: U.S. NRC, Office of Nuclear Material Safety and Safeguards, November 1993), xxiii; hereafter cited as Draft EIS.

39. EIS, 4–86.

40. Beauchamp and Childress, PBE, 78–113; Shrader-Frechette, BU, 200ff.

41. Beauchamp and Childress, PBE, 110, 215; H. K. Beecher, "Editorial: Some Fallacies and Errors in the Application of the Principle of Consent in Experimentation," *Clinical Pharmacology and Therapeutics* 3 (March–April 1962): 144–45.

42. Beauchamp and Childress, PBE, 101.

43. Beauchamp and Childress, PBE, 111; see also Shrader-Frechette, RR, 153–56.

44. See EIS, 4–77 through 4–84.

45. EIS, 4–77.

46. EIS, 2–11.

47. See EIS, 2–12, 2–14.

48. EIS, 2–14.

49. EIS, 2–11.

50. EIS, 4–46, 4–77 through 4–86.

51. EIS, 4–53, 4–54, and 4–56. See also Shrader-Frechette, RR 71, for discussion of risk regulation.

52. See R. D. Bullard, "Commentator No. 5," in EIS, vol. 2, 1–20. See also Bullard, "Overcoming Racism," 39.

53. EIS, 2–3.

54. See EIS, ch. 4.

55. See NEPA, Sec. 101.(b)(2), Sec. 101.(c), Sec. 102.(B).

56. EIS, 4–42, 4–44, 4–78, 4–79, 4–83, 4–84. See also Draft EIS, 4–79.

57. See Sierra Club Legal Defense Fund, Inc., "Commentator No. 41," in EIS, vol. 2, 171.

58. E. J. Mishan, *21 Popular Economic Fallacies* (New York: Praeger, 1969), 235.

59. See Shrader-Frechette, SPEEM, 227.

60. EIS, xxvi, 4–35.

61. EIS, 4–35.

62. W. K. Frankena, "The Concept of Social Justice," in *Social Justice,* ed. by R. B. Brandt (Englewood Cliffs, N.J.: Prentice-Hall, 1962), 15; Shrader-Frechette, BU, 184; Shrader-Frechette, SPEEM, 226; Shrader-Frechette, RR, 142.

63. See I. Kant, *Groundwork of the Metaphysics of Morals,* trans. H. J. Paton (New York: Harper and Row, 1964), 95–98; Shrader-Frechette, RR, 142.

64. EIS, 1–5 and 4–77.

65. See U.S. Congress, *National Energy Strategy (Part 2)*. Hearings before the Subcommittee on Energy and Commerce, House of Representatives, 102d Congress, first session (Washington, D.C.: U.S. Government Printing Office, 1991); hereafter cited as U.S. Congress, NES; and *Energy Policy Act of 1992* (EPA), P.L. 102-486, 24 Oct. 1992; hereafter cited as EPA.

66. See U.S. Congress, NES.

67. EIS, 1–5.

68. See EPA, Sec. 1502, Sec. 1601.

69. See U.S. Congress, NES, 141–42.

70. See U.S. Congress, NES, 151.

71. EIS, 1–5.

72. EIS, 1–7.

73. EIS, 1–5.

74. See, for example, J. L. Campbell, *Collapse of an Industry: Nuclear Power and the Contradictions of U.S. Policy* (Ithaca: Cornell University Press, 1988); hereafter cited as Campbell, *Collapse*.

75. See Campbell, *Collapse*, 3; U.S. General Accounting Office (GAO), *Electricity Supply: What Can Be Done to Revive the Nuclear Option?* (Washington, D.C.: U.S. GAO, 1989), 10, 23; hereafter cited as GAO, ES.

76. GAO, ES, 14.

77. See Shrader-Frechette, BU; N. Lenssen, "Confronting Nuclear Waste," in *State of the World 1992*, ed. by L. R. Brown (New York: W. W. Norton, 1992), hereafter cited as: Lenssen, CNW; GAO, ES, 4.

78. See GAO, ES, 22–25.

79. U.S. General Accounting Office (GAO), *Nuclear Science: U.S. Electricity Needs and DOE's Civilian Reactor Development Program* (Washington, D.C.: U.S. GAO, 1990), 3, 17.

80. Lenssen, CNW.

81. Draft EIS, 4–75.

82. See EIS, 4–76 through 4–86. See also Draft EIS, 4–80.

83. See note 62.

Part Three

Racism in Africa

9

The Political Economy of the African Environment

Omari H. Kokole

Africa, with the highest rate of population growth, suffers from the ecological hazards of water pollution, desertification, deforestation, and urban sprawl, but it would be a mistake to say that population growth *causes* these problems.

Samuel Kim, *The Quest for a Just World Order*

There exists a significant environmental dimension to the current "African crisis." In its broadest sense the environment is "everything that surrounds us. It is the air we breathe, the water we drink, the soil that grows all our food, and all living beings."[1] However, in this analysis environment transcends the merely physical, for it also encompasses the socioeconomic context as well. It (the environment) interacts with a variety of other forces—all in a nonsimple way. In this chapter we limit our investigation to the reciprocal interplay between politics, economics, culture, and the African environment.

In size the second largest in the world, Africa is also the most centrally located of all the continents on planet earth. Possessing a total area of 11,596,000 square miles (or 30,149,600 square kilometers), the continent is virtually bisected by the equator. As such, the tilt of the earth never determines the sun's rays on Africa. Much of Africa is centrally exposed to the sun and therefore gets direct solar rays permanently. This exposure has both its environmental benefits and costs.[2]

Africa is also traversed by both the tropic of Cancer and the tropic of Capricorn. No other part of the world is more centrally located than Africa though equally true is the observation that perhaps no other continent is currently more environmentally challenged.

Africa also contains the largest desert in the world—the Sahara (an expanding reality) in the north. As Kenneth Davis has remarked about this desert, "it is by far the world's largest, most desolate, and hottest desert . . . stretches across North Africa from the Atlantic Ocean to the Red Sea, covering an area of more than 3.5 million square miles dwarfing the other great deserts of the world."[3]

In the southern portion of the continent, the Kalahari desert is also not insubstantial. With an area of over 120,000 square miles, the Kalahari traverses several countries in the subcontinent. Other parts of the continent are either arid or semiarid and to that extent are agriculturally marginal or irrelevant.

Considering the fact that the total population of the world stands at 5.7 billion and that Africa represents a quarter of the world's land area, Africa's current total population estimated at roughly 700 million is rather modest.[4] Yet Africa's population is the fastest growing in the world. The current average rate of population growth of 3 percent is not only the highest worldwide, but according to the World Bank's 1989 seminal study on Africa, "the highest seen anywhere at any time in human history."[5] If this persists, the current African population will balloon to 9.5 billion people by the end of the next century alone.[6]

This is a pace of population expansion that is much faster than over the 2 percent average for the entire Third World (Africa, Asia excluding Japan, and Latin America taken together). It is also a pace that far outstrips the annual growth rate of world population estimated at 1.63 percent by 1986.[7] In addition, it is way ahead of the 0.6 percent rate of expansion for the developed societies of the Northern Hemisphere (First and Second Worlds).

Should current trends continue unabated, Africa's population will double approximately every two decades. Meanwhile Africa's economies have been seriously ailing.[8] For example, in 1987 Africa had a total gross domestic product of $135 billion, roughly the equivalent of the GDP of Belgium alone (the population of Belgium is barely ten million).[9] What is more, the collective external debt of the continent itself is now larger than $500 billion.

Economic growth has basically lagged behind population growth. Averaging 3.4 percent a year since 1961, aggregate economic growth has managed to be only a fraction above population growth. The effects of this poor economic performance are exacerbated by other problems, infrastructural decay, unsanitary living conditions, and lack of clean water.[10] What this means is that living standards have not only failed to improve since independence, but have actually deteriorated. The serious implications of a poverty-stricken continent filled with too many Africans and too little of the resources necessary to sustain life are alarmingly obvious.

This chapter seeks to identify and analyze various factors, political, economic, as well as cultural (and their complex interrelationships) and to illustrate how these forces are distressing the African environment and impeding its sustainable development. A major argument advanced here in light of the evidence available is that there is a case to be made for cultural re-Africanization as one of the major solutions to Africa's current environmental crisis.

A Methodological Note

Needless to say, the complex set of factors and the nonsimple interaction between, and their cumulative impact on the African environment are best analyzed interdisciplinarily. This is necessary because of the close interconnectedness between the relevant factors and partly because this investigation is explicitly concerned with the *political economy* of Africa's environment and the implications and effects thereof. At the same time, however, for purely analytical purposes we shall discuss the various dimensions separately and sequentially beginning with the political.

Politics And Environment

Africa comprises well over fifty nation-states. Almost all of these countries are enclosed in colonial boundaries. The Europeans who drew these boundaries in the last quarter of the nineteenth century paid little attention to historical and/or cultural considerations as they divided up their African subjects. Consequently, many Africans who should have been together due to historical and cultural reasons found themselves scattered or dispersed—sometimes several ways as in the case of the Somali, the Kakwa, the Yoruba, and many others.[11]

Internal conflicts in Africa sometimes spill over into neighboring territories in defiance of the arbitrary frontiers the Europeans established. For example, in the 1970s Uganda's violent politics involved external dimensions partly because the president of the country at the time, Field Marshall Idi Amin Dada, came from an ethnic group (the Kakwa) that had been divided three ways by the Europeans.[12] The Kakwa were part Ugandan, part Zairean, and part Sudanese. Under Amin it really did not matter whether a particular Kakwa was Ugandan or not. Amin looked at all the Kakwa as his ethnic compatriots and many non-Ugandan Kakwa people reciprocated the gesture. Many sought economic and career opportunities in Amin's Uganda regardless of their national origins.

The Tanzania/Uganda war of 1978–79 that finally brought down Amin's regime in Kampala cost Uganda dearly infrastructurally as well as environmentally. Much of the vegetation, the flora and fauna, were destroyed. Game parks or national game reserves were virtually decimated by the fighting and fighters. But one of the major factors behind Amin's surprisingly long stay in power was his capacity to reward his supporters, non-Kakwa and Kakwa alike. The coffee boom of the mid-1970s was critical in this connection. The 1970s were also the heyday of OPEC, an external generous benefactor for Idi Amin. The internal (coffee) and the external (petrodollars) were relevant factors in sustaining Idi Amin in power for over eight years. But to grow coffee is not to fulfill the dietary needs of any society. Rather, it diverts attention and resources from more fundamental activities for Uganda or any other country. Yet the global economy had trapped the country in that peripheral role. But in principle the export-bias here is not environmentally friendly. Many Africans have been encouraged to engage in a wide variety of export-driven economic activities that ultimately are environmentally detrimental. These activities include the raising of beef-cattle for export, especially to European Union (EU) countries, on marginal land as in Botswana—an activity that also contributes to the expansion and deepening of the Kalahari desert. And yet only a very tiny fraction of the population of Botswana benefits from beef exports.[13]

The growing of coffee, tea, sugar, and other primary products for export also diverts attention, energy, and resources away from the growing of more fundamental food crops even as it disables and disempowers the African masses by exacerbating their need for, and dependence on, food imports.

Many Africans (and these represent the vast majority) who should not have been together again for the same historical and cultural reasons found themselves imprisoned within the walls of the same prison (read "nation-state").[14] Basil Davidson's latest volume, entitled *The Black Man's Burden: Africa and the Curse of the Nation-State*, aptly captures some of the pernicious consequences and contradictions of Africa's inherited colonial state.[15]

Africa's numerous armed internal conflicts in the postcolonial era are, at least in part, a direct result of the artificial nation-states created and left behind by the European colonial masters and the often ruthless competition and rivalry between the various groups within

them. These conflicts have carried considerable environmental implications and consequences. As a result, in spite of its small continental
population, today Africa possesses approximately 50 percent of the
world's refugees and displaced persons. The vast majority of Africa's
refugees flee from one poor country to another poor, if not poorer,
country. In global terms this is basically a unidirectional southern flow
of refugees. Only a small fraction moves to the rich North.

Refugees by definition place stress on the environment not only
because they crowd out their hosts and consume resources not of their
own but also because they are rendered less productive by their very
predicament. The violence entailed in their uprooting also involves
ecological devastation.[16] In conflict-ridden places as diverse as the
Sudan, Uganda, Angola, and Mozambique, there is evidence to suggest the increasing employment of the environment as a "weapon" of
war.[17] This includes the burning of food crops, the destruction of gra-
naries and seeds, and the baring of forests, thick bushes, and jungles
all in the effort to make the "enemy" vulnerable and force a surrender. Africa's refugees are often fleeing from violence, tyrannical rule,
and general chaos as well as economic difficulties. The global nation-
state system, which began as a European experience but has now come
to encompass Africa and the rest of humanity alike, is based on organized violence and the legitimate use of that power. It was the German sociologist Max Weber who described the state as virtually the
only entity that was entitled to the "monopoly of the legitimate use
of physical force."

In Africa the state has often been ruthless in its application of that
monopoly with serious environmental effects. For example, currently
the militarized repression of dissent and manipulation of ethnic rivalry as in the Rift Valley Province of Kenya is rendering the relevant
environment less wholesome than it once was.[18] The burning of Rift
Valley forests in order to flush out "undesirable aliens" (or fugitives)
is by definition a process of environmental degradation whose full
impact has yet to be computed. The turbulence in Kenya in the early
1990s was followed by a sharp decline in the tourist industry of the
country, a lesson that dependence on tourism was risky, even unwise.
We shall return to tourism and how it relates to environment deterioration and decay later in this analysis.

Military and Security Forces

The institution of a professional or standing army is almost alien
to Africa. Its current presence on the continent is mainly a direct re-

sult of European intervention. While militarization might have aided industrialization and general socioeconomic transformation elsewhere, in Africa the military has at best been a consumptive force and at worst a destructive entity. What is more, Africa's armies consume a considerable proportion of the GNP and foreign reserves (or hard currency) of their respective societies. Almost all of Africa's military gear, equipment, weaponry and, yes, even uniforms, are imported from the outside world.[19] This means Africans have to sell their primary products and minerals overseas in order to pay for these destructive paraphernalia. And because African economies are essentially agricultural, this implies major stress on Africa's environment to produce more primary products every year.

What is more, sometimes the military hardware imported into Africa, including land mines, contributes to the shrinkage of Africa's useable and cultivatable land. Vast parts of the continent have been land mined and thus rendered unsafe for agricultural work let alone human habitation.[20] Perhaps Samuel Kim overstates the case when he describes the war system as "the greatest environmental predator and polluter of the earth," but Kim was touching on a fundamental point nonetheless.[21]

Military expenditures also contribute toward Africa's mounting indebtedness. Africa's debt burden in turn compromises African states in their negotiations with the major global financial institutions, preeminently the International Monetary Fund (IMF) and the World Bank (WB). The ruthless so-called Structural Adjustment Programmes (SAPs) foisted upon the debt-burdened societies of Africa carry serious environmental implications and consequences. As many Africans are rendered economically desperate and as they are neglected (not so benignly) by their SAP-implementing governments, wanton exploitation of the ecology inevitably follows.[22]

SAPs are basically capitalist prescriptions imposed by Western-dominated financial institutions that call for, *inter alia*, expansion of exports, privatization of the economy, separation of the polity from the economy. As Osita Ogbu and Gerrishon Ikiara have put it, "These [SAP] programmes focus on the reduction of the direct role of government in economic activities, the removal of price controls and subsidies, the liberalization of exchange rates, the reduction or elimination of foreign exchange controls, the promotion of the role of the private sector and reduction of the government regulatory structures and policies. "[23] These are measures believed to cure distressed economies, but there is evidence to suggest that these prescriptions carry a heavy environmental cost. The experience of Ghana, where the timber industry has devastated the tropical forests of that West African country in the 1990s, is a case in point.[24]

Wood remains the major source of energy in most African countries, accounting in many cases for up to 80 percent of the gross national energy supply.[25] Food preparation consumes most of the energy. The increasing demand for fuelwood, and the inefficient way wood is both harvested and spent result in considerable environmental damage.

Across much of Africa, firewood and charcoal are cheaper than either electricity or gas, and as such there are many cash-strapped Africans who have resorted to the former because of the ramifications of SAPs. The selling of firewood and charcoal is a major form of self-employment for many Africans. Domestically Africans use that same source of energy for themselves as well. However, the felling of trees for firewood and charcoal contributes to deforestation, and in turn topsoil erosion; in other words, environmental deterioration follows.

Evidence from Tanzania, Ethiopia, and elsewhere in Africa suggests that urban fuelwood demands on neighboring rural areas contribute to environmental deterioration and soil erosion. This is partly manifested in escalating prices for fuelwood and charcoal, which suggests the ever-expanding distance that needs to be traversed to obtain these resources.[26] And in Africa often when energy-starved refugees have been resettled in well-wooded communal lands as has been the case with Mozambican refugees in Zimbabwe, for example, experience has proved that "No-one today would describe these areas as well-wooded, least of all a local . . . living within their vicinity."[27]

Africa's Elites

Africans are sometimes described as people who "produce what they do not consume and consume what they do not produce." Generally, it is true that Africa's food self-sufficiency has been increasingly compromised since the 1960s, and more and more Africans have been consuming imported food. Nevertheless, it remains substantially accurate to observe that Africa's elite (or intelligentsia), many of whom are culturally westernized, consume a disproportionate share of that which their societies do not produce both in terms of exotic foods from abroad and in terms of industrial or manufactured goods, all at a considerable cost to Africa's ecology.

Some of what the elites import to facilitate the good life introduce environmental problems—automobiles, air conditioners, and refrigerators are potentially pollutants in their own right. Chlorofluorocarbons

(CFCs) and other gases used in these facilities evaporate and undermine our protective ozone layer. These imported items are generally purchased in hard (or foreign) currency, which means Africa has to sell ever more agricultural goods and minerals in order to afford them. This all implies increasing exploitation of the environment without reference to fulfilling basic human needs in Africa itself. It is true that a baby born in the Northern Hemisphere will consume several hundred times more resources than another baby born in the global South. But it is also true that babies born to the elites of the South consume far more than the babies born to the masses in the same global South.

Politics and Numbers

Africa's elites, especially the political elite, are generally also not overly enthusiastic in their support of programs for reducing human fertility or family planning. In Africa south of the Sahara especially, political allegiance remains closely related to ethnic identity and solidarity. Clearly, it is not in the interest of many politicians to encourage the "depopulation" of his/her own ethnic group precisely because this is his/her most dependable political constituency.

Population control (or population planning), therefore, is not effectively encouraged and every new year there are more hungry mouths to feed than there were the previous year. The age distribution, or structure, of this rapidly expanding population is more alarming than the sheer numbers. The preproductive proportion of the population, those below the age of fifteen, in many African countries is considerable. Kenya topped the list in 1985 with 52 percent of its population reported to be under fifteen.[28] The population of toddlers or babies within this 52 percent while difficult to ascertain must be considerable. Kenya is reputed to have the highest rate of population growth in the world—4 percent a year. By the year 2025, it is estimated that Kenya's population will be about 79 million, up from its 24 million in 1990.[29] If current trends persist, approximately 40 million of these Kenyans will be under fifteen years old.

The raging AIDS pandemic has complicated the situation even further. Currently, there is a growing number of children dubbed "AIDS orphans" in Africa—children too young to fend for themselves, left behind by parents who have succumbed to AIDS. Also increasing in numbers are "AIDS grandparents," often elderly people or senior citizens who have had to inherit the parental responsibilities and obligations of their AIDS-stricken young adult progeny. This postproductive sector of society combined with the preproductive sector of AIDS orphans further widens the gap between population growth and economic productivity (or growth) in Africa. The social impact is potentially serious.

Cruel Nature

Nature, too, has played havoc with Africa's environment and societies. Drought and the closely related famine in various parts of the continent have exacerbated hunger, poverty, misery, and health problems. African countries like Ethiopia, Somalia, the Sudan, Mali—generally many of those in the Sahel region and in Southern Africa—have experienced serious drought and famine in recent years.[30] As a result, the people in those areas were forced to be environmentally more destructive than they would otherwise have been.

For example, many African pastoralists have been forced to cut down trees so that their livestock may graze on the fallen leaves.[31] Yet these trees take a long time to grow. As the trees gradually disappear, the pastoralists need to traverse ever-longer distances in order to find sustenance. That movement itself compounds the environmental degradation, especially the damage to topsoil as the heavy animals trample on it. The Sahelian experience in the 1970s and 1980s was a dramatic illustration of desertification exacerbated by human degradation of the environment.

It is self-evident that in Africa water shortage is a major source of environmental stress. Malin Falkenmark has estimated that by the end of this century over 66 percent of the African people may be living in "water-stressed countries."[32] Currently many Africans spend a lot of prime time fetching water—several hours every day, and it is unclean water, which poisons and kills many Africans every year. The time and energy spent in collecting water could be put to better use under different circumstances. No wonder some have begun to talk about "water aid" for Africa.

Additionally, some parts of Africa are simply ecologically vulnerable. These are areas that are prone to floods, soil erosion, and other environmental dangers. These "critical zones" can hardly sustain the present generation of inhabitants, let alone their descendants.[33]

Corruption

The sad realities of Africa are not helped by the corruption and mismanagement perpetrated by many African politicians and bureaucrats. It would be absurd to suggest that Africa has a monopoly on corruption but corruption in Africa has even more pernicious effects than it does elsewhere. This is because at its highest levels it does often involve "capital flight" out of Africa—often hard currency banked in the North with the latter's tacit complicity, which means no spin-offs redound from the corruption to the benefit of the African society victimized. Even aid intended for refugees and internally displaced persons has been known to be sold by the very officials who were supposed to distribute it. But because these are either politically influential or politically well-connected people this corruption occurs with depressing impunity. African politicians especially are notoriously self-aggrandizing. Many who enter politics poor, soon become wealthy.

These corrupt activities contribute to the impoverishment, if not endangerment, of the African environment. This is true whether the corruption provokes a revolt and an ecologically devastating civil war ensues, or whether these politicians permit themselves to be bribed by foreigners to allow industrial wastes (which may be radioactive and toxic) from northern countries to be disposed of in their surroundings, or whether they squeeze more agricultural exports out of their hapless compatriots, or whether they permit (for a price) multinational or transnational corporations (MNCs/TNCs) to exploit Africa absent any environmental ethics whatsoever.[34]

All these are political factors that impinge on the African environment affecting prospects for its sustainable development. Next, let us turn to the economic domain before pulling these variables together and advancing some tentative remedies for Africa's distressing condition.

Economy And Environment

Since African polities (or nation-states) were externally imposed, Africa's economies have been externally oriented, again as a result of Western intervention. The asymmetrical incorporation of Africa's economies into the global economy, on fundamentally unequal and unfair terms, has chronically shortchanged Africans and dealt them a raw deal not just historically but up to contemporary times. It will also influence future economic prospects.

Initially the West needed labor from Africa, cheap unskilled labor to work on the plantations of the so-called New World, hence, the Atlantic slave trade. Second, the West moved to the territorial conquest of Africa, hence, European colonization of Africa. Third, the West needed raw materials, more cheap labor, and captive markets, hence, the still-continuing economic exploitation of the continent. Some describe this as "neocolonialism"—a new way of retaining control over former subjects.[35]

In the postcolonial era, the West wants Africa's raw materials and minerals at prices ultimately dictated by Western consumers even as it remains stubbornly uninterested in the manufactured or industrial goods originating from Africa. Indeed, it is arguable that it is not in the interest of the West to help in the industrialization of Africa and because of that fact the West has effectively sabotaged or discouraged Africa's industrialization. To be sure, schemes like the European Union's Stabilization of Export Earnings (STABEX), the insurancelike arrangement designed to compensate primary producers for shortfalls in export earnings, and the similar arrangement to stabilize earnings from the sale of minerals (SYSMIN) represent basically an incentive for Africans to continue in their traditional role as producers of raw materials and as secure sources of strategic minerals for Europe, essentially serving as "hewers of wood and drawers of water" for westerners.[36]

External trade is critical for many African countries and yet the list of exports from any African state remains dangerously short (in fact, for Zambia it is basically a single commodity, copper; for Uganda it is basically coffee; and these illustrations can be further extended). In addition, the prices the primary products fetch fluctuate wildly, plummet often, and are generally unfair and unjust in sharp contrast to the prices of the industrial/manufactured goods they are often utilized in producing.

In some cases, Africans earn less for the primary products on the world market even when they produce more. In his doctoral work, Dal Didia has persuasively demonstrated a clear negative relationship between export prices and tropical deforestation.[37] Africa's ever-enlarging external debt has immense implications for its environment. The pressure to earn the hard currency with which to handle the debt encourages African governments to adopt policies, including the maximization of agricultural and mineral exports, which wreak environmental deterioration and decay.[38] As the costs of manufactured goods shoot up while the prices of primary products keep on plummeting, primary producers deforest and ravage their environment even more recklessly in order to pay their debts and to survive.

As a result, some young Africans lay down their implements in frustration and head toward towns and cities where many languish unemployed. This is the phenomenon of rural-urban migration in Africa.

Urbanization without Industrialization

Africa's rapid rate of urbanization (without much industrialization) has many implications and consequences. In 1950 there were only two African cities with more than one million inhabitants. By the 1990s, the number of such cities had jumped to over 40.[39] It is conceivable that rather than stimulate development, urbanization in Africa is likely to hinder it instead. Economically, urbanization expands the ranks of the unemployed and the underemployed. Politically, it creates a potentially explosive situation especially because those affected the most are young, modestly educated, and deprived. Declining health standards, hunger, pollution, crime, violence, drugs, prostitution, and many other social ills abound as the rural-urban migration continues unabated.[40] For example, during the heady days of OPEC petrodollar power, hundreds of thousands of Nigerians flocked to towns and cities in optimistic expectation of finding "paradise" there.[41] But even after the OPEC euphoria had fizzled out, many Nigerians still continued this rural-urban migration, and Lagos, for one, may qualify as "being possibly the world's worst city" as a result.[42]

Poor health services, food shortages, traffic congestion and the related pollution, inadequate housing, water shortages, poor sanitation and sewage facilities, and massive unemployment are only some of the consequences of this relentless rural-urban migration.[43] The United Nations Population Fund (UNFPA) estimates that by the end of the century, some 40 percent of Africa's "absolute poor" will consist of residents of towns and cities.[44]

SAPs and Ecocide

I mentioned earlier the SAPs imposed on the vast majority of African countries. SAPs often encourage the export orientation in African economies. What this means is that Africans are forced or encouraged to increase their exports, including the export of timber, which means potential deforestation, soil erosion, and subsequent ecological decay.[45]

Deforestation also occurs because farm lands have to be carved out of rain forests. Many experts in the field concur that the demand for agricultural land is the single most important factor instigating deforestation in the tropics.[46] This upsets the ecological balance and enhances the possibility of future drought and other hazards. And because

Africa's exports are basically agricultural or mineral, this means too much exploitation of Africa's environment perpetrated too quickly. Debt-burdened and under-industrialized African countries are usually the ones forced to ravage their environment.

Africa's debt burden has also helped to elevate tourism to a new level of national significance in many instances, thus introducing a new, even riskier form of dependency for some African countries. Many African countries (including Kenya, Gambia, Tanzania, Tunisia, and Egypt) now derive a substantial portion of their foreign exchange earnings from the tourist industry. Tourism has implications for ecological balance. As certain lands are set aside as "game reserves" for tourist entertainment and as the Hiltons, InterContinentals, and Sheratons replace farms, factories, and industries, the relationship between human beings and their environment is naturally changed for the worse. Animals may be valued more than human beings in some cases and some lands denied to desperate citizens.[47] One consequence is the exacerbation of Africa's disturbing rural-urban migration as land-hunger continues to displace many. It is estimated that approximately 70 percent of the fast urban growth in many African cities is precisely due to rural-urban migration.[48]

Protecting Africa's wildlife may benefit animal rights and conservation groups, but it creates additional difficulties for the already hazardous survival of Africa's poverty-stricken peasants. What is more, the tourists, often Northerners themselves, come with a cultural baggage that is consumerist, materialist, even extravagant and some of their ways may rub off on locals partly at an environmental price. Where touristic sex is involved, the work ethic is considerably undermined quite apart from the possibility of being infected by sexually transmitted diseases, including deadly HIV and AIDS.[49]

Upon their departure, many tourists take back home with them a part of the African environment. "Tourist art" is a corollary of the tourist industry.[50] Many Africans find it gainful to sell souvenirs to the tourists, mostly objects obtained from the environment, in order to make a living. Some resort to "poaching" to acquire ivory and tusks for sale. On the whole, this new precarious dependence on tourism shifts attention from production to service; long-term basic needs are sacrificed at the altar of short-term quest for foreign exchange. Nor does the wildlife remain constrained in its conserved territory. It has been known to wreak extensive damage on food crops, property, and even cause loss of human life in areas adjacent to the game reserves. What also ought to be remembered is that because many Africans operate on diminishing land as some of it is reserved for wildlife, they are *ipso facto* forced to place ever-greater pressure on the remaining land simply to survive.

Culture And Environment

Traditionally, Africans did not sharply distinguish humanity from nature. The environment was not perceived as intended to serve human beings nor were the latter superior to the environment. Indeed, it was not easy to tell where nature ended and humanity began in the indigenous worldview of many African peoples. Because of this lack of separation between nature and humanity, many African cultures carried a deep respect, even affection, for nature.[51] Land especially had deep psychological, emotional, and spiritual meaning for many people.

Indigenous religious systems neither anthropormophized God, nor royalized God, nor centralized God. Under traditional religious paradigms, it was therefore possible to have divine rivers, divine lakes, divine trees and mountains, or even animals. In other words, aspects of nature were even superior to humanity, or at least they did not exist for the satisfaction of people's pleasures or needs. Then came the intervention of Islam and the West in Africa altering the relationship between humanity and nature. The new cultures were more materialist and consumerist than the indigenous ones. People, after all, were conceived in the image of their Maker. As such people were not coordinate, let alone subordinate, to nature but rather superordinate to it. The ecological implications are obvious.

As indicated, the export bias encouraged by Europe in Africa resulted in economies that produced for strangers regardless of the environmental and human consequences. Conversely, some Africans acquired foreign tastes and when politically or otherwise influential in their respective countries, those African elites were determined to satisfy these acquired tastes regardless of the implications (environmental and otherwise). Peter Wenz refers to this entire process as "cultural pollution."[52] Taste transfer through the global communications revolution and even through the physical movement of Northern tourists is creating a breed of Africans with foreign wants, tastes, aspirations, and dreams. Africa's youths, being the most impressionable segment of society, constitute the majority of the victims of cultural pollution. As many of them flock to tourist resorts, night clubs, and towns, they cease to be productive members of society, and are even tempted to commit crimes, including violent crimes on the tourists. Africa's fast expanding population means the ranks of the culturally polluted will continue to swell with those whose cultural orientation is increasingly out of step with their environment.

For some, to partake in one's traditional dish or food is to manifest residual backwardness or primitiveness. For many it is important to dress, eat, walk, and talk like westerners. This cultural self-contempt has had a deleterious socioeconomic impact as Africans stagger into the twenty-first century.

Remedies For Environmental Decay

Although the following suggestions are tentative and need further elucidation and elaboration, they present remedies for environmental decay.

1. Increase food production in order to reduce the need for food imports purchased at a high environmental price (export of timber, of incidental crops, of Mazrui's "dessert and beverages" economies).

2. Inculcate traditional respect for nature and relay the message that in the final analysis humanity and nature need each other and are fundamentally interdependent. Environmental consciousness needs to be raised.

3. Reduce the traditional dependence on external trade especially the dominant North-South variety with all its massive inequities, injustices, and imbalances. How? Partly by cultivating South-South trade.

4. Curtail or moderate militarism, especially the institution of a "professional army." The modern African soldier should be taught and encouraged to grow his or her own food, erect his or her own barracks, learn to build roads, bridges, and schools for society almost like a pre-colonial ancestor who was a warrior only when there was a war to fight. In other words, African soldiers should be taught to be functionally versatile so that their burden on the African environment is reduced.

5. The infusion of foreign tastes needs to be discouraged partly by exposing its victims as essentially culturally self-contemptuous. This condition is neither necessary nor healthy.

6. Since Africans have been reducing their infant mortality rates and can reduce them even further, this "death control" could be enhanced and exploited to reduce birth control. This indirect method to population planning might help to balance the lopsided relationship between demography and ecology on the continent.

Notes

1. UN, *Teaching about Environment and Development* (New York: UN, 1991), 10.

2. Kenneth C. Davis, *Don't Know Much about Geography: Everything You Need to Know about the World but Never Learned* (New York: William Morrow, 1992), 279.

3. Davis, 280.

4. UNESCO, *UNESCO Statistical Yearbook* (Paris: UNESCO, 1993).

5. Ibid.; see also World Bank, *Sub-Saharan Africa: From Crisis to Sustainable Growth, A Long-Term Perspective Study* (Washington, D.C.: World Bank, 1989), 40.

6. Davis, 301.

7. UNFPA (United Nations Population Fund), *State of the World Population Report* (New York: UNFPA, 1993).

8. Omari H. Kokole, "The Politics of Fertility in Africa," chapter in Jason L. Finkle and C. Alison McIntosh (eds.), *The New Politics of Population: Conflict and Consensus in Family Planning* [*Population and Development*: A Supplement to Volume 20, 1994] (New York: The Population Council, 1994), 73–88.

9. World Bank, 2; and Barry James, "Economic Crisis in Africa: State-Led Plans as Failure," *International Herald Tribune*, 22 November 1989, 13 and 16.

10. Mathew Connelly and Paul Kennedy, "Must It Be the Rest against the West," *Atlantic Monthly* 274, no. 6 (December 1994).

11. See, for example, A. I. Asiwaju, ed., *Partitioned Africans: Ethnic Relations across Africa's International Boundaries* (London and Lagos, Nigeria: C. Hurst and University of Lagos Press, 1985).

12. Major C. Hugh Stigand, *Equatoria: The Lado Enclave* (London: Frank Cass and Company, 1923, 1968), 57–58.

13. Susan Turner, "Botswana: Economy," *Africa South of the Sahara, 1990* (London: Europa, 1989), 272–78.

14. See, for example, Basil Davidson, *The Black Man's Burden: Africa and the Curse of the Nation-State* (New York: Random House/Times Books, 1992), and Jacques Depelchin, *From the Congo Free State to Zaire (1885–1974): Towards a Demystification of Economic and Political History* (Dakar, Senegal, and Oxford: CODESRIA, 1992).

15. Ibid.

16. See, for example, Aristide R. Zolberg et al., *Escape from Violence: Conflict and the Refugee Crisis in the Developing World* (New York: Oxford University Press, 1992).

17. Steve Lonergan, "Population Movements and the Environment," *Refugee Participation Network* (RPN) 18 (January 1995): 4.

18. See Africa Watch, *Divide and Rule: State-Sponsored Ethnic Violence in Kenya* (New York: Human Rights Watch, 1993).

19. See Alfred Maizels and Edward Dommen, "The Military Burden in Developing Countries," *Journal of Modern African Studies* 26, no. 3 (1988):

377–401; and Robert E. Looney, "Military Expenditures and Socio-Economic Development in Africa: A Summary of Recent Empirical Research," *Journal of Modern African Studies* 26, no. 2 (1988): 319–25.

20. "Landmines: Africa's Deadly Legacy," *Africa Confidential* (London) 34, no. 23 (19 November 1993): 1–3; and Africa Watch, *Land Mines in Angola* (New York: Human Rights Watch, 1993).

21. Kim, *The Quest for a Just World Order*, 268.

22. See, for example, Simon Commander, ed., *Structural Adjustment and Agriculture: Theory and Practice in Africa and Latin America* (Portsmouth, N.H.: Heinemann, 1989).

23. See Osita Ogbu and Gerrishon Ikiara, "The Crisis of Urbanization in Sub-Saharan Africa," *Courier* (Brussels) 149 (January-February 1995): 53.

24. See J. S. George, "A Forest beyond the Trees: Tree Cutting in Rural Ghana," *Human Ecology* 20, no. 1 (1992); and Alexander Sarris and Hadi Shams, *Ghana under Structural Adjustment: The Impact on Agriculture and the Rural Poor* (New York: New York University Press, 1991).

25. The World Bank, *Sub-Saharan Africa: From Crisis to Sustainable Growth*, 131.

26. See Jonathan Baker, "Urban Development and Rural Change," *Courier* 149, (January-February 1995): 59.

27. Gus Le Breton, "Stoves, Trees and Refugees: the Fuelwood Crisis Consortium in Zimbabwe," *Refugee Participation Network* (RPN) 18 (January 1995): 9.

28. Connelly and Kennedy, 76.

29. UNFPA, *1993 One World Almanac* (New York: UNFPA, 1993). See section entitled "Basic Indicators."

30. Consult also Ezekiel Kalipeni, ed., *Population Growth and Environmental Degradation in Southern Africa* (Boulder, Colo.: Lynne Rienner Publishers, 1994).

31. Basil Davidson, *Africa*, an eight-part TV series (London: Beazeley, 1984).

32. Malin Falkenmark, "Rapid Population Growth and Water Scarcity: The Predicament of Tomorrow's Africa," *Resources Environment and Development Review* 16 (1990): 92–94.

33. UNFPA, 7.

34. World Bank, 22.

35. See, for example, Kwame Nkrumah, *Neo-Colonialism: The Last Stage of Imperialism* (London and New York: Panaf Books and International Publishers, 1968).

36. See Omari H. Kokole, "STABEX Anatomized," *Third World Quarterly* (London) 3, no. 3 (July 1981): 687–702; and Maxwell Owusu, "Agriculture and Rural Development since 1935," in *Africa Since 1935*, ed. by Ali A. Mazrui General History of Africa, vol. 8 (Oxford, England, and Berkeley, Calif.: Heinemann and University of California Press, 1993), 317–56.

37. See Dal O. Didia, "The Interaction between the Sustainable Sector, Non-Sustainable Sector and the International Economy: Implications for Trop-

ical Deforestation," unpublished doctoral dissertation, SUNY-Binghamton, 1993.

38. J. R. Kahn and J. McDonald, "Third World Debt and Tropical Defor-estation," *Ecological Economics* (1994): and Konrad Von Moltke, "Interna-tional Issues in Tropical Deforestation." Paper presented for the "Workshop on Climate Change and Tropical Forests," Sao Paulo, Brazil, 1990.

39. UNFPA, 5.

40. Richard E. Stren and Rodney R. White, eds., *African Cities in Crisis: Managing Rapid Urban Growth* (Boulder, Colo.: Westview Press, 1989), and Catherine Coquery-Vidrovitch, "The Process of Urbanization in Africa (From the Origins to the Beginning of Independence)," *African Studies Review* 34, no. 1 (April 1991): 1–98.

41. For the housing implications of rural-urban migration, consult Peter Amis and Peter Lloyd, eds., *Housing Africa's Urban Poor* (Manchester and New York: Manchester University Press, 1990).

42. Davis, 303.

43. Ibid.

44. UNFPA, 11.

45. Tim Lang and Colin Hines, *The New Protectionism: Protecting the Future against Free Trade* (London: Earthscan, 1993).

46. See, for example, D. J. Mahar, *Government Policies and Deforesta-tion in Brazil's Amazon Region* (Washington, D.C.: World Bank, 1989); S. Postel and L. Heise, *Reforesting the Earth* (Washington, D.C.: World Watch Institute, 1988), World Watch Paper #83; and World Resources Institute, *Tropical Forests: A Call for Action* (Washington, D.C.: World Resources Institute, 1985).

47. See, for example, Cynthia Enloe, *Making Feminist Sense of Interna-tional Politics: Bananas, Beaches, and Bases* (Berkeley and Los Angeles, Calif.: University of California Press, 1989), especially 19–41.

48. See Ray Bonner, *At the Hand of Man: Peril and Hope for Africa's Wildlife* (New York: Knopf, 1993). Also see Nomsa D. Daniels, *Protecting the African Environment: Reconciling North-South Perspectives* (New York: Council on Foreign Relations Press, 1992). Richard E. Stren and Rodney R. White, eds., *African Cities in Crisis: Managing Rapid Urban Growth* (Boul-der, CO: Westview Press, 1989): 68.

49. See, for example, Norman Miller and Richard C. Rockwell, eds., *AIDS in Africa: The Social and Policy Impact* (Lewis, N.Y.: Edwin Mellen Press, 1988).

50. Jan Vansina, "Arts and Society Since 1935," in Ali A. Mazrui, ed., *Africa Since 1935*, 582–632, and *Africa Events* (London) 1990s and *The Cou-rier*.

51. It has been claimed that one of the major stimulants of African stud-ies in Japan is indigenous African orientations to the environment. See Philip M. Peek, "Japanese Anthropological Research on Africa," *African Studies Review* 133, no. 1 (April 1990): 93–131.

52. Peter S. Wenz, personal communication to the author, 17 December 1994.

10

Somalia: Environmental Degradation and Environmental Racism

Hussein M. Adam

The Somali people share a common language (two main dialects), religion (Sunni Islam), physical characteristics, oral literary traditions, legal and informal rules and procedures, as well as pastoral and agro-pastoral customs. They constitute a widely spread "ethnic community," which is divided into clan-families, clans, and subclans—all the way down to lineages. At the top level of segmentation, Somalis are divided into five unranked clan-families: Hawiye, Darod, Isaq, Dir, and Digil/Mirifle under which comes the Rahanwin clans of agropastoralists occupying the interriver areas around the southwestern town of Baidoa situated between the country's two main rivers—the Juba and the Shabele. Somalia has its minorities: there are people of Bantu descent living in farming villages in the south, and mixed Arab-Somali populations living in urban enclaves in the coastal cities.

Before the civil war, the population of Somalia was estimated at ten million people. It is estimated that four hundred thousand were killed as a result of current civil wars and war-induced famine or disease. Nearly 45 percent of the population was displaced inside Somalia or fled to neighboring countries (Ethiopia, Kenya, Djibouti), to the Middle East, or to the West. Today, about one million Somalis live in diasporas scattered in several countries.[1]

The Cold War as well as elite manipulation of clan consciousness principally by the Siyad military regime have played a crucial role in instigating the current clan-oriented civil wars. The central challenge facing Somalis is how to channel clan conflicts into peaceful democratic politics. The collapse of the Somali state has brought out the worst in Somali clan violence, but it has also provided the opportunity for experimentation with indigenous forms of governance.

181

Imposing and sustaining a colonial state and militarist neocolonial state on Somali civil society and culture constitutes, broadly speaking, a form of environmental racism. This chapter will analyze this aspect within a historical overview that discusses colonial and neocolonial environmental degradation. Civil wars and state collapse have exacerbated these problems and given a window of opportunity for additional international environmental racism—attempts to dump toxic wastes on the Somali environment while plundering its fishery resources. This historical perspective on Somalia's environmental problems will also analyze examples of traditional Somali attitudes toward the environment.

The Tree, the Camel, and Environmental Balance

Somalia covers an area of about 638,000 square kilometers, roughly the size of Texas. It is situated on the Horn of Africa, bordered by Kenya in the south, Ethiopia in the west, Djibouti in the northwest, the Gulf of Aden in the north, and the Indian Ocean in the east. Somalia's physical setting consists of three major zones. To the north, a low-lying, coastal plain runs parallel to the Gulf of Aden. In the central region, a high plateau rises from the coastal plain and drifts into Ethiopia's Region Five (the so-called Ogaden) where it forms the major watershed for Somalia's two large rivers. In the south, several smaller plateau ranges and valleys run down to the Indian Ocean.

The northern and central regions provide some of the best grazing land in the country. The northwest region, but especially the southern zone, is the best suited for agriculture. Colonially introduced banana plantations are a significant farming activity in the area. Although some parts of the south receive up to 500 mm annual rainfall, the variability is extensive, making long-term rain-fed agriculture a relatively risky venture. Before the civil wars, about half a million Somalis practiced rain-fed agriculture. At that time estimates indicated that more than half the population were pastoralists or agropastoralists who raise camels, cattle, sheep, and goats. There were farmers, mostly in the south and northwest and, except for a small number who rely on fishing, the rest of the population were urban dwellers.

Situated in the south, the Juba and Shabele rivers constitute the country's larger underdeveloped potentials. Potential irrigable land for the Shabele is 80,000 ha. and for the Juba 160,000 ha., yet actual land use before the war amounted to only 34,000 ha. and 14,000 ha.,

respectively. One hopes that in future, the choice of irrigation strategies will avoid large-scale projects with their economic, social, and
environmental problems. The semiarid climate has given Somalis extensive experience in dealing with drought. Migration constituted one
reliable response to lessen drought's harsh impact. The Ethiopian presence in the Ogaden limited the migration option during years of Ethio-
Somali hostilities. The region today enjoys Somali autonomy within
Ethiopia, and the possibilities for resuming traditional migration patterns look better.

Ben Wisner notes, "Nowhere is the contrast between Eurocentric
rationalism and African philosophy greater than where the environment is concerned." He goes on to argue that simplified concepts such
as "carrying capacity" which reflect "highly pervasive mental images
bear no relation to vernacular thought and action."[2] Our main argument: future progress on environmental soundness will have to draw
upon the detailed indigenous knowledge of local environments and the
active participation of the people. To be able to engage the people in
a transforming praxis, it is important to understand their language and
thoughts. By drawing on selected Somali proverbs and poetry, this study
will offer glimpses of environmental consciousness experienced at mass
levels, an aspect that remains invisible to those who ignore expression in the Somali language. To facilitate this task, we have decided
to analyze a body of Somali literature that deals with trees and camels, key features of rural Somalia.

Somalis are aware of the importance of trees as forage for camels,
building material, honey production, medicinal herbs used in traditional
human and veterinary medicine, and domestic fuel wood. In Bari and
Sanag regions, certain trees are valued for the commercial production
of frankincense, myrrh, and gums. Somali villagers are also fully aware
that the indiscriminate cutting of trees (relatively sparse given the
semiarid climate) leads to strong dusty winds and flash floods. The
presence of trees indicates water sources, usually underground.

As in most semiarid environments, the contrast between trees and
grass during the dry and wet seasons is quite remarkable. As soon as
rains fall, the arid yellow grass suddenly turns green. A number of
poetic love songs use this change in vegetation to symbolize the beauty
of women:

> The growing buds and leaves mature,
> The fresh and ungrazed grass are you.[3]

The tree symbolizes various things in Somali poetry: in love poetry it
is often a metaphor for a young woman's beauty, for it is tall and

straight; sometimes it is used to conjure up an image of traditional Somali law (*xeer*), to allude to the actual or potential presence of water, and as a general source of protection. The umbrella-shaped Somali Acacia tree provides shade for juridical sessions of elders. There is a saying that roughly translates: "Somali law (*xeer*) is like a thick tree, one cannot bypass it from below or from above." A famous Somali poet once composed a poem about a special tree that offered relief "from poverty." Here is a brief example of the tree-love image:

> Ah, O Beloved, the tree in the village:
> you possess its most beautiful color.[4]

Another love song-poem, composed in 1958, reads:

> Ah, you are the branch of a tree, which
> grows in a cool place,
> Often completely covered with flowers,
> The moment I saw you, I felt something
> strange inside myself;
> Take my word for it, at times I shiver for you.[5]

In 1968, composer Mohamed Suleyman Bidde praised his lover for her spiritual and physical features in the following manner:

> You are like a tree hidden from view
> by its leaves and flowers;
> And each separate branch has a cluster
> of fruit,
> Which, on every side of the branch,
> has reached over-ripeness.
> And the fruit leans downward in its ripeness,
> And dips its sides into a cool pool of water.
> And you are like a tree which does not lose
> its color in *Gu* or *Jiilaal*.[6]

These poems show that Somalis love trees and vegetation, but they love camels even more. During most of Somali history, they seem to have achieved some sort of balance between these passions. The introduction of Somalia into the peripheral capitalist markets of the global imperialist system ruptured this delicate balance. A Somali proverb states, "no camels means no milk, no milk means no life."[7] Like trees, camels serve multiple purposes. The economic side of camel husbandry points to their value as sources of milk and meat and as the means of transport for seasonal migrations and for water and trade caravans.

Their use in various social transactions include a form of payment in kind, such as bridewealth given to the family of a bride, compensation for death or injury, and gifts of prestige. In these and other aspects, camel herding functions as a source of social cohesion and solidarity. Somalis compare the walk of a beautiful woman to that of a "graceful camel." The worst curse is said to be: "may you get no camels, nor sire sons!"[8] One poet captured the nutritional value of camels thus:

> milk and hump-meat the camel gives to people
> with milk it feeds its calf too
> delicious fermented milk
> from young lactating camels we enjoy
> by Allah, miserable would always be
> the man who owns no camels.[9]

In the following lines, a poet points out the fact that camels could procure for a man the costliest bride:

> the prettiest and costliest of brides
> though she be secluded and guarded by a jealous father
> her hand is readily given to him
> who brings virgin camels as brideprice. [10]

Traditional Somali law stipulates that the close kinsmen of a murdered man should receive one hundred camels as blood-compensation (*diya*). The camel watering-song quoted below relates an incident in which a respected man was killed, creating bitter enmity between the relatives of the deceased and those of the culprit. The payment of camels as blood-money to the bereaved party had, however, restored concord between the two sides. Due to the high social and economic values society places on the payment of camels as compensation for murdered persons, this often resolves bad blood existing between communities and individuals. No other category of livestock could play this role. Camels, therefore, constitute a significant element in traditional Somali peacemaking and peacekeeping:

> O camel mine
> as blood price you are
> acceptable to the relatives
> of a respected black-bearded man
> whom our clan had slain. [11]

Historically, camels and trees coexist in a complementary manner. It is the colonial and postcolonial distorted commercialization of livestock exports leading to overstocking that has produced serious contradictions between trees and camels captured in the following poetic riddle subject to multiple interpretations:

> Whenever one looks, the life of this
> world depends on water
> But if the water itself feels thirsty,
> From what well can one quench
> its thirst?[12]

No livestock are as supremely adapted to the arid and semiarid Somali environment as camels. They are capable of living without water for long periods, able to survive, even thrive, on scanty and forbidding vegetation. "As for pasture, the camel does not compete with sheep or cattle. Where the latter accept even the dry grasses on the ground, camels predominantly browse bushes. They are constantly on the move, biting one twig here and another there, thus utilizing the vegetation evenly. When on the move the camel walks softly with its big soft two-toed feet, keeping trampling at a minimum."[13] A camel produces more milk a day than other livestock: about twelve litres of vitamin C-rich milk underlining the Somali belief that man can live on camel's milk alone. Camel's milk does not get spoiled as fast as milk from other domestic animals. It turns into sour milk through a natural process and, in that form, can be enjoyed for several weeks. Unlike cattle or goats, camels could be ready for milking within an hour of the previous milking or suckling period.

Traditionally, a person in possession of one hundred camels was considered rich. Endemic labor shortages indirectly limited livestock size in the previous domestic-oriented economy. Camel-herding could not be conducted by a man working alone. Milking camels requires at least two people, while such tasks as driving a herd to water or to pasture, protecting it against robbers and beasts of prey, or recapturing it if it has been looted, certainly require a team of strong men dependent on one another for mutual support and cooperation. The tree and the camel symbolize how the Somali pastoral economy made good use of its modest natural resource base. A most striking sense of the traditional Somali ethos of environment nurturing is provided by Somali girls' poetic witticisms. In one of these, the first girl boasts: "As for me, where my father is, the land which has deteriorated, he causes it to recover!" The second girl responds: "As for me, where my father is, the land has no cause to deteriorate!"[14] The natural conservationist provides the role model.

The Imposed State and
Environmental Degradation

The era of colonialism (from the late nineteenth century till 1960) can be best conceptualized as a period of transition, directed by imposed colonial states (the British in the north and the Italians in the south), from precapitalist relations to peripheral capitalism. Eventually this guaranteed the permanency of pastoral participation—livestock exports—in both the colonial and postcolonial economies. European colonialism laid the seeds for the future horrendous clash of cultures manifested during current civil wars: it introduced the theory and practice of frontiers, the standing army, and the centralized state with a monopoly on the physical use of violence. Politically, the British colonial state followed the pattern of indirect rule; the British needed the colony mostly to supply Aden (on the route to India) with meat and other supplies. Italy hoped to turn southern Somalia into a settler (bananas, sugar) colony. Under Mussolini this area experienced a direct, brutal form of fascist colonialism.

Abdi Samatar points out, "The political structure of pre-colonial Somali society reflected the decentralized nature of the production base. . . . pre-colonial Somalis never developed any centralized authority."[15] Professor Ali Mazrui argues that the centralized European-imposed colonial state—later inherited at independence—is even more alien and unbearable among pastoralists ("lovers of animals") than among settled agricultural farmers ("lovers of land"):

> Lovers of land have sometimes had experience of elaborate political and social hierarchy even before the impact of the modern state. Lovers of animals, on the other hand, had ordered anarchy ruled through consensus rather than coercion. . . . In pre-colonial times Somalia was a nation without rulers. Its system of government was ordered anarchy within a culture of consensus—order without government.[16]

Precolonial Somalia was involved in regional trade networks. The following table shows the 1840 exports from Berbera, the main northern port, which did not export livestock, though it included livestock products.[17] Coffee exports included in the table originated from the Ethiopian hinterland. The British proclaimed a protectorate over northern Somaliland in 1884. "During the first fifteen years there were no major trade or economic changes in the protectorate, although livestock began to account for a large share of the value of this trade. According to one estimate, the Somali coast as a whole exported to Aden 4,000 camels, 50,000 sheep and goats, and 6,000 horses and mules a year before the end of the century."[18]

The colonial and postcolonial economy began to take shape so that

Table 10.1	
Exports of Berbera: 1840 (in kilos)	
Commodity	Quantity
Coffee	240,000
Gum Arabic	200,000
Myrrh	100,000
Ivory	40,000
Ostrich feathers	200
Civet	50
Wax	100,000
Hides	8,000
Goatskins	4,000
Sheepskins	5,000

by 1990, for example, agriculture/livestock contributed 65 percent of the GDP (gross domestic product), of which livestock exports were responsible for over 50 percent, crop exports (mostly bananas) contributed 38 percent, and forestry and fisheries about 1 percent each.[19] Samatar argues that these trends led to (1) neglecting the development of the productive forces in the rural sector; (2) the intensification of trade between the rural sector and the regional mercantilist system; and (3) the rise of merchant and bureaucratic elites that had a claim on rural production.[20] These and related factors—rising costs of needed imports—induced pastoralists to accumulate livestock to mitigate the effects of drought and other natural disasters. With the changes of the pastoral economy when incorporated into the colonial economy, the delicate balance between pastoralist and environment was upset. Thus began the process of environmental degradation that has continued ever since. Privately owned cement-lined water catchments mushroomed all over the place leading to livestock concentrations and rangeland degradation.

Over the ages, colorful tales have been created by the Somali popular mind involving wildlife who inhabit the same environment. The jackal is considered the most intelligent, while the lion and elephant are feared as possessors of superior physical strength. In many Somali folk tales, the hyena is endowed with supernatural powers, such as the ability to transform itself into a man. Most Somalis shun wildlife meat (as they have fish until recently) and therefore giraffes, antelopes, ostriches, and other herbivorous species have been free to roam without fearing human hunters. Among the beasts of prey the most harmful ones are the lion, the leopard, the cheetah, the hyena, and the jackal. Somalis felt obliged to kill them whenever they threatened people and/or livestock. Colonialism did not appreciate this notion of hunting as a limited defensive necessity. It introduced and legalized the practice of hunting for sport, prestige, and profits. This has continued during the postindependence era with devastating consequences to Somali wildlife.

The European scramble for Africa divided Somalia into five parts: we have already referred to British Somaliland and Italian Somaliland; another part became French Somaliland (now the Republic of Djibouti); Ethiopian Somaliland (the Ogaden, now Ethiopia's Region Five), and the Northern Frontier District (NFD) in the British colony of Kenya. For the Somali pastoralist the imposition of colonial frontiers and borders constituted a severe constraint placed on his delicate, spread-out ecosystem. Colonial partitions ignited Somali anticolonial struggles and when independence came, it took the form of unifying Italian Somalia and British Somaliland into the Somali Republic. The Italians imposed a modified version of their parliamentary system onto the Somalis. Residual Pan-Somalism in the postindependence years led to a buildup of the Somali military under the Soviets, and ultimately to war with Ethiopia and fighting in northern Kenya. The inefficient and corrupt political elites created a situation bordering on anarchy, which gave the military under Gen. Mohamed Siyad Barre the opportunity to intervene on 21 October 1969 and to dominate Somali politics until he was overthrown by the civil wars in 1991.

At first, the military regime showed some environmental awareness. It released a series of media propaganda on tree planting and declared 21 April each year as National Tree Planting Day. The most well-known campaign was against shifting sand dunes in the areas around Merca, where the dunes were encroaching into agricultural land, threatening power lines, and submerging coastal roads. Prickly pear cactus planted by hundreds of volunteers were used to stabilize the dunes. Very soon, the regime turned its attention to other media-attractive events and the follow-up was left to the bureaucratic National Range Agency and its army of full- and part-time employees. It is not surprising, therefore, that out of 5,000 square kilometers of shifting dunes, the campaign dealt with only 50 square kilometers.[21]

The military regime reinforced with a vengeance the commandist approach, the top-down export/plantation model inherited from colonialism. Its rigid centralist, militarist approach further alienated it from the residual culture of consensus that has sustained Somali society and politics over the centuries. The regime survived for about twenty-one years due to (1) Siyad's Machiavellian personal rulership, (2) the military and militarism, (3) the poisoning of clan consciousness and relationships, and (4) the Cold War with its large amounts of economic and military assistance. Siyad had the devilish ability to manipulate his domestic and external audiences. At first he pretended to be a "prophetic" ruler with a vision—"scientific socialism." Elected as OAU chairman in 1974, he declared himself a Pan-Africanist who would not attack another African country. Proclaiming his Pan-Arab sentiments, he got Somalia to be among the first non-Arab members of the Arab League. By 1977, he became a Pan-Somali nationalist, sending his army into Ethiopia to redeem "the Ogaden." The USSR backed Mengistu's Ethiopia, and he appealed to President Carter for support. He spent his remaining years manifesting his true nature, that of a tyrant.

> Siad Barre's policies had elements in common with Pol Pot and the Khmer Rouge in Cambodia. Pol Pot wanted to agriculturalize the urban population, send them back to the farm, in a kind of brutal re-ruralization. Barre also wanted to agriculturalize Somalis, but not urban Somalis; he focused on the Somali pastoralists. He wanted to take them from pastoral nomadism to the field for cultivation—a form of brutal modernization, a blow to the ancient ways of the Somali people.[22]

In 1964, the Soviets agreed to raise the Somali army from 3,000 to about 12,000. Pleased with the 1969 Siyad coup, they trained and equipped an army of 20,000. By the time Siyad ordered the army to "liberate the Ogaden," it had reached a size of 37,000. After the war, the United States and the USSR agreed to prevent their new clients from crossing each other's borders. Somalia no longer needed a large army. However, the United States continued to provide it with defensive weapons as Siyad increased the size of the army to 120,000 by 1982. During this period, the seeds were laid for catastrophic clashes between a centralized European-trained and equipped standing army and decentralized, autonomy-seeking pastoral civil societies. Within and outside the official army, Siyad created clan-based paramilitary and security forces. These forces were involved in various forms of urban and rural terror. For example, in July 1989, at least forty-seven young northern civil servants were taken to an empty Mogadishu beach and massacred by Siyad's Death Squads.[23]

Clan consciousness among Somalis is a product of the stateless material conditions of pastoral society. Historically, clans practiced the politics of mutual recognition regulated by the traditional law (*xeer*).

Elites—the Siyad clique in particular—have been able to transform peaceful clan competition into violent clan conflicts. From the 1980s onwards, Siyad poisoned clan relations by instigating rural clan conflicts in various parts of the country. He singled out northern Somalia—where he placed the bulk of the army—for particularly brutal, fascist types of punishment. He allowed no room for loyal, peaceful opposition groups. Clan-based armed and decentralized opposition groups rose to challenge his military dictatorship. The northern opposition group developed fast and was able to invade northern Somalia in May 1988; that date marked the beginning of the intensive phase of the Somali civil wars.

The durability of the Siyad regime is very much a product of the Cold War. The superpowers turned Somalia into a massive dumping ground for all types of conventional armaments—weaponry pollution. With the help of Arab petrodollars, Siyad was about to augment the weaponry stockpile through direct purchases from various arms markets. The United States provided a great deal of economic assistance, including food aid for refugees. The EEC and Italy provided substantial assistance, as did the World Bank, the United Nations, the rich Arab states, and China. As the civil wars heated up and Siyad's human rights violations became too obvious to hide, the regime began to receive less and less foreign assistance. The United States and other Western powers cut most of their assistance by 1989/1990, and the Siyad regime fell early in 1991.

In 1969, the Siyad regime banned the international export of charcoal from Somalia, but by the mid-1970s it removed the ban in order to open up a lucrative source of revenue for its patron-client networks. It is ironic to witness Somalis cutting trees in a semiarid environment to satisfy not only urban woodfuel needs but also to export them to East African countries with ample reserves of forests. The disastrous Ogaden war of 1977–78 resulted in over a million refugees who entered Somalia and were settled in large urban-type camps in five regions of the country. Each region hosted about six to seven huge camps. The refugees needed wood for housing and fuel. By the late 1980s, there was almost total devegetation in areas surrounding the camps as a result of such needs.

For the period 1984–87, Italy gave Somalia $1 billion for a series of projects: the Garowe-Bosaso Road, Bosaso Port, fisheries, and some agricultural projects. A former minister in the Siyad regime explains how this aid program was removed from the normal jurisdiction of the ministry of planning and placed under the foreign ministry headed by the president's brother, Abdirahman Barre: "All procedures and norms for project planning, implementation, review and monitoring were completely dispensed with. No standard accounting records were kept. . . . Regretfully, this blatant private appropriation of public resources made the state a *cosa nostra* for the Barre family."[24]

It was during this period that rumors about toxic dumping in Somalia became rife. There were those who claimed that Italian sources provided the funds for a road in the remote desert region of Bari in order to use road construction activities as a cover-up for toxic dumping. The Somali regime had been approached by brokers, according to informed sources, but there was no concrete proof of actual commitments and implementation.

During his desperate last years, Siyad did orchestrate a systematic wildlife poaching project to raise funds for his family and loyalists. He facilitated the collection of evidence about his poaching activities by being brazen enough to carry them across international borders—the border between Somalia and Kenya in particular. Professor Richard Greenfield maintained in a presentation at a recent Congress of Somali Studies that there is sufficient evidence to convict Siyad in a court of law for destruction of such wildlife as elephants, rhinos, leopards and cheetahs.[25]

Early in 1986, a ship on the way to South Africa ruptured while at Mogadishu harbor and spilled toxic chemicals. At first it seemed like a repeat of the Bhopal, India, accident, and there was talk of evacuating the city. The ship's captain claimed that there was no danger from nuclear wastes since they were stored in stronger metal cases. Most of the elites moved their families from the city. It was never fully ascertained what happened and with what consequences, because the Siyad regime cashed in on the neat tragedy and went out of its way to provide an elaborate cover-up. In addition to the toxic chemical spills, the ship also caused an oil spill that polluted Mogadishu and surrounding beaches for months.[26] It is only a matter of time before Somalia experiences a catastrophic oil spill. It is, after all, situated on the heaviest oil tanker traffic route in the world—about 475 million metric tons each year. As of 1991, when the Siyad regime collapsed, Somalia had no oil pollution fighting equipment.[27]

State Collapse and International Environmental Racism

The result of the Somali state disintegration in the 1980s, and final collapse early in 1991, was not just a staggering human tragedy. It also signalled the need for a paradigm-shift in theories of political science and African studies. Aspects of the Somali tragedy and attempts at state restoration may well mirror Africa's images in the twenty-first century. Africa will enter the next century confronting the deeper question that involves the compatibility between ancient African civil societies and the relatively recent postcolonial state. It should not surprise anyone to witness Somalia as the pioneering instance of total state collapse. This is a consequence of the extent and sharpness of the mismatch between the European derived postcolonial state and the nature and structure of Somali pastoral and agropastoral society. The heavy-handed, highly centralized, Siyad military dictatorial regime became the perfect agent of history necessary to ignite the implosion of the Somali state, and therefore of this contradiction. It is as if Somali society could no longer tolerate the cultural-political pollution imposed by European colonialism, and then inflated and perpetuated by the Cold War. On the positive side, there is a glimmer of hope that Somalia might also be the first to experiment with novel principles of restructuring state/civil society relationships.

Somalia is about to enter its fifth year without an internationally recognized polity; no national administration exercising real authority; no formal national legal system; no banking and insurance services; no telephone and postal systems; no national public service; no reliable, organized educational and health systems; no national police and public security services; no electricity or pipe water systems. In southern Somalia in particular, disruptive violent bands of armed youths have perpetuated a state of episodic chaos and semianarchy. Although Somalis have had to contend with many a hard time before, the present is exceptional in both intensity and pervasiveness. "Catastrophe, or *burbur*, then, captures a state of affairs—one characterized by a constellation of crises, the full impact of which is a severe depletion of the material, moral, and intellectual resources of Somalia."[28]

The Cold War—involving a U.S./Soviet strategic tug-of-war—was primarily responsible for prolonging the life (twenty-one years) of Siyad's atrophied state. The militarization of state instruments, Siyad's diabolical personal rulership, and his megalomaniac insistence on retaining power at all costs, played critical roles in state inflation during the early years and, ultimately, the unprecedented state implosion that followed. Poorly organized and led, decentralized armed opposition groupings contributed to a prolonged state of civil war. The group that captured Mogadishu, the United Somali Congress (USC, Hawiye clan-family dominated) broke into two warring factions led by Gen. Mohamed Farah Aidid and Ali Mahdi Mohamed. As happened once in Chad, factional war erupted among the USC victors who turned Mogadishu into another Beirut divided by a so-called green line. Unlike Liberia, where the capital never fell into rebel hands, chaos and anarchy engulfed Mogadishu itself. In most of Africa, with weak but nominal authorities in the capital city, civil wars caused the state to retract its effectiveness, functioning, and legitimacy, but not collapse altogether.

Siyad Barre escaped from Mogadishu to his clan homeland southwest of the city; from there his deranged insistence on challenging those who have phased him out of power led him to pursue RENAMO (Mozambique spoiler rebels)-type tactics for most of 1991 and 1992. The tug-of-war between his forces and those of General Aidid devastated the livelihood of the Rahanwin clans situated around Baidoa, between Siyad's clan base and Mogadishu. This led to a man-made famine that attracted global media attention and an international humanitarian intervention led by the United States (Operation Restore Hope, ORH) under United Nations auspices (December 1992). The mission did provide humanitarian assistance to famine victims, especially in and around the Baidoa zone, most of whom have since gone back to their traditional agropastoral activities. ORH and the follow-up UN missions, UNOSOM I and II, have found the task of national reconciliation, state restoration, and nation building as elusive as ever. It is estimated that 350,000 have died since the inception of full-scale civil war in 1988; about two million have been displaced internally and almost 4.5 million Somalis have been kept alive through international emergency assistance.[29]

Somalia today presents a country with two differing political cultures: in the southern parts, armed strongmen dominate the political landscape, the so-called warlords, including Ali Mahdi Mohamed (northern Mogadishu), General Aidid (southern Mogadishu and parts of central Somalia), General Morgan (Siyad's son-in-law who controls the southern town of Kismayu) and Col. Omar Jess (who controls southwestern areas surrounding Kismayu). The northeastern and northern parts of the country have enjoyed relative peace and stability. Since May 1991, former British Somaliland has established its own Somaliland Republic with a separate government that enjoys *de facto* but not *de jure* recognition. The British had ruled Somaliland through indirect rule, which strengthened the role of traditional religious and secular elders.

The Italians ignored clan elders and, during Mussolini's epoch, actively persecuted and humiliated them. In southern areas, political and military leaders were much more enmeshed within Siyad's corrupt military regime, while northern elites were often shunned and the northern people generally adopted a defensive, hostile stance toward the regime. The northern armed opposition movement (mostly Isaq clan-family dominated), the Somali National Movement (SNM), adopted democratic procedures from its inception. It held periodic congresses and peacefully rotated its leaders at each congress. It shunned military leaders and, except for one brief instance, regularly elected civilian leaders. Following its 1988 attack on Siyad forces in all major cities of the north, Siyad used indiscriminate air and ground bombardments to chase about 500,000 northerners into refugee camps within Ethiopia. This gave the SNM the opportunity to merge with the populace and to work closely with traditional secular and religious elders. In the south, armed opposition groups formed late and rushed to capture Mogadishu without political preparation, pursuing narrow-minded clan revenge policies.

As soon as Siyad was chased out of Mogadishu in late January 1991, Ali Mahdi Mohamed declared himself interim president of Somalia. This arbitrary action was rejected, not only by the other USC leader General Aidid, but also by all the other factional leaders in all parts of the country, including the SNM, which used this new instance of "southern arrogance" to declare independence for the north. The Superpowers, who had dumped lethal arms into the country for years, now decided to dump and forget Somalia altogether. As the Siyad regime fell, a U.S. helicopter from a U.S. warship off the Somali coast ferried both the U.S. and the USSR ambassadors from Mogadishu. The two powers, especially the United States, missed a golden opportunity to contain the civil wars through timely, strategic interventions—political and diplomatic, as well as economic and humanitarian assistance. The Italians and Egyptians backed the Mahdi faction and sponsored two conferences in Djibouti, in June and July 1991, to give legitimacy to Ali Mahdi and his self-declared interim government. The United Nations, now headed by former Egyptian state minister of Foreign Affairs, Boutros Boutros-Ghali, backed this Italian/Egyptian initiative. General Aidid, the SNM, and some other factions refused to attend. This arbitrary foreign interference simply sparked civil war between the Ali Mahdi and Aidid factions of the USC (both within the Hawiye clan-family).

State collapse and factional disputes made Somalia a tempting site for the dumping of unwanted hazardous waste. In industrialized nations, popular pressures for better protection of public health and the environment prompted official regulations that have led to accelerating costs for waste disposal. "A major element of the new international division of labor, the new round of imperialism is the export of hazard. . . . And when such toxic waste disposal is put into an imperial context, quintessentially a racialist context, the export of hazard is nothing short of toxic terrorism."[30] During mid-1992, media coverage carried stories concerning negotiations to dump toxic chemicals and hazardous wastes in Somalia. A Swiss broker apparently negotiated a deal on behalf of Italian companies with a Dr. Nur Elmi Osman, a minister of health in Ali Mahdi's factional, unrecognized government.[31] As the media coverage increased in scope and frequency, the executive director of the Nairobi-based United Nations Environmental Program (UNEP), Dr. Mostafa K. Tolba, felt obliged to issue a forceful press release on 9 September 1992:

> Information has reached this office on incidents concerning chemicals and hazardous wastes in Somalia. A number of European firms are believed to be involved. Negotiations between UNEP and the governments of the countries in which the firms concerned are located are now in progress. UNEP's object is to ensure that the planned disposals do not occur. We would prefer not to comment on the substance of these negotiations at this stage.[32]

The contract between Italian and Swiss firms trading in hazardous wastes and Ali Mahdi's minister allowed for the export of various types of toxic waste to Somalia for twenty years, 1991–2011. The value of the first phase of the contract was believed to be in the order of eighty million U.S. dollars. Shipments—each of 100,000 to 150,000 tons— were to have yielded a profit of eight to ten million dollars each, while the Swiss broker firm involved in the transaction was to take a profit of two to three million dollars per shipment. UNEP sent a two-man team to Somalia to investigate reports that waste consignments have already been dumped along the Somali coast. It is difficult to see how much such a brief mission could accomplish. Somalia is a relatively large country with vast expanses of its territory hardly occupied by human populations. The mission included a Somali UNEP director. While in Somalia the team was also asked to report on a separate incident: a warehouse containing 81,200 liters of toxic chemical pesticides used to combat locusts was set ablaze earlier in 1992. The damaged chemical containers had reportedly leaked into a nearby dry riverbed that is used for the meager water supply of Hargeisa, capital of Somaliland.

Somalia's long coastline—about 3,300 kilometers, the longest in Africa—has been vital to its trade with the Middle East and the rest of East Africa. It has also contributed to Somalia's coveted location within the Cold War strategic competition. The ocean fisheries off the coast of Somalia have great potentials; however, the aversion to eat fish afflicts many Somalis, especially the pastoralists. As part of its Treaty of Friendship and Cooperation, the Soviet Union had a large fishing fleet permanently exploiting Somali fishery resources. "During 1992, there were alarming reports that in the vacuum created by the fall of the Barre regime—which meant the absence of a central government to enforce rights over territorial waters—fishing ships from as many as two dozen countries were plundering the marine catch offshore."[33] Alarmed by such reports, a group of Somali and non-Somali scholars meeting in Geneva during the summer of 1992 issued the following recommendation to the international community: "The illegal exploitation of Somali marine resources by foreigners should be denounced, and all forms of foreign environmental opportunism in the absence of a Somali state should be prevented."[34]

Future Prospects and Pitfalls

A discussion of the future relations between Somali society and its natural environment can only be undertaken by making certain assumptions. Obviously, peace is a prerequisite for undertaking any meaningful human effort. The activities suggested below must therefore be viewed from the perspective of restored peace, stability, and collective institutions—a goal that is yet to be attained. Whether a Somali state or two states arise from the present catastrophe does not affect our speculations, since issues of environmental degradation concern both the northern Somaliland Republic and the rest of Somalia. We have treated issues in a comprehensive, boundary-transcending manner throughout this study. It can also be safely assumed that the future Somalia (or Somalia/Somaliland) will feature a thriving private sector—the state will certainly not be able to control and dominate the Somali economy the way the Siyad state did.

The concept of crisis implies both danger and opportunity; Somalia today stands at crossroads: one path leads to peace and a great opportunity at indigenous restoration; the other confronts serious pitfalls and the slippery slope toward more violence and warlordism as a system. For the most part, we shall assume that Somalia—at least in the long run—will be able to tap its deeply rooted consultative democratic political culture. This will be the best way Somalia can truly combat the cultural and political pollution of the colonial and Cold War neocolonial periods.

Between 1991 and 1994, the Somaliland Republic has been able to create an incipient—albeit fragile—indigenous democracy. Before analyzing this delicate experiment, let us provide as sociopolitical background a significant historical antecedent. The current situation is one in which, with the full collapse of the state, Somalis have been obliged to rely on traditional *xeer*. A similar situation occurred in the sixteenth century when the Islamic state of Adal collapsed.[35] From its coastal capital of Zeila, its famous leader, Ahmed Gurey, waged several successful wars against the Christian Abyssinian kingdom. In 1542 his highland enemies defeated his armies leading to the decline and collapse of Adal. Oral traditions record the recurrent wars, famine, chaos and banditry (*shifta*) that followed. A common response to the decline of public law was to revive and revitalize the *xeer*. The Issa clan (Dir clan-family) in particular produced an elaborate constitution (*Xeer Cisse*).[36] The constitution bound together six subclans—three related by blood kinship and three "adopted" subclans. Having lived under the pluralistic state of Adal, they decided to transcend the concept of kinship based solely on "blood." Although blood kinship is pervasive, Somali genealogies also indicate examples of kinship by "contract" and through "fictitious" stories of origin. This is an example of a rational social contract used to create "kinship"; Max Weber notwithstanding, an example of reversed modernity.

All the six subclans came to constitute the Issa clan through this legal instrument—all of it composed in poetic style to assist memorization. It was decided that the traditional clan leader, the *Ugaas* (other Somalis use *Suldan* or *Bogor*), would be chosen from the numerically smallest subclan of the six—which happens to be of the three adopted sub-clans in the original contract. The leader is a first among equals. The constitution provides detailed provisions concerning choosing the right *Ugass* as well as dethronement. A nonthreatening subclan was given, through the *Ugaas*, special prestige, recognition, and responsibility in adjudicating claims and disputes objectively and fairly. It is claimed that this specially crafted social contract carried the Issa through the chaos and turmoil of the sixteenth century and continues to minimize and resolve intra-Isse conflicts. The *Ugaas*, like other Somali traditional leaders, presides over the decision-making body or assembly, the *shir* (open to all adult males of the clan). Since the decision taken would bind the whole *shir*, including opponents, the good leader seeks to accommodate the opposition along consociational practices to avoid pressures that might later divide the group. Above all, given the cultural obsession with pride, every effort is made to avoid a loss of face.

Similarly, in Somaliland reconciliations legitimize and facilitate political cooperation. Northerners have taken a grassroots approach to the process. Traditional secular and religious (local) elites, modern elites, representatives of nongovernmental organizations, and ordinary citizens have participated in peace and reconciliation conferences held in virtually all the main towns: Berbera, Burao, Sheikh, Hargeisa, Erigavo, and Borama. Elders play a leading role. Siyad's wars brought conflicts to civil society, and unless these are resolved, there will be no mutual trust necessary to reestablish embryonic state organs. The traditional approach has won the support of most non-Isaq clans, and the SNM was therefore able to transform Somaliland from a clan to a multiclan or territorial project. The trust and social solidarity being created rests on a multiclan foundation. There are three Somali clan-families represented in Somaliland—the Isaq (the largest) and parts of the Dir (Issa and Gadabursi) and Darod (Dulbahante and Warsangeli) clan-families. The Isaq clan-family is itself subdivided into six clans at least.

The Somaliland social contract is being forged in stages. The Borama Peace and Reconciliation conference lasted from January until May 1993. At first, it set out to reconcile outstanding clan conflicts and on 30 March adopted a communal and territorial Peace Charter.[37] The Borama Conference went on to provide a more detailed social contract in the form of a National Charter adopted on 3 May 1993.[38]

The National Charter establishes a polity with a legislative body divided between a seventy-five-member House of Elders (*Guurti*) and a seventy-five-member Constituent Assembly; an executive headed by a president, vice-president, and cabinet of ministers; and an independent court system headed by a Supreme Court. The government has already lost cases involving ordinary citizens that came before the Supreme Court. Members of the interim National Assembly (both houses) are elected indirectly through intensive communal (clan) consultations and intricate mechanisms of proportionality. The government tried to block the sitting of one new assembly member, and he took the matter all the way to the Supreme Court where he won the case. The 150-member interim assembly meeting in Borama went on to elect former premier Ibrahim Mohamed Egal the new Somaliland president (by ninety-nine votes), and SNM veteran Abdurahman Au-Ali from Borama, the new vice-president. The then incumbent President Abdurahman Tour and former foreign minister Umar Arte both ran, but lost the election. Freedom of expression and freedom of the press thrive. This transitional administration was given until May 1995 to prepare a detailed constitution—a formal social contract for Somaliland—and hold a national referendum.

The evolving sense of communal solidarity enhanced by a social contract established by mutual consent facilitates the critical task of disarmament and demobilization. UNOSOM in southern Somalia, with immense financial and logistical resources, has failed to accomplish what the Somaliland communities have achieved through mutual trust. The Council of Elders (*Guurti*) is specifically charged to focus on peace and disarmament issues. The Peace Charter lays out policies to be pursued and establishes district and regional Guurti organs to concentrate on conflict resolution, peace, and disarmament. The National Demobilization Commission (NDC) has been set up to work with the various committees of elders. The commission coordinates the surrender and assembly of weapons (disarmament) and the registration and organization of demobilized personnel (demobilization, including the setting up of special training camps).

In the northeastern zone of southern Somalia, the communities involved have enjoyed relative peace since 1991—except for a brief period in 1992 when an Islamic fundamentalist group tried to capture regional power. In July-August 1994, tensions rose as the protopolitical organization of the region tried to hold a Congress and elect its leader. In an effort to bypass the two protagonists—Col. Abdulahi Yusuf and Gen. Abshir Musa—the Elders Council of the region recommended former premier Abdirazak Hussein as a compromise candidate, but Abdulahi Yusuf refused to accept their decision. Both Abdulahi Yusuf and Abshir Musa claim to be the SSDF leader. However, so far, there has been no outbreak of significant violence and conflict. Ever since late 1994, Abdulahi Yusuf has joined Gen. Aidid in Mogadishu in a final UNOSOM-backed attempt to impose a state on Somalia. They are joined by Col. Omar Jess of the SPM and former Somaliland president Abdurahman Tour. Factions loyal to Tour provoked Egal's government into a major conflict in and around Hargeisa in November/December 1994. Somaliland has faced and resolved several clan manipulated conflicts before, but it now faces its major challenge since its self-declared independence in 1991.

Somalia/Somaliland are in a perpetual tug-of-war between consociational democracy and warlordism. Ironically, the UN entered Somalia not only to feed the hungry, but to combat warlordism and restore democracy. In a desperate effort to impose another artificial state on the Somalis before its March 1995 withdrawal deadline, UNOSOM became allied with the Aidid faction of warlords (after fighting him during June–October 1993) and seems implicated in efforts to destabilize the more peaceful, stable areas, such as Somaliland.

Nevertheless, in what follows, we continue to assume—at least in the long run—the establishment of a deeply rooted democracy. This is critical in that sound measures to combat environmental degradation imply local citizens' and community participation. During the postindependence period, Somali pastoralists have shown willingness to participate in sand dune stabilization programs; the building of enclosures to conserve forage and grass; other pasture improvement programs; the dipping of livestock and related veterinary programs; as well as the construction of bunds to plug gullies. Ongoing community participation is also necessary to finally clear all land mines and undetonated explosives. One of the horror aspects of the Somali civil war was the planting by Siyad's army of over a million land mines in the cities, towns, and roads of what became the Somaliland Republic. The thousands of maimed victims in those areas bear witness to this policy of environmental pollution through mines and related explosives.

A new Somali order will have to reinstitutionalize data-gathering programs and thoroughly review the experiences of pastoral cooperatives and all previous "rural development" programs and projects. The Siyad government, for example, had earmarked a dozen areas to be preserved as wildlife conservation areas, but went on to devastate Somalia's wildlife for profit, as discussed above. Armed gangs during the civil wars destroyed wildlife with impunity. Forest and wildlife conservation require much greater attention than in the past.

A new Somali order must take full advantage of regional cooperation frameworks. An ironic twist of the Somali civil wars is that, while it has created hostilities and fractured the once united Somali people, it has also paved the way for harmony and cooperation between the Somalis and Ethiopia. All the armed dissident factions opposed to the Siyad regime (SSDF, SNM, USC) sought and obtained Ethiopian support to use Ethiopia to launch their armed raids against the Somali army. The new order in Ethiopia has created a federal system, and the Somalis in Ethiopia finally have autonomy to run their own affairs. Somalia and Ethiopia also need to cooperate to provide land-locked Ethiopia with Somalia's ample port facilities, while safeguarding Somalia's need for the waters of the Juba and Shabele rivers, both of which flow from the Ethiopian hinterland. Long-term cooperation could be achieved through bilateral agreements, as well as through participation in the existing Inter-Governmental Authority for Drought and Development (IGADD)—consisting of Ethiopia, Djibouti, Eritreal Kenya, Sudan, and Uganda. The current situation provides excellent prospects for Somali pastoralists to resume long-established seasonal patterns of livestock movement back and forth across the Somalia/

Ethiopia border, which was brutally disrupted with the coming of colonialism and territorial partitions. The new Somali order will achieve greater progress by prioritizing fishery development, tree and forestry development, and camel and livestock development.

Somali development and environmental protection call upon the future order to fully exploit the over 3,000 kilometers of coast and highly productive fisheries. Minority communities of coastal Somalis have traditionally eaten fish. The Somali pastoralist "aversion" to fish is superficial; it is even opposed by Islamic dietary regulations, which recommend fish eating. Experience has shown that Somalis within the army, police, boarding schools, and related institutions ate fish whenever it was offered at meal times. Over the years, the Somali diaspora community in Aden not only ate fish willingly, but consider it a staple of their diet. Following the 1974 drought, the Siyad regime settled over one hundred thouosand former nomads in agricultural and fishing settlements. These former nomads not only ate fish but also became "instant" fishermen. They learned that fish provides an ample drought resistant food source. Most urban Somalis would consume more fish than meat if the problems of pricing and availability could be resolved. Technical problems dealing with boats, refrigeration, and transportation, as well as organizational and marketing issues, will have to be dealt with to assure cheaper prices and dependable supplies. Somalia needs to develop fisheries not only for the domestic market, but also for export to neighboring countries.

The tree and forestry crisis is very much related to the fuelwood crisis. Poor Third World countries are much more affected by the fuelwood crisis than by the oil crisis, which seriously affects the balance of payments of many industrial countries (and most developing countries as well). Donor assistance to refugees in Somalia introduced alternative energy sources—wind and solar. Solar power was introduced to a much greater extent than wind power; however, both sources tend to produce electricity, whereas the main energy required by households is in the form of fuel. Donor assistance also allowed certain refugee camps to establish fuel plantations. Experience showed that most of the newly planted trees—imported fast growing trees as well as some of the local trees—can be utilized for fuelwood after only two or three years. In 1982, an energy expert estimated that in the year 2000 at least 75 percent of the whole woodfuel demand in the cities and towns, agricultural settlements, and refugee camps could be obtained from plantations and woodlots. He also estimated that an area of 0.6 million ha. would be necessary for this purpose.[39] Serious and sustained attention should also be given to improving charcoal production. A community oriented new Somali order needs to take all necessary legal and practical steps to ban the export of charcoal. As for domestic needs, it will be necessary to measure the efficiency of charcoal production and, if necessary, to improve production techniques.

A mid-1970s estimate of Somalia's livestock suggests a general figure of 21 million to 34 million: 15 million goats, 9.5 million sheep, 5.3 million cattle.[40] Somalia is reputed to have more camels than any other country; nevertheless, export-oriented commercialization has led to a decrease in the ratio of camels to cattle with dire consequences for the environment. Middle Eastern markets have dramatically increased the demand for Somali sheep and cattle. Ben Wisner analyzes the phenomenon and consequences thus:

> Increased commercialization in the last few decades not only has had a possibly negative impact on the land, but it has also reduced the ability of the nomads to cope with occasional droughts. Commercial pressures have resulted in a change in the composition of herds. A comparison of 1944–1951 with 1973 shows that the ratio of camel to cattle decreased from 5.4:1 in the North and 1.4:1 in the South to only 1.8:1 in the North and 0.5:1 in the South. This change increased the risk of drought because it reduced the effectiveness of time-tested coping strategies such as mobility. Cattle are not only less resilient than camels and more dependent on a constant water supply, they are also less mobile.[41]

A revived Somalia will need to restore and expand at least one project within this theme undertaken during the 1980s by the Somali Academy of Sciences and Arts and the Swedish Agency for Research Cooperation with Developing Countries (SAREC): the Somali Camel Research Project. The project included study of the camels: browsing behavior in relation to vegetation and the environment; diseases and health; breeding and reproduction; milk production and preservation; subspecies; and role in folklore. Somalis need to recall their rich camel folklore to restore the traditional balance between the ratio of camels to cattle: "He who does not own camels lives under the protection of others." For the sake of Somalia's improved environmental future, Somalis must recall that no other domestic animal can utilize the Somali environment as efficiently as the camel does.

Let me conclude by underlining the very urgent tasks that a restored Somali order will have to undertake immediately: enforcing Somali rights and sovereignty over territorial lands and water—preventing the plundering of coastal resources and banning the dumping of any and all forms of toxic waste. There is, after all, an eternal Somali optimism based on communal praxis: "A united, cooperating people can even stitch a broken sky, even if the rupture be a foot wide!"

Notes

1. Diana Briton Putnam and Mohamood Cabdi Noor, *The Somalis—Their History and Culture*. Washington, D.C.: The Refugee Service Center—Refugee Fact Sheet Number 9, October 1993, 1.

2. Ben Wisner, "Jilaal, Gu, Hagaa, and Der: Living with the Somali Land, and Living Well," in Ahmed I. Samatar, ed., *The Somali Challenge—From Catastrophe to Renewal?* ed. by Boulder, Colo.: Lynne Rienner, 1994), 31.

3. Cited in John W. Johnson, *Heelloov, Heelleelloov: The Development of the Genre Heello in Modern Somali Poetry* (Bloomington: Indiana University Publications, 1974), 60.

4. Ibid., 74.

5. Ibid., 97.

6. Ibid., 153. *Gu* and *Jiilaal* are Somali words for the rainy and dry season respectively.

7. Axmed Cali Abokor (translated by Axmed Arten Xange), *The Camel in Somali Oral Traditions* (Uppsala: Scandinavian Institute of African Studies, 1986), 49.

8. Ibid., 47.

9. Ibid., 53.

10. Ibid., 41.

11. Ibid., 39.

12. Excerpt from a play poem by Hassan Sheikh Mumin cited in K. S. Loughran et al., *Somalia in Word and Image* (Bloomington: Indiana University Press, 1986), 2–3.

13. Tiiariitta Hjort in Abokor, iv.

14. A popular saying, commonly recited when Somalis discuss the natural environment.

15. Abdi Samatar, "The State, Agrarian Change and Crisis of Hegemony in Somalia," *Review of African Political Economy* 43 (1988), 29.

16. Ali A. Mazrui, "Crisis in Somalia." Paper delivered at the Fifth International Congress of Somali Studies at the College of the Holy Cross, 1–3 December 1993, 2–3.

17. Richard Pankhurst cited in Abdi Samatar, 30.

18. Ibid., 31.

19. Putnam and Noor, 4.

20. Abdi Samatar, 29.

21. Wisner, *53*.

22. Mazrui, 6.

23. Ali K. Galaydh, "Notes on the State of the Somali State," *Horn of Africa* 13, no. 1 and 2 (Jan.–Mar., Apr–June 1990), 23.

24. Ibid., 26.

25. Richard Greenfield, "The Siyad Barre Regime and the Fauna of North-

east Africa," a paper presented at the Fifth International Congress of Somali Studies, College of the Holy Cross, 1–3 December 1993.

26. Communications with eyewitnesses.

27. Wisner, 53.

28. Ahmed Samatar, 8.

29. Ibid., 3.

30. Phil O'Keefe, "Toxic Terrorism," *Review of African Political Economy*, 42 (1988), 86.

31. Wisner, 54.

32. Mostafa Tolba, "Disposal of Hazardous Wastes in Somalia," United Nations Environmental Program (UNEP) News Release, Statement by UNEP Executive Director, Nairobi, 9 September 1992.

33. Wisner, 52.

34. Cited in Ahmed Samatar, 254–55.

35. Harold D. Nelson, *Area Handbook SoTaalia.* (Washington, D.C.: GPO for Foreign Area Studies, The American University, 1982).

36. Ali Moussa Iye, *Le Verdict De Liarbre* (Dubai: International Printing Press, 1991).

37. *Axdiga Nabadgalvada Ee Beelaha Soomaaliland (Peace Charter),* Boorama, 30 March 1993 (mimeographed).

38. *Shirweynaha Guurtida Beelaha Soomaaliland Axdi Oarameed* (National Charter), Boorama 25, April 1993 (mimeographed).

39. Keith Openshaw, "Somalia: The Forest Sector—Problems and Possible Solutions," Mogadishu, 1982 (mimeographed).

40. Cited in Wisner, 43.

41. Ibid., 46.

11

South Africa: Environmental Sustainability Needs Empowerment of Women

R. J. A. Goodland

Environmental sustainability has recently become a priority in economic development almost entirely because of social concerns. Lack of environmental sustainability harms people, especially poor people, and thus is inequitable and non-democratic. South Africa suffers inequity due not only to environmental degradation, however, but also due to apartheid government policies of the past that have left significant income gaps between the white minority and others in society. The government now has to raise average per capita income of poor people. But it must do this without compromising environmental sustainability, which is also needed for the welfare of the poor.

Relationships here are reciprocal. The welfare of the poor is needed for environmental sustainability. Social stability provides the social scaffolding of people's organizations that empower self-control and self-policing in people's management of natural resources. Social stability of this sort is impossible in the context of enormous gaps between rich and poor, because in that context poor people are often too desperate to practice self-restraint. Thus, environmental sustainability requires social stability, which requires income redistribution to ameliorate the current effects of apartheid practices.

One popular approach to economic redistribution is to promote general economic growth from which all will benefit. In general, however, present levels of resource consumption in industrial countries cannot possibly be generalized to all currently living people (i.e., the South), much less to future generations. Given South Africa's fragile environment, as well as current and projected populations, this generalization applies to South Africa. So the social and economic problems of inequitable income distribution cannot be addressed adequately by policies designed only to extend affluence to the poor. Rather, emphasis must be placed also on population reduction.

Unfortunately, in its current plans, South Africa devotes all attention to increasing income, and little to stabilizing population. The first overriding broad assumption of South Africa's Rural Restructuring Program (RAP) states: "In all instances, priority must be given to sustainably increasing household incomes for the rural poor." There is no mention of decreasing population.

The present work argues that a necessary means of achieving both environmental sustainability and the social stability that comes with reducing extreme poverty is population stabilization and reduction. Empowerment of women, which is required on moral grounds related to human rights, is required also if population stabilization is to have a real chance of success.

This chapter has four parts. Part one relates poverty to apartheid and to problems of environmental sustainability in South Africa's particularly fragile environment. The second part applies a general resource model to the South African context. Part three concludes that despite possibilities of marginal technological improvements, South Africa requires population stabilization. However, past racism and current poverty make this difficult. Part four relates traditional oppression of women to population issues, concluding that women's empowerment is essential for population stabilization. However, success regarding both women's empowerment and population stabilization is uncertain.

Poverty and the Environment

Poverty and Apartheid

South African society is hurtling away from environmental sustainability, largely because of apartheid, environmental racism, widespread inequity (the worst in the world in 1978), poverty, inadequate consumption per capita, and rapid population growth that undermines future consumption per capita. South Africa's black 76 percent majority earns only 36 percent of the national income, whereas the white 13 percent minority earns 54 percent of the national income (Table 11.1). Black[1] income averaged $670 in 1990, whereas white income exceeded $6,500. Approximately 50 percent of all South African households and 60 percent of all blacks (80 percent of those living in reserves) lived below the minimum living level, whereas in 1989 40 percent of the population lived below that level.

Table 11.1 Income Distribution in South Africa

Income level (Rands)	population (%)	white (%)	black (%)	Coloreds and Asians (%)
100,000 +	0.61	0.54	0.05	0.02
50,000--100,000	1.96	1.68	0.17	0.10
10,000--50,000	16.12	7.08	6.47	2.57
1,000--10,000	30.32	2.26	23.34	4.72
Less than 1,000	49.24	4.44	38.91	5.89
Unspecified	1.75	0.29	1.23	0.23

Source: Development Bank of South Africa, Economist Intelligence Unit, 1992-93.[1]

Note: Total national population: 30,796,474 persons.

More than half of the blacks (55.45 percent) earning less than R1,000 means the society is not only inequitable, but also violence-prone (e.g. land invasion) and unsustainable. A conservative 20–40 percent of South Africans are unemployed. Only 2 percent of national school leavers in 1992 managed to find employment in the formal sector. The following year's level was expected to be zero.

Poverty and Sustainability

Poverty alleviation is essential for environmental sustainability.[2] In recent decades, poverty and environmental degradation have been increasingly linked. The poor have not only suffered disproportionately from environmental damage, but have been forced to become a major cause of ecological stress themselves. Pushed onto fragile lands due to high-input and export-led agriculture on the fertile lands, by population growth, and by uneven income distribution patterns, many of the developing world's poor are forced into over-exploiting local resource bases for daily survival, sacrificing the future to salvage the present. Short-term strategies, such as slash-and-burn agriculture, shorter fallow periods, harvests exceeding regeneration rates, depletion of topsoil, and deforestation, permit survival in the present, but place enormous burdens upon future generations.

Poverty alleviation, on the other hand, reduces pressure on the environment, through reduction in overharvesting, overgrazing, or overfishing to meet short-run subsistence needs.[3] By generating additional output and purchasing power, poverty alleviation widens domestic markets. Local markets offer greater potential for employment creation and increased self-reliance upon local resources to produce local needs.

Resource Problems

It is essential that environmental stress be reduced in South Africa because it is a fragile, vulnerable environment.

Consider first agriculture and water. Only 45 percent of South Africa receives more than 500 mm of rain, the generally accepted minimum for dryland crop production. The long-term productivity of most of the entire Karoo region has been substantially reduced[4] whether this is called desertification or not. Only 13.5 percent of surface area in the whole of the country is suitable for cultivation; only 3 percent is considered to have high potential. Irrigated products account for 4 percent of GDP, and this may not increase when water is put on a full cost-pricing basis. The predominantly arid nature of South Africa was seen very early on as the major constraint to development. In the 1960s, concern with aridity combined with rapid population growth translated into serious population and land management programs.

Consider also rural fuelwood and deforestation. Heavy reliance for cooking and heating by seventeen million people on fuelwood collected from natural woodlands has led to severe and worsening deforestation. Annual collection of 8 million tons of fuelwood[5] is one of the leading causes of environmental degradation, along with overpopulation in homelands, poverty, overgrazing, and inappropriate agricultural expansion. Most South African households, possibly over 59 percent, use wood for cooking and heating. Fuelwood contributes nearly two thirds of total energy use by the rural and urban poor. In this respect, South Africa's energy patterns resemble those of other African developing economies, rather than those of industrial economies. Deforestation has led to acute soil erosion, especially in Natal and Transkei where it exceeds 300 million to 400 million tons per acre. While it is difficult to disaggregate causes of deforestation and erosion, fuelwood collection and overgrazing probably top the rank, with forced overcrowding and poverty in homelands, fencepost collection, and land clearance for agriculture and settlements also leading causes.

General Resource Model

Carrying capacity,[6] the impact of human activities upon a resource base, is largely synonymous with environmental sustainability. The impact of any population or nation upon environmental sources and sinks is a product of the damage done by the particular technologies (T) used, the levels of affluence (A), and the population (P). The relationship between them may be expressed as

$$I = T \times A \times P$$

where (T) technology refers to technological efficiency defined in terms of the number of units of output or consumption produced per unit of environmental cost: the impact intensity of income. Thus, one MW (megawatt) from a dirty coal-fired thermal plant will increase T more than one MW from solar generation. Affluence (A) as used here is the per capita GNP. The impact due to increased levels of affluence consists of the material flows needed to maintain each form of capital, as well as consumption. Population (P) refers to human numbers. Each human needs an irreducible biophysical minimum of throughput in the amount of 1,500 to 2,000 calories of daily food, in addition to fuel to cook it, shelter, and minimal clothes.[7]

There are only three means of reducing environmental impacts of human activities upon an already-stressed environment. These are (1) improving technology, thereby reducing throughput intensity of production; (2) limiting affluence; and (3) limiting population growth. South Africa's predicament is so serious that progress or improvements on all three fronts will be necessary.

However, as we have seen, below a certain level of affluence, that is, under conditions of extreme poverty, people tend also to degrade environments. So in South Africa, "limiting affluence" must mean that of the wealthy, while simultaneously redistributing income and wealth to the poor. This is why in South Africa limiting affluence cannot be the major component. Population control has increasing importance in this context.

Table 11.2
Environmental Sustainability:
General Guidelines (Modified Constant Natural Assets Rule)

OUTPUT RULE:
Waste emissions from a project should be within the assimilative capacity of the local environment to absorb without unacceptable degradation of its future waste absorptive capacity or other important services.

INPUT RULE:
Renewables: Harvest rates of renewable resource inputs should be within regenerative capacity of the natural system that generates them.

Nonrenewables: Depletion rates of nonrenewable resource inputs should be equal to the rate at which renewable substitutes are developed by human invention and investment. Part of the proceeds from liquidating nonrenewables should be allocated to research in pursuit of sustainable substitutes.

Population Problems

Population Projections

South Africa is unusual in that it has, or had, a national goal, set by the cabinet in 1983 (and published in 1984), for its total population size by 2025. This was set at 80 million, and exceeds most views of a population seen within South Africa's carrying capacity. The World Bank's World Development Report (WDR) of 1993 calculates, however, that South Africa's theoretical population size at stability will be 103 million.

Person-to-land ratios are worsening fast.[8] Homeland agricultural density (1.2 ha/family) is already too low for full-time farming. But there is not enough land even at that improbably low (1.2 ha) level outside homelands for all settlers likely to request land, or who are restituted with land.

Total black fertility rates exceed five children per woman for 1985 to 1990. Urban fertility rates have fallen gradually since about 1960, and more steeply since the early 1970s[9] because contraception and sterilization were used for occupational reasons. Employers required contraceptive use before hiring, and were permitted to fire an employee for pregnancy. Job loss jeopardized a woman's right to stay in the urban area instead of returning compulsorily to a homeland. In addition, live-in domestics had to send any children back to their homeland—with unacceptably high mortality rates following therefrom. Caldwell and Caldwell suggest that urban program results have reached a plateau.[10] This puts into doubt the chances of a similar transition in rural areas. It is also uncertain that the urban transition will persist in urban areas now that apartheid and many related policies have been repealed.

Black rural women want 20 percent more children than do black urban women.[11] There is a clear urban-rural difference in implied demand for contraception—5.7 living children per urban woman, and 6.1 for rural women. Rural fertility rates may not be falling. Rural areas have few fixed birth control clinics; users rely on irregular mobile services; a full 80 percent of black women use a monthly pill or injection, both of which require highly regular, steady supplies and precisely timed use, which are not yet practical in rural areas. Because a relatively large proportion of contraceptive use is for spacing rather than for limiting numbers of births, users are not likely to be consistently scrupulous in contraceptive practice, especially in view of the problematic methods used.

No Technological Fix Is Possible

What would it take to raise living standards of the poor majority in South Africa to present levels of affluence of the rich? Returning to the assumption that population will double in the next forty years, white per capita income (U.S. $6,530) is nearly ten times greater than that of blacks (U.S. $670). To raise the consumption of the poor to today's level of the rich (holding impact and white affluence constant) implies improvements in technological efficiency by 2 (for the doubling of the population) × 10 (for current income disparity between blacks and whites), or twenty times. However, annual historical improvement rates in technological efficiency of 1 percent to 2 percent are considered good. While technological improvements in agriculture, energy, transportation, and urban planning may radically reduce the environmental damage caused by current systems, a twentyfold advance just does not seem to be at all feasible. In short, even with the wildest technological optimism, it will be exceedingly difficult for poor segments of South African society to even approach current living standards of their rich compatriots.

For these reasons, limiting South Africa's population growth is an essential enabling condition toward an acceptable standard of living. Of course, slowing the population growth rate is just an essential first step. Population stabilization as quickly as possible is the prudent goal. But attaining population stability prohibits even a 1 percent rate of population growth, as this permits a population to double every seventy years. Population stabilization requires families to be limited to 2.1 children per family on average. South Africa's current 4.0 children per woman makes an income increase to narrow the equity gap practically impossible.

Population and Racism

In South Africa's deeply divided society, community and political resistance is high to a program perceived as imposed by the minority population with a clear political agenda. The government's specific aim under apartheid of reducing the size of the black population— and increasing the white—is responsible for the mistrust that confuses present discussions of population policy.[12] However, even steeply declining black fertility would make little difference to the country's racial proportions over the critical near to medium term.[13] Political leaders on all sides are probably already convinced that smaller families and slower rates of increase would benefit the black population.

Slowing the momentum of population growth in South Africa will not be an easy task. In South Africa, roughly 50 percent of the population is under the age of sixteen. Age structures so heavily skewed toward the young, who have yet to live their reproductive years, generate tremendous demographic momentum, particularly as modern medicine lowers death rates (i.e., infant mortality) in South Africa.[14]

Population and Poverty

Social security is one of the most effective means of reducing the pressure for the poor to engage in short-term environmental damage. Direct support for poverty alleviation, such as "safety nets," reduces the need for large families to help on the farm during harvest and at other times of high labor demand. Old-age pensions reduce reliance on large numbers of children to support their elderly parents. China's achievements over the last few decades in lowering total fertility rates so fast were, in large measure, due to social security of various forms, combined with conventional family planning campaigns. Racism has in the past constrained sharing with blacks the benefits of social security. B. Klugman sums up the situation thus: "It is not the poor themselves who have caused their poverty by having many children, but the practice of discrimination—which has denied them access to resources and security and in so doing, has caused the birth rate to increase."[15] In sum, blaming the victim—the poor are responsible for their own poverty because they have too many children—should be rejected. At the same time, however, as 38 percent of South Africa's population have yet to enter reproductive ages, population stability is urgent.

Four Implications

Four implications can be drawn from the environmentally fragile nature of South Africa's land:

1. Land reform, however widely implemented, will not be sufficient to alleviate fully all the rural poverty problems of blacks.
2. The available supply of land is simply not sufficient to grant a useful quantity of land to all, or even the majority, of non-whites wanting it.
3. Due to population pressure, as much or more effort will need to be devoted to generating nonfarm employment opportunities to meet the needs of future population growth.[16] These will have

to be in rural (i.e., farm services, traders, fuelwood, water provision), urban, and especially peri-urban areas.

4. The most effort, concurrent with or even before land reforms, needs to be focused on reducing population pressures directly. Otherwise all investments will rapidly be overwhelmed.

Oppression of Women

Women's Legal Liabilities

In South Africa until now, racial oppression obscured female oppression. However, most black women remain subordinate in home and society, with severely limited autonomy.[17] (Even women from the dominant groups have in the past largely accepted secondary roles.) This is an unacceptable waste at the very least. Women transmit tradition and spark innovation and change, precisely the values so much needed.

Of the two concurrent legal regimes in South Africa, Roman-Dutch and traditional, the latter normally consigns women to the legal status of minors until menopause or even later.[18] This situation will severely hamper empowerment of women and environmental sustainability until it is democratized. Minority status (i.e., under twenty-one years of age) makes access to bank loans, other credit, mortgage, landownership, and many other essentials either difficult or impossible. This undemocratic situation is starting to be modified, especially in KwaZulu. But local magistrates are unlikely to countermand traditional law in favor of Roman-Dutch law. Customary law is now protected by clause 8 of the draft constitution on gender. The draft constitution thus fails to redress historic discrimination against women. While South Africa's "Age of Majority" Act has not applied to women, an appeal may be made for extension to females.

However, the rights of traditional leaders are confirmed by the draft constitution and will be managed by regional (not national) institutions that have less regard for the rights of women than do national institutions. Local (not national) courts will adjudicate between the two legal regimes if they conflict.

Women's Disproportionate Suffering

Lack of population stability harms women more than it harms men. Rapid population growth within subsistence economies intensifies maternal health problems and increases infant mortality. It also compounds environmental degradation (i.e., soil erosion, depletion of soil fertility, deforestation, and indirect effects on watersheds, irrigation, etc.), thereby increasing the impact of human activities on the local resource base.[19] And women suffer most from this, too.

Unsustainable amounts of time and energy are currently allocated to two activities essential to all households—acquisition of water and fuelwood. These activities are carried out almost entirely by women (although to a significant extent by children as well). More of women's time spent on these activities means less time is available for child care, education, wage labor, and other activities. Because the main aim of development is helping people up out of subsistence, any facilitation of water and fuelwood supply will be enormously beneficial, especially to the poorest of the poor, namely women. That gastroenteritis is the leading cause of mortality suggests that water scarcity hampers hygiene.[20]

Although as much as 60 percent of South Africa's households use fuelwood, about 40 percent of the South African population depends almost exclusively on fuelwood for their energy needs. Because practically all fuelwood is collected by women, its scarcity means more of women's time is spent in collection. One headload costs three to five hours to collect. As most households need two to three headloads per week, seven to nine hours are needed for gathering fuelwood. Many women walk 6–19 kms per headload. Headload weight (averaging 21 to 38 kgs) is increasing, and headloads as heavy as 67 kg have been recorded. This means less time is available for education and childcare. This penalty also probably translates into less cooking, more food storage (cooked and uncooked), more food spoilage, and gastroenteritis.

Women and Birth Control

South Africa has achieved an impressive urban "demographic transition" (although more in declining fertility than mortality). By 1991 there were 57,240 (later 60,200) "clinical family planning service points," twice as many locations as there were for health care. South Africa has lower fertility rates and lower preferred family size than any other country in Sub-Saharan Africa. Unlike health services, family planning is free. Mobile family planning teams visit factories, mines, and at times, even some rural villages. This is by far the most effective such program in Africa, and one of the better-funded ones in the world. Although the average advice time at such clinics is only two minutes,[21] even this intensity exceeds anything ever seen in countries associated with the Organization for Economic Cooperation and Development (OECD).

The extent of malpractice and coercion, which is partly responsible for the negative view of family planning on the part of many South African clients, needs to be ascertained, and future programs monitored to prevent any such happenings in the future. Use of Depoprovera injectable contraceptives further politicized the issue under apartheid. It can only be resolved by women themselves in a society that empowers them with equal status.

By 1991, official statistics on South African contraceptive usage ran as high as 86.5 percent in sophisticated urban communities and 50.5 percent in some rural communities. As these figures seem to exclude homelands and unmarried women (childless single women?), they overstate the success rates. Annual expenditures by 1987 were U.S. $10 per eligible woman or $40 million (80 million Rand) according to the *South Africa Official Yearbook, 1991–1992*. Caldwell and Caldwell's[22] main question is, will this qualified achievement survive democratization? The question becomes, will current urban fertility declines be repeated in rural areas, as women become empowered and living standards rise, or will urban fertility declines reverse in rural areas as ex-homelanders resume farming after generations away from the land?

In spite of widespread access to free birth control, black urban women want smaller families than they in fact have. An average of 42 percent–52 percent of births are unwanted (1989 data). Practically all (79 percent) low income/high fertility respondents in the Human Services Research Department's 1992 survey said South Africa's population was growing too rapidly, and 75 percent said some form of intervention is needed.

Empowering Women is Essential

The "Tamil Nadu Miracle" suggests that the most productive path toward population stability and reduction is through empowerment of women. In India, the Tamil Nadu instituted noon meals for school children in 1975. This had the effect of getting girls out of households (where they cared for infants, fetched water, etc.) and into the school room, at least until lunch was over. Just as soon as the new cohort reached reproductive age about fifteen years later, the total fertility rate plummeted from 35/1,000 to 20/1,000. This seems to have been accomplished by school attendance alone.

South Africa has begun the process of women's empowerment. The first comprehensive statement on women's emancipation released by any political party or organization in South Africa was that of the African National Congress (ANC) on 2 May 1990.[23] It acknowledges women's contribution to the political struggle, which has brought South Africa to the eve of change; it acknowledges the persistence of gender discrimination in all spheres and urges: "Women's right to democratic participation in all decision-making must be there in principle and in practice." Another statement—"Within apartheid ideology, African women have been perceived simply as the breeders of future generations of labor"—does not yet have the complement that any ideology that perceives women first as reproducers and only second as equals will cause injustice to women as great as apartheid has. *The argument for environmental sustainability also has to avoid that reductive tendency.*

Priorities for Women's Empowerment

South African priorities for empowerment of women, environmental sustainability, and population stabilization, as found in the literature,[24] include the five points outlined below, which constitute an approach toward a definition of women's empowerment:

1. *Women's Empowerment*: This is the ability to take control over their own lives. Women should have equal opportunities for development as soon as possible.[25] Women's opportunity for informed decision making about matters affecting themselves and their families is essential. The means for fulfilling women's goals should be under female control. Women are agents for economic and environmental change, and must be recognized for their role in managing resources and families. Equal rights for women on wages, ownership, land and so on is widely sought in the South African literature, and may be fundamentally effective. The ANC's land manifesto specifically mentions equal gender rights to all land-related issues. Replication of discrimination under apartheid against urban women (e.g., fired when pregnant) must be avoided by specific measures for empowerment. As all women are different, it is their decision making that is the key, rather than any blanket principles. The most effective empowerment recognizes that some classes of women are more vulnerable than others (e.g., household heads, disabled, unemployed, pregnant, aged).

2. *Girls' Empowerment*: Increased educational opportunities for girls, as well as increased and meaningful employment opportunities for

women, are integral parts of their empowerment. As incomes, education, and employment opportunities for women improve the quality of life, the need for more children declines. Education of girls, at least up to that now enjoyed by boys, has been demonstrated to reduce fertility and increase income. Thus, girls' education is arguably the most cost-effective investment to improve the human condition. Noon meals help greatly. Community-level literacy and tutoring campaigns can be highly effective in education, and in expanding girls' choices and opportunities. Women want truancy rates decreased, especially of their own children. Many girls do not attend school because they have to gather fuelwood or water; fuelwood lots and well drilling, or similar arrangements, have high payoffs. Women with even an elementary school education raise living standards in developing countries. Such women are thus empowered to have fewer children, take better care of those they have, and earn more when they take a job or market their products.

3. *Protection of Women's Rights*: Human rights policies are needed to prohibit gender discrimination. The Interim Constitution outlaws unfair discrimination on the basis of gender and sex, among many other factors (Bill of Rights, ch. 3, 19 Nov. 1993). Historic discrimination against women needs to be rectified, and some of this may imply strengthening the law. Financial, agricultural, and banking arrangements may be included. Universal access of women is needed to primary health care, including maternal and child health care, through programs that are woman centered and women managed. In addition, empowerment of women will halt involuntary, coercive, or discriminatory family planning programs.

4. *Women's Unmet Needs for Reproductive Health*: Support for rural women's desires will reduce teenage, schoolgirl, adolescent, accidental, premature, and extramarital pregnancies; will delay marriage and defer the birth of the first child; and will help women space their children. Black women want to reduce today's 62 percent single motherhood.[26] Apparently, easy concealment of contraception is desired. Urban young women want to prevent premature childbirth and marriage from interfering with their education and employment.[27] National programs admit reduction in teen pregnancies as a goal, but are silent on abortion (as of 1988). In sum, meet women's unmet demand for family planning, family size, and spacing planning.

5. *Women's Equality*: Rectify today's situation in which women bear

most of the financial burden of raising children, while men have most of the decision-making powers on fertility. Prevention of sexually transmitted diseases, especially AIDS, is crucial for survival as well as for empowerment. To the extent traditional law continues to force women to remain minors until menopause, or treats them more importantly as group members than as individuals, equality will be impossible. Patriarchy and apartheid interacted to compel black women to accept contraception under circumstances that reduced their choices.[28] Klugman[29] investigates the assumption underlying the concept of overpopulation. Massive participatory information campaigns (radio, musicals, "green" theater like the protest drama that grew from Port Elizabeth) are called for, directed toward both women *and* men, particularly addressing the links between women's empowerment, redressing historic imbalances, and economic impoverishment.

Uncertain Prospects

Although greatly to be welcomed, prudence dictates that not too much reliance be put on an expectation of an automatic demographic transition to solve the rural predicament of excessive people/land ratios.[30] Two countervailing tendencies occur. Undercapitalized families will start farming and will not be able to afford much labor-saving machinery. They will need much labor but will not be able to pay wages. This is likely to strongly promote a desire for larger families. In addition, when women obtain land and no longer are forced to be wage-earning domestics, they cannot be fired if pregnant, and hence may want larger families. The countervailing tendency is that people with freehold tenure eventually may feel secure, and hence will not need large families to care for them in their old age. This tendency may be weaker than the need for more labor for three reasons. First, changing perceptions of one's future take time, possibly more than one generation. Second, homelanders have been so repeatedly abused that confidence in the new South Africa may be slow in coming. Third, only a fraction of people will enjoy freehold tenure; many will be wage earners.

For these reasons, population growth seems likely unless specific measures are put in place from the start to promote family planning. If women remain subject to the legal status of minors until menopause, the tendency to larger families may be more pronounced. The two countervailing tendencies also act at different times. The need for more labor starts as soon as farming or planting starts. It is especially acute at harvest times and is felt repeatedly. Perceptions of confidence in freehold tenure are more likely to become engendered mainly by time. A historically based skepticism will become confidence in the future.

In sum, women's empowerment is no panacea. But given the fragility of the South African environment, poverty-induced environmental degradation, and current demographic trends, it is imperative to create a context of racial justice and more equitable income distribution that facilitates population stabilization. The empowerment of women is an essential means to both population stabilization and greater income equity, even if it does not, by itself, assure success.

Notes

In addition to World Bank colleagues Herman Daly and Gus Tillman, I want sincerely to thank Craig McKenzie of DBSA, Anton Eberhard, Clive van Horen, and John Raimundo of the University of Cape Town. Tom Merrick, Kobus Oosthuizen, and Professor O. Chimere-Dan kindly commented on the demographic and population sections. Peter S. Wenz gave special editorial assistance.

1. Clarification is needed on "black." Throughout this chapter, black is used almost entirely in the strict sense excluding coloreds, Asians, and Indians. However, Ramphele defines black as "the widely accepted term to describe all non-white South Africans" (M. Ramphele, ed., *Restoring the Land* [London: Panos, 1993]). Clearly, disaggregation of data into four categories would be greatly preferable. The data show, however, that coloreds and Indians fall between the two extremes of black and white. For example, infant mortality per 1,000 live births in the first year of life: white 13, Indian 20, colored 57, black 68. Similarly, TFR: white 1.9, Indian 2.5, colored 2.9, black 4.6. Racial share of national income is similar: black 37 percent, Asian 4 percent, colored 10 percent, white 48 percent. But lumping colored and Asian data together can severely mask important differences, especially as South African Indians are progressing fast socioeconomically, while coloreds are not.

2. R. Goodland and H. Daly, "Poverty Alleviation is Essential for Environmental Sustainability," World Bank Environment Department, Working Paper 42, 1993.

3. Ibid.

4. J. Yeld, *Caring for the Earth: South Africa, a Strategy for Sustainable Living* (Stellenbosch: Southern Africa Nature Foundation, 1993).

5. M. V. Gandar, "The Imbalance of Power," in *Going Green: People, Politics and the Environment in South Africa*, ed. J. Cock and E. Koch (Cape Town: Oxford University Press, 1991).

6. Carrying capacity is a measure of the amount of renewable resources

in the environment in units of the number of organisms that those resources can support. Thus, it is a fraction of the geographical area and the organism. It should be noted that carrying capacity is difficult to estimate for humans because of major differences in consumption (affluence) and technology on national and international levels.

7. The statement $I = T \times A \times P$ clearly is a simplification, but it is also inclusive. The terms can be greatly subdivided or disaggregated, but there is nothing else. Early studies of environmental limits to human activities emphasized the limits to environmental resources (i.e., petroleum, copper, etc.). Experience has shown, however, that the sink constraints (i.e., waste assimilation such as air and water pollution, greenhouse gases, and ozone depletion, etc.) are more stringent.

8. M. Roth, *The Economics of Agricultural Land Use and Redistribution in South Africa* (Madison, Wis.: Land Tenure Center, The World Bank, 1992).

9. W. P. Mostert and J. M. Lotter, eds., *South Africa's Demographic Future* (Pretoria: Human Sciences Research Council, 1990).

10. J. C. Caldwell and P. Caldwell, *The Relevance of the South African Fertility Decline* (unpublished manuscript, 1993).

11. Mostert and Lotter, *South Africa's Demographic Future.*

12. O. Chimere-Dan, "Population Policy in South Africa," *Studies in Family Planning* 24, no. 1 (1993): 31–39.

13. J. C. Caldwell and P. Caldwell, "The South African Fertility Decline," *Population and Development Review* 19, no. 2 (1993): 225–62.

14. See T. W. Merrick, "Demographic Momentum," *Integration* 33 (August 1992): 57–64; and T. W. Merrick, *Population Dynamics in Developing Countries* (Washington, D.C.: World Bank manuscript, 1993).

15. B. Klugman, "Population Policy for South Africa: A Critical Perspective," *Development Southern Africa* 8 (1991): 19–34.

16. Roth, *The Economics of Agricultural Land Use and Redistribution in South Africa.*

17. Chimere-Dan, "Population Policy in South Africa."

18. T. W. Bennett, *Customary Law of South Africa* (Cape Town: Juta Publishing Co., 1991).

19. K. Davis, "Zero Population Growth," *Daedalus* (Fall 1973): 15–30.

20. M. V. Gandar, "Some Social and Environmental Aspects of the Use of Fuelwood in KwaZulu," in *Rural Studies in KwaZulu*, ed. N. Bromberger and J. D. Lea (Pietermaritzberg: University of Natal, 1982).

21. E. Kollstedt and S. Bergstrom, "Family Planning in South Africa: Coloreds and Blacks are Neglected Groups," *Lakartidningen* 89, no. 11 (1992): 854–57.

22. Caldwell and Caldwell, *The Relevance of the South African Fertility Decline.*

23. S. Bazilli, *Putting Women on the Agenda* (Johannesburg: Raven Press, 1991).

24. For example, Caldwell and Caldwell, "The South African Fertility Decline"; B. Bozzoli, "Life Strategies, Household Resilience and the Meaning of Informal Work: Some Women's Stories," paper presented at the Con-

ference on Women and Gender in Southern Africa, Durban, University of Natal, 1991; and Bazilli, *Putting Women on the Agenda.*

25. Chimere-Dan, "Population Policy in South Africa."

26. Kollstedt and Bergstrom, "Family Planning in South Africa: Coloreds and Blacks are Neglected Groups."

27. Caldwell and Caldwell, *The Relevance of the South African Fertility Decline.*

28. B. Klugman, "The Politics of Contraception in South Africa," *Women's Studies International Forum* 13, no. 3 (1990): 261–71.

29. Klugman, "Population Policy for South Africa: A Critical Perspective."

30. Roth, *The Economics of Agricultural Land Use and Redistribution in South Africa.*

Additional Reading

Bernstein, H. *For the Triumphs and for Their Tears: Women in Apartheid South Africa.* London: International Defence and Aid Fund, 1985.

Bozzoli, B., and Mmantho, N. *Woman of Phokeng: Consciousness, Life Strategy, and Migrancy in South Africa 1900–1983.* Portsmouth, N.H.: Heinemann, 1991.

Brown, B. "Facing the Black Peril: The Politics of Population Control in South Africa." *Journal of Southern African Studies* 13, no. 2 (1987): 256–73.

Budlander, D. "Women and the Economy." Paper presented at the Conference on Women and Gender in Southern Africa, Durban, University of Natal, 1991.

Clarke, J. *Back to Earth: South Africa's Environmental Challenges.* Johannesburg: Southern Book Publishers, 1991.

Durning, A. B. "Apartheid's Environmental Toll." Washington, D.C.: Worldwatch Paper 95.

Eberhard, A. A. "Shifting Paradigms in Understanding the Fuelwood Crisis: Policy Implication for South Africa." *Journal of Energy R&D in Southern Africa* 3, vol. 2 (1992).

Friedman, M., and M. Hambridge. "The Informal Sector: Gender and Development." In *South Africa's Informal Economy.* E. Preston-Whyte and C. Rogerson, eds. Oxford: Oxford University Press, 1992.

Fuggle, R. F., and M. A. Rabie, eds. *Environmental Management in South Africa.* Kenwyn: Juta and Co., 1992.

Fuggle, R. F., and M. A. Rabie, eds. *Environmental Concerns in South Africa.* Cape Town: Juts and Co., 1983.

Gandar, M. V. "Wood as a Source of Fuel in South Africa." *South African Forestry Journal* (June 1984): 7–8, 25.

Goodland, R., C. Watson, and G. Ledec. *Environmental Management in Tropical Agriculture.* Boulder, Colo.: Westview Press, 1984.

Rees, H. "Women and Reproductive Rights." In *Putting Women on the Agenda*, S. Bazilli, ed. Johannesburg: Raven Press, 1991.

Sachs, L. *Protecting Human Rights in a New South Africa.* Cape Town: Oxford University Press, 1990.

Simkins, C. E. W. "Population Pressures." In *Restoring the Land*, M. Ramphele et al., eds. London: Panos, 1993.

Wilson, F., and Ramphele, M. "Uprooting Poverty: The South African Challenge." Cape Town: D. Philip and New York: The Hunger Project Global Office, Paper 7.

Yollenhoven, S. "South Africa through Women's Eyes." *Ms.* (Sept.-Oct. 1993).

Index

Page references followed by *t* and *n* indicate tables and notes, respectively.

About the Contributors

Hussein M. Adam (Ph.D., Harvard University) is associate professor of political science at the Holy Cross College Department of Political Science and the Center for International Studies. His interests include development, state–civil society relationships, and the role and impact of voluntary development organizations. He taught at the Somali National University from 1974 to 1986, and as a UN consultant in 1985–86 he established the Intergovernmental Authority for Drought and Development in six African nations. He serves on the advisory Board of the Brown University Alan Feinstein World Hunger Program and has just been appointed to a three-year term as a member of the Council of African Advisors of the World Bank.

Elizabeth Bell is an environment protection specialist for American Indian affairs at the EPA. She began her work in the environmental justice movement over four years ago working with a grassroots organization on the south side of Chicago to block the siting of an incineration plant in this predominantly African American and low-income community. Over the past five years she has worked with a number of environmental organizations including Ohio Citizen Action and the Public Interest Research Group (PIRG). Most recently, she chaired the American Indian Outreach subcommittee for the interagency effort on the Comprehensive Environmental Response Compensation and Liability Act (CERCLA) reauthorization.

Robert D. Bullard is Ware Professor at the Department of Sociology at Clarke Atlanta University. His groundbreaking research has made him one of the leading experts on people-of-color grassroots groups and the environmental justice movement. His publications include *Dumping in Dixie* (Westview Press, 1994), *Confronting Environmental Racism: Voices from the Grassroots* (South End Press, 1993), and numerous journal articles and chapters in books.

243

Clarice E. Gaylord (Ph.D., Howard University) is the first director of the Office of Environmental Justice. Created in 1992, the office deals with environmental impacts on racial minorities and low-income populations. Under her direction, the office administers the Minority Academic Program and coordinates communication, outreach, education, and training of the public on justice issues. Prior to the EPA, Dr. Gaylord served as a health scientist administrator with the National Institute of Health and held several science administrator positions with the National Cancer Institute and the Division of Research Grants.

R. J. A. Goodland (Ph.D., McGill University) is an environmental adviser at the World Bank, which he joined in 1978. Before that he worked as an applied ecologist in many developing nations including Brazil, Costa Rica, Bangladesh, Malaysia, and Indonesia. He was chairman of the Ecological Society of America (Metropolitan) in 1989–1990; was the founding editor of the International Society for Ecological Economics; and in 1994 was elected president of the International Association of Impact Assessments. He has published seventeen books and approximately 70 other publications, mainly on environment and development in the Third World, including *The Race to Save the Tropics* (1990), *The Environmental Assessment Sourcebook* (3 vols., 1991) and *The Transition to Sustainability: Population, Affluence, Lifestyle* (1992).

Omari H. Kokole (Ph.D., Dalhousie University) is adjunct assistant professor of political science and Afro-American and African studies and associate director of the Institute of Global Cultural Studies at SUNY–Binghamton. He has published, coauthored, and edited many articles and books including *Dimensions of Africa's International Relations* (Caravan Books, 1993) and *The Global African: Portrait of Ali A. Mazrui* (Africa World Press, 1995).

Bill Lawson (Ph.D., University of North Carolina at Chapel Hill) is chairperson of the Department of Philosophy at the University of Delaware. He edited and contributed material to *The Underclass Question* (Temple University Press, 1992) and was coauthor of *Between Slavery and Freedom* (Indiana University Press, 1992) with Howard McGary. He writes in the area of African American philosophy and social and political philosophy.

Howard McCurdy, Jr. (Ph.D., Michigan State University) is a prominent Canadian political figure. He has been vice president of the Federal New Democratic Party, president of the Michigan State University Chapter of the National Association for the Advancement of Colored People (NAACP), chairman of the Conference of University Chapters of NAACP, and founding president of the National Black Coalition of Canada, as well as president of the University of Windsor Faculty Association and chair of the Biology Department. He received the Centennial Medal of Canada in 1967.

Richard Phillips earned an honours B.A. in philosophy and criminology at the University of Windsor and is now pursuing graduate work in criminology there.

Kristin Shrader-Frechette (Ph.D., University of Notre Dame), Distinguished Research Professor of Philosophy at the University of South Florida, earned degrees in mathematics, physics, and philosophy, and post-doctoral fellowships in ecology, economics, and hydrogeology. Since 1981, NSF and NEH have funded her research. Author of 185 articles in journals such as *Ethics, Environmental Ethics, Journal of Philosophy, Science, BioScience,* and *Philosophy of Science*, she has written 12 books on ethics, philosophy of science, risk assessment, and environmental policy, published by such presses as Cambridge, Oxford, and Yale. Winner of several university-wide teaching awards, Schrader-Frechette lectures throughout the world and has served as advisor to many international and federal agencies. She has been elected president of the Society for Philosophy and Technology, the commission on Ethics and Science, and the Risk Analysis and Policy Association.

Laura Westra (Ph.D., University of Toronto) is associate professor of philosophy at the University of Windsor. She is a founding member of the International Society for Environmental Ethics (ISEE) and is currently ISEE secretary. Westra is author of two books, *An Environmental Proposal for Ethics: The Principle of Integrity* (Rowman & Littlefield, 1994) and *Freedom in Plotinus* (Mellon, 1990) and coeditor of *Ethical and Scientific Perspectives on Integrity* (Kluwer, 1995) and *Roots of Ecology in Ancient Greek Thought* (University Press of North Texas, 1996). She has also published numerous journal articles and chapters in books, most on environmental ethics and ancient, Hellenistic, and medieval philosophy.

Peter S. Wenz (Ph.D., University of Wisconsin) is professor of philosophy and legal studies at Sangamon State University and adjunct professor of medical humanities at Southern Illinois University School of Medicine, both in Springfield, Illinois. His books include *Environmental Justice* (SUNY Press, 1988), *Abortion Rights as Religious Freedom* (Temple University Press, 1992), and *Hear the Grass Scream* (Temple University Press, 1996). His current work relates environmental philosophy to social justice and technological change.

Daniel C. Wigley holds a M.F.A. in painting and a M.A. in philosophy. For the last ten years he has taught undergraduate courses in both painting and philosophy at the University of South Florida. He specializes in ethics, aesthetics, and analytic philosophy, and expects to receive a Ph.D. in philosophy in May 1996. Winner of the 1992 Graduate Philosophy Award for his paper on Hume and taste, Wigley has also done environmental ethics research on projects funded by the National Science Foundation and the National Endowment for the Humanities. He and Kristen Shrader-Frechette have coauthored journal articles and book chapters on ethics, environmental justice, and epistemology.